Learning, Teaching and Assessment in Higher Education

Palgrave Teaching and Learning

Series Editor: **Sally Brown**

Facilitating Workshops
For the Love of Learning
Leading Dynamic Seminars
Learning, Teaching and Assessment in Higher Education
Live Online Learning
Further titles are in preparation

Universities into the 21st Century

Series Editors: **Noel Entwistle and Roger King**

Becoming an Academic
Cultures and Change in Higher Education
Global Inequalities and Higher Education
Learning Development in Higher Education
Managing your Academic Career
Managing your Career in Higher Education Administration
Research and Teaching
Teaching Academic Writing in UK Higher Education
Teaching for Understanding at University
Understanding the International Student Experience
The University in the Global Age
Writing in the Disciplines

Palgrave Research Skills

Authoring a PhD
The Foundations of Research (2nd edn)
Getting to Grips with Doctoral Research
Getting Published
The Good Supervisor (2nd edn)
Maximizing the Impacts of University Research
The PhD Viva
The Postgraduate Research Handbook (2nd edn)
The Professional Doctorate
Structuring Your Research Thesis

You may also be interested in:

Teaching Study Skills and Supporting Learning

Learning, Teaching and Assessment in Higher Education

Global Perspectives

Sally Brown

First published 2015 by
PALGRAVE

Palgrave in the UK is an imprint of Macmillan Publishers Limited, registered in England, company number 785998, of 4 Crinan Street, London N1 9XW.

Palgrave Macmillan in the US is a division of St Martin's Press LLC, 175 Fifth Avenue, New York, NY 10010.

Palgrave is a global imprint of the above companies
and is represented throughout the world.

ISBN: 978-1-137-39666-2

This book is printed on paper suitable for recycling and made from fully managed and sustained forest sources. Logging, pulping and manufacturing processes are expected to conform to the environmental regulations of the country of origin.

A catalogue record for this book is available from the British Library.

A catalog record for this book is available from the Library of Congress.

Printed in China

Contents

Acknowledgements

The author and publishers would like to thank Northumbria Assessment for Learning CETL for permission to reproduce Figure 7.1.

The author and publishers would also like to thank the following for permission to reproduce good practice accounts:

Priya M Vaidya, Jahirul Haque, Carolyn Roberts, Brian Shoesmith, Belinda Cooke, Sue Smith, Pauline Fitzgerald, Catherine Coates, Justine Simpson, Steve Jones, Simon Thomson, Stephanie Jameson, Ruth Pickford, Laura Guertin, Kalyan Banerjee, Danqing Liu, Sarah Gravett, Josef de Beer, Nadine Petersen, Hala F. Mansour, Geoff Hill, Christopher Hill, Ganakumaran Subramaniam, Biddy Unsworth, Alice Mauchline, Rob Jackson, Maya Bogova, Nadya Yakovchuk, Emma Coonan, Helen Webster, Ruth Pickford, Junxia Hou, Melanie Miller, Yvan Martinez, Darren Raven, Joshua Trees, Victor M. López-Pastor, Victoria Guzzo, Mark Glynn, Anita O'Donovan, Michelle Leech, Orla Murphy, Cath Fraser, Judi Honeyfield, Lynette Steele, David Lyon, James Derounian, Celia Popovic, Kathleen Winningham, Susan F. Stevenson, Kishwer Kingschild, Mike Cole, Bernadette van de Rijt, Mirjam Bastings, Marina Harvey, Phil Race, Hetty Grunefeld, Shrinika Weerakoon, Suki Ekaratne.

This book is dedicated to my sister Wendy Stainton Rogers who not only helped me become an academic but has enriched my practice by her ways of thinking and her meticulous scholarship. I would like to thank all the good practice account authors who have enriched this book and also Phil Race who has worked alongside me in the production of this book and provided the kind of support any author would be lucky to receive.

Series editor's preface

This series of books with Palgrave for all who care about teaching and learning in higher education has been developed with the express aim of providing useful, relevant, current and helpful guidance on key issues in learning and teaching in the tertiary/post-compulsory education sector. This is an area of current very rapid and unpredictable change, with universities and colleges reviewing and often implementing radical alterations in the ways they design, deliver and assess the curriculum, taking into account not just innovations in how content is being delivered and supported, particularly through technological means but also the changing relationships between academics and their students. The role of the teacher in higher education needs to be reconsidered when students can freely access content world wide and seek accreditation and recognition of learning by local, national or international providers (and may indeed prefer to do so). Students internationally are becoming progressively more liable for the payment of fees, as higher education becomes seen as less of a public good and more of a private one, and this too changes the nature of the transaction.

Texts in this series address aspects of these and other emergent imperatives. Among topics covered are volumes exploring student-centred approaches at undergraduate and post-graduate levels including doctoral work, the necessity to work in an internationalised and transnational, tertiary education context, the challenges of staff-student interactions where engagements are as likely to be through new technologies as face-to-face in the classroom and issues about the levels of student engagement, especially where study is in competition with other demands on their time including employment and caring responsibilities.

This book is especially close to my heart, as it is my own first contribution to the series and one which is concerned with an area of particular topicality, since it provides a variety of global perspectives on what comprises good university teaching, learning and assessment. I am very keen to showcase inter- and transnational approaches to higher education pedagogy and am keen to hear from further potential authors for inclusion in the series.

Sally Brown

1 Global approaches to teaching, learning and assessment

Introduction

There are many books on teaching and assessment at higher educational level, both scholarly reviews of academic practice and pragmatic guidance books offering advice to novices and others on how to be an effective student-centred academic. So why write another? My aim here is to use the best of the scholarship underpinning teaching and learning in universities in the last half-century or more while at the same time taking account of the changing nature of the student body, higher education institutions and potentially of learning itself. However, my particular ambition in this volume is to do so from a global perspective, recognising that many extant texts about tertiary teaching are written from the perspective of a single nation, or a very limited group of nations, usually within highly-advantaged, commonly English-speaking nations. What I have sought to do here is draw on good practice from six continents, supported by a framework of pedagogic discussion and review, which is designed to be of highly practical value to educators worldwide.

This book cannot provide comprehensive coverage of all national practices, nor do I claim that the good practices I include here are the only ones worth discussing. While I cover a wide range of teaching approaches across subjects and disciplines, and refer to undergraduate, masters level and doctoral education, it would be inappropriate to suggest that this is a complete compendium of global perspectives. What I can claim is that I am proud to celebrate here alternative voices, and to help to make them audible beyond their home nations through the good practice accounts (GPAs) I include from six continents. I chose to shun the arrogance of the term 'best practice', since it is impossible to judge what is 'best' without knowing all of the possible alternatives. In seeking international perspectives, I looked for descriptions of pedagogic practice that were regarded as strong in their own countries, without trying to impose my own quality judgements. I have been delighted with the range and scale of the accounts, and by the generosity of the authors in sharing them.

The chapters in this book are designed to provide a broad perspective on enhancing the diverse practices that comprise the design, delivery, assessment and support of the curriculum, together with some thoughts about how we can best support the people charged with undertaking those tasks, including academics, learning support staff and managers, and on how to work strategically to improve the ways we make it happen.

After exploring in this chapter some of the differences students and their teachers experience across the globe, and how we might respond to them, I next explore in Chapter 2 some of the theories and concepts that underpin successful teaching in higher education. Chapter 3 is concerned with translating these into the curriculum we offer our students, ensuring that everything we do is constructively designed (Biggs and Tang, 2007), by working out in advance what we need our students to know and be able to do at the end of the programme, then thinking through how to deliver this, assess whether the students actually can do what we anticipated they could and evaluate our success at doing so. This process is not something that can be undertaken and then continuously implemented, so the chapter also covers enhancement of the quality of provision, through review and refreshment. In Chapter 4 I move to discussing the concept of curriculum delivery and some of the ways we actually do deliver in a range of settings, particularly but not exclusively in lectures, and in Chapter 5, I consider other settings in which students work, within and beyond the campus. Chapter 6 focuses on students, the recipients of curriculum delivery, stressing the importance of fostering various literacies: academic literacy, information and digital literacy, assessment literacy and social and interpersonal literacies, which together are necessary to help students achieve their best. The next two chapters cover aspects of assessment: in Chapter 7 looking especially at how we can make it fit for the purposes it was designed to achieve, and in Chapter 8 considering how assessment can be fully integrated with the learning process, rather than being a separate activity tagged on to the end. Crossing all chapters, but particularly covered in Chapter 9 are thoughts on technologies to support learning and good examples of how these are put into practice. Looking towards the end of the student lifecycle, on graduation students move beyond the university, so Chapter 10 reviews how we can promulgate not just students' employability but also how they can integrate into the wider community, with a toolkit of knowledge, skills and capabilities to equip them to make the best of life opportunities. Recognising the importance of ensuring the effectiveness of those who help students learn, Chapter 11 examines initial and ongoing training and development activities for university teachers, so they can be competent and current in their practices. The final chapter offers some conclusions on what really matters in higher education and how those of us who work in it can practise to good effect in a global community.

At the outset, therefore, I want to raise a number of questions about higher education pedagogical approaches and practices, and to unpack some of the assumptions that are currently made about how teaching and assessment are actually undertaken in universities in different nations, since unsurprisingly academics commonly assume that the dominant discourses in their own nations are the ones that prevail worldwide.

Do we currently have a global higher education environment?

Do we have, for example, shared concepts of pedagogy, compatible technologies for learning, comparable learning contexts, shared languages for learning and shared concepts of student support between nations? I would argue that we do not, and that gaining greater mutual understanding in these areas can be enormously helpful in supporting the recruitment and retention of international students and staff, in improving success rates and satisfaction scores, and in helping to make universities supportive learning communities.

Do we have shared concepts of pedagogy?

Table 1.1 aims to tease out some of the underlying perceptions we each have about pedagogies in our own nations. Consider what your answer would be to each of the questions: 'Yes. Of course, without hesitation, what's the problem'; 'It depends. Possibly'; 'No. Under no circumstances. It would be completely inappropriate'.

Discussion

There can be significant variations in approaches to teaching and learning based on cultural factors. These can, according to Ryan (2000), centre on the extent to which historical texts and previously accumulated knowledge

Table 1.1 International perceptions of pedagogy

	Would you as a lecturer/ academic tutor:	Yes	Possibly	No	Comments
1	Accept your final year student's invitation to his wedding?				Would this depend on how long you had taught the student? On how lavish the wedding is expected to be?
2	Encourage your students to interrupt and ask questions in your lecture?				In some nations, lectures are encouraged to be dialogic, but in others they are formal occasions with very large cohorts where interruptions are strongly discouraged.
3	Accept gifts from your students?				Would it depend on the size of the gift? The timing (e.g. not just before an assessment period? After graduation?) Does your university have a policy on this?
4	Encourage your students to pose opposing views to your own?				Would your response be the same in relation to seminars, lectures, tutorials, private conversations?
5	Let your students 'friend' you on Facebook?				This might depend on how you are using your own Facebook page and what privacy settings you have on it.
6	Follow your students on Twitter? Encourage your students to follow you on Twitter?				Might this depend on whether you have a Twitter account solely for academic/professional purposes?
7	Meet up with your students in a bar after classes?				If you said no, is the issue meeting outside class, or is it the location (a place where alcohol is served)?
8	Advise your student on how to use the university toilets?				One of the GPAs in this book mentions doing this, as does one of the authors quoted in this chapter
9	Help your students with graduate job applications? Will you write references for them?				Does your response depend on how long and how well you know them?
10	Provide detailed feedback and advice on draft assignments?				Does this depend upon the stage within the programme? Some academics comment extensively on first assignments. In some countries very detailed feedback on drafts is an expectation at all levels.

Would you as a lecturer/ academic tutor:		Yes	Possibly	No	Comments
11	Routinely spend an hour with your students after a lecture discussing queries?				In some cultures, academics are timetabled for at least an hour after lectures to clarify issues. In others, it's normal to speed from one lecture to another.
12	Ask your students to call you by your first name?				Whether you do or not will depend on cultural mores and the power distinction between academics and students.
13	Require your students to participate in assignments where they are assessed as members of a group?				In some nations this is uncommon or indeed frowned on.
14	Allow your students to negotiate the mark you are awarding them?				Might it be possible for students to convince you that they deserved a higher mark? Or is this completely out of the question?
15	Timetable exams on Friday afternoons, Saturdays or Sundays?				This might be problematic for students with devout religious convictions.

is respected and how much students are expected to have their own ideas, how far authority figures, including teachers, are respected (or not) and in particular, how far it is acceptable to be overtly critical of authoritative texts or figures, whether a 'correct' answer is sought, and the extent to which alternative responses are acceptable.

Cultural mores can impact on expectations of behaviour and thereby can impact on assessment. For example, 'Eastern, Latin American and some Caribbean cultures can deem it rude to make firm eye contact: while in the UK it is often thought rude not to' (Grace and Gravestock, 2009, p. 61). Maori students in New Zealand similarly retain close eye contact for personal relationships (or to frighten enemies). An insistence on the desirability of direct eye contact can be problematic where the assessment criteria for a presentation specifically mention it, which may be difficult for some students, including female students from cultures where eye contact with males is considered brazen.

Expectations around participation in **group work** can similarly pose problems, with some students being thrown by expectations to do so as part of assessed activities if they have no experience of it to date. Until recently in Denmark assessing students collectively in groups was illegal in higher education, due to government ministers' uncertainties about assessment. In some nations, group work is an expectation of students throughout school education, so nothing strange to encounter at university, but for students from other nations, it may be a first! Students from cultures where the genders are usually strictly segregated may find participating in mixed groups challenging initially.

Asking and answering questions: in many Western nations, there is often an atmosphere of 'give and take' in lectures, with questions and interruptions welcomed, but in some Eastern European nations, for example, to stop a lecturer in full flow for a query would be considered quite rude. There can be issues in cultures where staff are almost venerated and students are not prepared to ask questions in class or seek support, for fear of 'losing face' themselves or causing the teacher to 'lose face'. These divergences are not problematic so long as the local contextual 'rules' are shared, otherwise some students can be regarded as inappropriately forward and others as excessively passive.

Similarly, the extent to which students expect academics to find time to talk to them personally, live or electronically, can vary across cultures. Some universities in Pacific Rim nations provide substantially more one-to-one support than students might expect in the UK, for example, acting almost *in loco parentis* to help students do well, so their students might feel short changed when arriving to study in a nation where fees are high and overall expectations of support are lower.

Some nations provide substantially less support than is common in the UK. For example, in some higher education institutions (HEIs) in Italy, it is not uncommon for the (very low) fees to cover only mass lectures, with seminars and personal tutoring available as extras.

There is diversity in the extent to which **robust discussion** is valued, with students from some cultures preferring to focus on the importance of harmony and co-operation within the group rather than the interests of the individual within it (Ryan, op. cit.), and others where challenge is more highly valued.

Diverse assessment approaches

There are likely to be differences in emphasis on unseen time-constrained exams (which are fairly ubiquitous, but vary in length from one hour on the Indian subcontinent commonly to nine hours in Norway!), multiple-choice questions (widely used in the US and many Pacific Rim nations) and oral defences, vivas and presentations, which are much more common in Northern Europe and Scandinavia than in the UK. What is actually assessed is variable too, since some national contexts prize accurately demonstrating the learning of content above all other elements, whereas in others, use of that information in context is the prime expectation. As Beetham proposes:

> 'When the focus is on accuracy of reproduction, learners will be given opportunities to practise the required concept or skill until they can reproduce it exactly as taught. When the focus is on internalisation, learners will be given opportunities to integrate a concept or skill with their existing beliefs and capabilities, to reflect on what it means to them, and to make sense of it in a variety of ways.'
>
> Beetham, 2007, p. 33

Group assessment is strongly encouraged in nations where problem-based learning is commonplace and is frowned on or banned in others. (Denmark, as mentioned earlier, has only recently repealed a law preventing higher education students being assessed in groups.) Negotiation of marks is considered part of the process in some nations, but is completely unacceptable in others.

The timetabling of exams can be problematic for some students if they fall at times which are traditionally set aside for religious observances, as can setting multiple exams on the same day if this coincides with days of religious obligation. For example, in further northern and southern latitudes, if Ramadan falls in high summer, fasting can last many hours after dawn, leaving devout Muslim students potentially debilitated towards the later part of the day.

Diverse expectations concerning feedback

There can be significant differences in expectations internationally about the type, timing and purpose of feedback. There is considerable diversity in the explicitness of criteria and the amount of support students can expect if they are struggling with assessed work, with academics in some nations taking a much more intense personal interest in students' progression than in others.

In some nations, multiple assessment opportunities are provided, and students failing modules simply pick up credits elsewhere (as in Australia and New Zealand for example), which is not the case in other nations, such as the UK, which have much more hidebound regulations on progression issues.

Carroll and Ryan (2005) note common problems about students complying with assignment length regulations: in some nations word limits are merely advisory, but in others they are strictly adhered to, which can cause real problems. For some African students, for example, starting into the main body of the essay without a personal preamble is considered impolite, meaning they frequently go considerably over required assignment word limits, while other students whose first language is not English comment on the problem of writing first-year assignments of say 3,000–4,000 words when their previous writing assignments have been around 1,000 words.

The nature of the **personal relationships** between academic staff and students is hugely variable internationally, with much more formal interactions expected in some nations than others. Knowing what to call your teacher can be a tricky issue: in the UK and US it is not at all unusual to be invited to use a lecturer's given name, but many continental European professors would be alarmed if anyone addressed them with other than their full title. Staff–student friendships outside the university can be either encouraged or regarded as suspect depending on the national context, while staff dating adult students would be considered gross professional misconduct in some nations and is completely acceptable in others.

Gifts to teachers are seen as unproblematic in many cultures, and are actually an expectation in others, for example, Japan. However, in the UK, for example, gifts other than small souvenirs from home nations of items of food or confectionery that can be shared with fellow students are frowned on, and it is a customary requirement in many universities for gifts of any other than trivial value to be recorded in the Gift Book and only acceptable if deemed so by a senior manager. Misconceptions in this area can cause embarrassment on both sides, especially if presents are given immediately before assessment activities.

▶ Teaching approaches

Students moving from one country to another to study can expect different modes of curriculum delivery. The traditional lecture, delivered from behind a lectern or from a podium, with little interaction between the lecturer and students is much more common in some nations than others and students may find it difficult to readjust to new contexts. A similar diversity exists in the level of provision of support materials students can expect to receive, including handouts, electronic texts and postings within social learning environments, depending on where they are studying.

▶ Do we have shared learning and communication technologies?

This is patently not the case, since there are huge differentials between universities in terms of access not just to kit (mobile devices, laptops, PCs, reliable servers) but also to infrastructure (networks, broadband speeds, liberty to access social networks and so on) and expertise (some academics are much better enabled to support their students through digital and social media than others, for example). This is not just a matter of the wealthiest nations having more of all of these than the less advantaged, since a number of these issues are politically rather than exclusively economically determined. In terms of kit and infrastructure, the near ubiquity of mobile phones and mobile devices in nations without the infrastructure (and reliable power supply) effectively to support fixed IT devices has radically changed some of the assumptions formerly made about access to technology.

Next are some questions to help us consider the extent to which we can say we have shared learning technologies. All of these questions are offered without making value judgements about which is best (or at least aim to do so!):

- Do your students principally write with pens or keyboards? Do they read screens or paper books primarily? Do they physically carry assignments to you or submit electronically? Do your students write notes in lectures? Do you permit/encourage/ban audio/video recording of classes?
- Do students primarily 'access content' (see other chapters for discussion of the issues underlying this seemingly straightforward term) through face-to-face lectures, seminars, lab practicals, studio work, online, through technology-mediated discussions, via Open Access resources or Massive Open Online Courses (MOOCs)? Are these issues a matter for discussion among your complement of teachers?
- Do your classrooms make it possible for students to access and use the internet, or is Facebook, for example, seen as a distraction from learning and (perhaps futilely) banned?
- Do you permit/encourage the use of Twitter for academic purposes?
- Do you expect your students to bring their own prescribed IT equipment? Do you advocate Apple or Microsoft® or other suppliers? Do you give them laptops? Do you tell them to 'Bring Your Own Device' (BYOD)? Do you work across media and platforms to ensure everyone can access equivalent learning materials?

- Are your teaching staff qualified, enthusiastic advocates for using technology to support learning? Are they techno-tentatives? Refuseniks?
- Do you use an assessment management system across the university for alignment of assignments to learning outcomes, submission and return of work, recording and presentation to exam boards of marks? Or do you rely on hard copy approaches?
- Is communication to and between staff (plans, policies, developments, initiatives) mainly done face-to-face in meetings and committees, by telephone and voicemail, or paper-based memos and documents, or using email, departmental bulletin boards, text messages for important snippets of information, email attachments for longer documents, and so on?
- How do staff mostly contact students when necessary, and vice versa, about issues such as changes to class venues, cancellations, tutorial appointments, assignment briefings, deadlines, marks/grades, and other such information? By mail and paper-based memos and notes? At face-to-face group meetings? By individual one-to-one appointments? By notices on boards? By phone? By voicemail? By email? Using text messages? Using Twitter? Using bulletin boards on course or departmental web pages?

Do we have shared learning contexts?

It certainly is not the case that learning contexts are the same worldwide, although technological advances are whittling away at some of the differences. Class sizes can be highly variable, with lecture rooms holding over a thousand students very common in some nations (see, for example, the good practice account from Egypt in Chapter 4), whereas in others lecturers regard class sizes of over about 60 students as being unacceptable. The trend internationally is, however, strongly towards the massification of higher education: whereas formerly perhaps 5–10% of the age cohort might be expected to study at university, in many nations this exceeds 50%, moving it from a privilege of the elite to a benefit for the many. However, how that benefit is perceived varies from nations where higher education is regarded as a public good, with society benefiting from having a highly educated populace (and hence state-supported), to nations, such as England at the time of writing where higher education is seen principally as a private good leading to higher employability and thus ultimately to a financial lifelong advantage (and hence high fees being charged).

The series of questions in Table 1.2 (pp. 12–13) is designed to enable us to interrogate the extent to which aspects of the learning context which we might regard as 'normal' are actually not as ubiquitous as we might imagine. As students studying and staff teaching away from our home nations, we are likely to encounter, on occasions, learning situations very different from those we normally experience. The learning context in which you work is likely to cause you to tick items in either column and also to add modifying/qualifying comments like 'This applies to most universities in this country, but not all', 'It used to be like this until relatively recently', 'This is a situation that is currently changing rapidly' and so on. They are presented here as a way of thinking about different international learning contexts, but sometimes items from both columns may be found concurrently in a given context or nation.

Do we have shared languages for learning?

Even when people from nations who share a language (English or Spanish for example) discuss pedagogy, it is not always the case that the words they use mean the same things to them both. Contested terms I've come across in the English language which do not automatically translate to different parts of the English-speaking world include:

- **Assessment** and **evaluation**: in the UK, assessment means the marking and grading of student work and evaluation means the commentaries and the ratings and feedback about teaching given by students, for example, through course evaluations of the National Student Survey. In the US it is usually the other way round. This can cause confusion – for example, when I invited an expert on classroom assessment from the US to speak at a UK Assessment conference! In my experience, in Australia and New Zealand the way they use the terms tends to depend on which side of the Atlantic they use as their principal resource-base.
- **Compensation** in the UK implies the regulatory framework through which students who for reasons of illness or due to other causes miss or fail assignments and can remediate the problem by undertaking re-sit examinations or alternative tasks. It can also be implemented on rarer occasions when the student's overall work can be deemed to have demonstrated that they have achieved a standard that merits the award, and they are given an aegrotat (from the Latin s/he is ill), meaning an award may be given without further work if the student is deemed likely to

Table 1.2 Questions relating to international work contexts

Aspects	Do your students:	Or do they?
Curriculum	Study a generic curriculum at undergraduate level as at the University of Melbourne in Australia, where specialisms are pursued at post-graduate level, or undertake Liberal Arts programmes as is the case in many US institutions?	Specialise from the first year of study in higher education, e.g. Law, Medicine, English Literature?
Gender mix	Study in single-sex environments as in Saudi Arabia?	Study in mixed-gender environments as in Europe (although some subject areas e.g. Physics and Nursing may be taught in de facto single-sex groups where there are few applicants other than from the dominant gender)?
Inclusivity	Study where any disabled students are protected against discrimination on the grounds of disability, as with the UK Special Educational Needs and Disability Act?	Experience direct or indirect discrimination as was being challenged in Indonesia in 2014? (*THES*, 20–26 March 2014, p. 18).
Institutional size	Study in small higher education institutions (5,000 students or fewer)?	Or large ones (30,000+ students)?
Retention	Mostly drop out (retention of less than 50% of those who start undergraduate programmes)?	Mostly complete? Are your national attrition rates relatively low (less than 15%)?
Curriculum	Study curricula that are mandated at a national level?	Study curricula that are devised at an institutional level, with considerable local autonomy over issues like validation, quality assurance, integration with professional body requirements, nature and scope of assessments and so on?
Proportion entering higher education	Represent up to 50% of school leavers as in Ireland?	Represent a minority of the age cohort?
Financial arrangements	Study without fees for home students for undergraduate study as in Scotland? Get financial support for other expenses e.g. living costs, accommodation, travel from home?	Pay substantial fees for undergraduate study as in the US and England?

Qualifications of teaching staff	Experience (mainly) being taught by permanent senior academics including lecturers and professors?	Mainly experience being taught by Graduate Teaching Assistants, Doctoral Students, part-time and sessional teachers?
Training for teaching staff	Experience being taught by academics who are normally expected to have training in how to teach and/or accreditation and/or CPD expectations as in UK?	Study in an institution where there are no expectations of training or accreditation for university teachers, so long as they are appropriately qualified in their subject areas (e.g. Masters degree/Doctorate)?
Estate and services	Have on-site catering? If so, is it subsidised? Do they have social learning spaces in which to do group work and individual tasks informally? Are your lecture theatres comfortable and well equipped? Are your teaching rooms heated/air conditioned with enough seats for all students, good sight lines and audibility? Is the estate spacious and landscaped?	Study on a university estate offering basic learning facilities only?
Learning resources	Have to buy all their own books and learning materials, IT equipment and devices? Are they expected to BYOD (Bring Your Own Devices)?	Have access to an extensive and up-to-date library containing books and other resources? Do they have ready electronic access to texts and journals on site/at home? Do they have access to loan laptops?
Classroom equipment	Learn in classrooms which contain fairly basic equipment (blackboard, whiteboards etc.)? Is maintenance of equipment and spaces a low priority?	Learn in classrooms equipped with effective audio-visual devices (microphones, data projectors, personal response systems ('clickers'), audio loops for hearing impaired students, connection points for electronic devices for each student etc.)? Are laboratories and other specialist learning spaces including studios well equipped and well maintained?
Political context	Study on campuses which are frequently disrupted by civic disturbances, warfare and so on? Do your students (and staff) feel safe on campus and travelling there?	Study on normally undisrupted campuses, with a calm atmosphere of mutual tolerance?
Status of being a student	Regard being a student as a right, and see themselves as customers?	Regard being a student as a privilege?

have otherwise passed exams if not incapacitated. In at least one nation to my knowledge, compensation alternatively means the legitimate process by which students pay extra to progress from one level to another without passing the assessments, in recognition of the extra work teachers will need to do to bring them up to the required standard.

- **Faculty/staff/administration**: 'Faculty' in the UK is an organisational term to describe groups of subjects or departments, for example, The Faculty of Arts and Humanities, but in the US the term means academic teachers. The term 'instructor' is widely used in the US for staff who teach undergraduate students, but would not be used for academics in the UK, although it could perhaps be used to describe technicians who provide technical instruction. A Professor in the UK is a status only reached after extensive application processes, but the title 'Professor' is given to all senior academics in some nations. University *staff* in the UK tends to mean everyone employed by the university, but in the US it applies to people termed 'administrators' in the UK who support the roles of teachers through professional and clerical services. Those termed Administrators in the US would normally be called Senior Managers in the UK!
- **Direct translations** from one language to another can be confusing too. When working in Spain I once stopped a keynote I was giving to discuss the term that was being to translate the word 'feedback'. The first word used was 'correcciones' (literally, corrections), then 'retro-alimentations' (literally, being sick), then 'commentarios' (comments), none of which were entirely satisfactory to convey the formative function of feedback I was trying to describe. In the end, we fell back on the term 'feedback' with a gloss in Spanish.
- The term '**internationalising the curriculum**' in some universities means ensuring all students are exposed to a variety of experiences and topics within their studies so they can gain global perspectives. In other contexts it means working hard with non-home students to support them in understanding the learning context of the place where they are studying. Much of what is written about internationalising higher education focuses on how universities can maximise income by being welcoming to students who will come to universities paying high international fees. In many nations it can be seen by some as the answer to financial problems rather than an opportunity to enrich the learning environment. It is commonplace for some universities and university staff to regard international students as 'other' and problematic, and advice given to them may sometimes come across as paternalistic. In writing

about 'the welcome package' to be used when inducting international students Humfrey advises:

> 'Most problems occur when mores are misunderstood or their importance misinterpreted. An institution confident in its own concern and care for international students can talk to newcomers with insight, frankness and kindness about bathroom and toilet habits, and what is likely to give rise to friction and offence. It is just as important, but easier, to discuss for example, the British view on the use of 'please' and 'thank you' (they [British people] like frequent repetition of these words); the attitude to women in authority (it is the person, not the gender that matters); the approach to manual or catering staff (they are employees, not servants); the expectation on receiving a social invitation (reply and then stick to it); and the custom with regard to punctuality (lectures, appointments and meals begin on time unless otherwise stated).'
>
> Humfrey, 1999, pp. 89–90

It is important in my view that a university's response to international students concentrates on the benefits to staff and students of working in a cross-cultural context, rather than emphasising the negative aspects. As Leask argues:

> 'The international classroom requires teachers to be skilled managers of a complex teaching and learning environment. They must not only possess the abilities associated with "good teaching" but be efficient intercultural learners who use cultural diversity in the classroom as a learning resource.'
>
> Leask, 2007, p. 87

An internationalised curriculum implies more than simply tweaking elements of the taught content:

> 'The features of internationalised curricula reflect the varied rationales behind them: early and less developed models will focus exclusively on content, but more complex models encompass references to knowledge and skills, sometimes to behaviours and, where the rationale is values-based, to attitudes.'
>
> Jones and Killick, 2007, p. 112

Do we have shared concepts of student support?

It is more common in some nations than others to adopt a highly caring and nurturing approach to higher education students. In France and Italy, for example, students tend to be regarded as independent, autonomous adults, capable of making their own decisions on how much and how hard to study, and the principal contact students are likely to have with their lecturers will probably be in the lecture theatre. In many Asian nations, there is a different transactional relationship between teachers and students, with teachers adopting a higher level of responsibility for students' success. The role of parents is seen as more central to the transaction in Singapore, say, than it is in many European nations, where parents enquiring of university staff about the progress of their sons and daughters are likely to be referred to Data Protection legislation and told that student grades can only be supplied to the students themselves.

The availability of student support services like language support, crisis support, buddying/befriending, financial advice, counselling and so on is highly variable according to the national context.

Throughout this book I include good practice accounts that illustrate truly diverse international practice, sometimes surprising, often providing different perspectives on familiar areas and always thought-provoking. The account that follows provides a perspective on learning that some might find unfamiliar but which illustrates a holistic outlook on the learning experience.

Experiential learning and Yoga education

Priya M Vaidya, Department of Philosophy, University of Mumbai, India

Introduction

Pedagogic practices reveal the approach of a country towards development of education in general and the progress of individuals in particular. Global providers of higher education have advanced the scope and significance of progressive practice. This has helped learners to move beyond prejudice and to develop varied skills necessary for empowerment and employability. Access to all kinds of information has improved tremendously, acquainting learners with the dimensions of the external world and its materialistic framework. But it has hardly helped learners to become aware about the 'world within' or helped them be proactive in preventing erosion of basic human values in the society. Higher education in many countries has been guided by technological innovation but is rarely directed by cultural or moral dimensions.

Issues that concern holistic development of individuals, including physical, mental, emotional, social and spiritual factors, are barely addressed within higher education curricula. The potential to nurture peaceful co-existence is not normally integrated within higher education teaching.

Consequently, it is currently important to collate experiential best practice in universities to establish self-empowerment to bring about progress, peace and prosperity. It is essential to reflect upon aspects of higher education which emphasise the transformative dimensions of education, going well beyond simple dissemination of information. The basis of such transformative education is unique to the culture of each country.

Yoga education as a pedagogic practice in India

Aspects of Indian culture are reflected in the core contents of the subject matter of schools of Indian philosophy where the spiritual framework of Indian philosophy is the hallmark, together with a broad theoretical base and high pragmatic relevance. Indian philosophies have guided the people of India for the last five thousand years in direct and indirect ways. Philosophical elements of Yoga, which is practised today not only by the people of India but also widely internationally, underpin Indian transformative frameworks.

The philosophy of Yoga is a complete way of living. For centuries, it has made a significant contribution to humanity through its method of physical, mental, intellectual, emotional and spiritual development. It has retained its relevance and has proven its usefulness in the modern life.

Yoga has passed the test of thousands of years of trials of intellectual research by many great sages and saints who have actually lived, practised and refined it. Recently, researchers in psychiatry at Harvard Medical School, led by John Denninger, reported that they are coming close to demonstrating that Yoga and meditation can prevent stress and disease. A five-year study on how these ancient mind-body techniques affect genes and brain activity in the chronically stressed provides some evidence of their value (*Times of India*, 2013).

Transformative education can be illuminated through the study and practice of Yoga. Holistic development of the individual is possible due to constant and consistent practice of Yoga, which includes mastery over maintaining some physical postures for fitness, following breathing exercises, meditative practices and of course practising ethical and moral norms to lead a positive life. Its experiential essence and value-based approach has tremendously benefitted learners to be better human beings and peace-loving global citizens.

continued overleaf

Experiential learning and Yoga education *continued*

Effective pedagogic practice

Yoga education is promoted in some schools and colleges as well as universities in India and is also practised daily by ordinary people. It has wonderful effects on the body, emotions, intellect and psychological makeup. It can open up channels of creativity essential for nurturing basic human values. Modern research in the field of education has laid emphasis on the training of the mind. Methodology in learning based on Yoga practices should be taught not only to teachers but also to students. For instance, it is through study and understanding of Yoga that self-knowledge is possible. Silence in classrooms can have pedagogical impact. It enhances learning and meaningful living. Several techniques based on the philosophy of Yoga to enhance body–mind awareness are regularly practised by many learners.

The Department of Philosophy at the University of Mumbai has for many years received excellent responses to its different post-graduate and undergraduate level Yoga study programmes. Its certificate and diploma programmes are found to be extremely beneficial to professionals, home-makers and students who do not have a background of academic study of philosophy. It has brought people with diverse backgrounds together to experience unique aspects of transformative education and the enhancement of the quality of their lives. Yoga education can be incorporated as an important aspect of transformative education in different universities. Establishment of Yoga study centres can help teachers and students to learn and practise techniques to be healthy, happy and members of a peace-loving world community, and this will be relevant not only for a few decades but for centuries ahead.

References

Times of India (2013) 'Harvard scientists have proof yoga, meditation work', *Times of India*, Mumbai, 24 November, p. 17. Available at http://timesofindia.indiatimes.com/home/science/Harvard-scientists-have-proof-yoga-meditation-work/articleshow/26288574.cms (accessed 23 May 2014).

Conclusions

Working in a global context as university teachers and senior managers, we need to familiarise ourselves with diverse expectations and practices in relation to assessment, learning and teaching if we are to offer a truly internationalised environment within the global context, one in which students can choose to study wherever they like, at least virtually if not *in situ*. The more we can share perspectives about the purposes and expectations of higher education teaching, learning and assessment, the greater the likelihood there will be that staff and students can avoid misapprehensions and unpleasant surprises while teaching and studying. Learning more about international higher education practices and context is likely to illuminate and enhance our own practices, hence the aspiration of this book to open up discussion of pedagogic practices across six continents. Collecting and sharing good practice from around the world has been highly enjoyable and illuminating for me, and I trust this will be the case for users of this text also.

2 Changing paradigms underpinning higher education learning internationally

Introduction

Promoting effective student learning in higher education is often spoken about as if it is a straightforward and unproblematic matter, but those concerned with doing so find that this is clearly not the case. Students have lives beyond the learning context, and we discount this at our peril. As Jean Lave argues:

> 'Traditionally, learning researchers have studied learning as if it were a process contained in the mind of the learner and have ignored the lived-in world'
>
> Lave, 2009, p. 202

For many years, Kolb's view has held sway, that '[l]earning is the process whereby knowledge is created through the transformation of experience' (Kolb, 1984, p. 38), and in 1987 Jarvis described his understanding of learning as 'the transformation of experience into knowledge, skills and attitudes' (Jarvis, 1987, p. 3). More recently, he further encapsulated his perspectives on learning as follows:

> 'Human learning is the combination of processes throughout a lifetime whereby the whole person – body (genetic, physical and biological) and mind (knowledge, skills, attitudes, values, emotions, beliefs and senses) – experiences social situations, the perceived content of which is then transformed cognitively, emotively or practically (or through any combination) and integrated into the individual person's biography resulting in a continually changing (or more experienced) person.'
>
> Jarvis, 2009, p. 25

It is the nature of these multiple transformations and how we as educators can best bring them about that is the focus of this chapter.

Designing for 21st century learning

Post-millennial technologies have indubitably changed the nature of pedagogy, since learning contexts nowadays encompass a wide variety of electronic and mobile technologies alongside traditional hard copy media including books, lecture notes, handouts, blackboards and other resources. Incidentally, I am with Beetham and Sharpe (2013, p. 1) in using 'pedagogy' throughout this book to describe activities focused on promoting learning, rather than andragogy (with its male connotations) or gynogogy (which just sounds silly!). As they argue, 'pedagogy embraces an essential dialogue between teaching and learning' (op. cit., p. 2) which is more helpful than setting the two terms in opposition to one another.

The diversity and ubiquity of social and digital media are changing the nature of interactions between learners and curriculum content, with a greater emphasis on *learning how* and *learning why* than on *learning what*. While content remains important, in many subjects where material dates fast, the ability of graduate practitioners to access up-to-date information on which to make informed decisions and to take appropriate action (for example, in medical practice, where research can change appropriate prescriptions and drug dosages over a matter of months), alongside the ability to filter and prioritise data, become as important as retention of a basic knowledge base. Pedagogies need to take this into account if they are to remain relevant.

In the past, the concept of instructional design underpinned much computer-based design in the early days, requiring competence to be systematically built from simpler skills and knowledge into progressively more complex and advanced capabilities and understanding. Although many will argue instructional design is an excellent basis for skills training, this approach seems less relevant today, when learning is not so much linear as acquired through multiple sources including the web and can be self-constructed, eclectic, haphazard, and serendipitous. Arguably, Biggs' emphasis on constructive alignment (Biggs, 2003b) is more helpful for 21st century learning, since he argues that we should be aiming to align (constructively!) what we reckon the students need to know or do at the end of a programme of learning, with the content we deliver, the pedagogies we use, the ways in which we assess their learning and how we evaluate our own teaching.

The available technologies don't change the essential processes of learning, but potentially alter the opportunities for engagement with them. Mayes and de Freitas describe effective learning as combining associationist approaches, which model learning as the gradual building of associations and skill components, with cognitive perspectives, using learners' attention, memory and concept formation processes, and situative perspectives, involving influences from social and cultural settings (Mayes and de Freitas, 2013). They suggest that:

> 'As technology-enhanced learning tools become truly powerful in their capability, and global in their scope, so it becomes more feasible to remodel the educational enterprise as a process of empowering learners to take reflective control of their own learning.'
>
> Mayes and de Freitas, 2013, p. 28

The key strengths of the currently available technologies, I would suggest, are that they:

- Enable learners to access huge volumes of information without requiring intermediaries to locate and interpret it for them, as was formerly the case when academics had privileged ready access to books and libraries, and had advanced expertise in using canonical knowledge to inform their lectures.
- Remove time barriers and drudgery from the task of accessing data. Whereas in the past those seeking to locate and make connections between academic texts often had to wait to physically find and use books and papers through citation indices, inter-library loans and the like, learners with access to the internet through fixed or mobile devices can undertake tasks in moments that took weeks or months in previous eras.
- Provide occasions for networking with others that can span national, geographic and intellectual boundaries.
- Offer peer-to-peer learning opportunities, so information-sharing and peer critique can occur at a local and global level.
- Reduce barriers for students with disabilities to learn and interact with one another. Technologies can allow students with visual impairments or dyslexia, for example, to access texts in alternative formats on their own devices, without waiting as in the past for others to supply Braille books or audio recordings. Students with mobility or confidence issues, or those with caring commitments, similarly can participate in classes without physically attending a particular building at a particular time.
- Potentially democratise learning, so that students with financial constraints can freely access Open Educational Resources and Massive Open Online Courses.

Making learning happen in universities

Educators supporting learning with tertiary-stage students in most nations are normally working with adults over the age of 18 whose day-to-day lives offer multiple occasions through which they can encounter experiences which lead to learning (particularly nowadays when technologies can ubiquitously provide data and information at the touch of a finger).

Lave proposes that:

> 'It is difficult, when looking closely at everyday activity, to avoid the conclusion that learning is ubiquitous in ongoing activity, though often unrecognised as such. Situated activity always involves changes in knowledge and action and "changes in knowledge and action" are central to what we mean by learning.'
>
> Lave, 2009, p. 201

It is a mistake, however, to expect that learning necessarily occurs without active agency, engagement with others and supportive guidance. Robert Kegan advises:

> 'Adult learners are not all automatically self-directing merely by virtue of being adults, or even easily trained to become so. Educators seeking self-direction for their adult students are not merely asking them to take on new skills, modify their learning style, or increase their self-confidence. They are asking many of them to change the whole way they understand themselves, their world, and the relationship between the two.'
>
> Kegan, 2009, p. 51

Such changes occur not just to the ways that learners act but also to the ways they think and how they construct their worldviews.

> 'Genuinely transformational learning is always to some extent an epistemological change rather than just a change in behavioural repertoire or an increase in the quantity or fund of knowledge.'
>
> Kegan, 2009, p. 41

He further suggests that learners are likely not only to be facing technical challenges that might be termed informative learning, but 'adaptive challenges, the kind that require not merely knowing more but knowing differently' (Kegan, op. cit., p. 49).

Making learning happen is a complex and highly nuanced process, Race argues, which takes time and agency to occur:

> 'We learn by doing – practice, repetition, trial and error. We reduce the vast sea of information down to manageable proportions – summarizing it. We try to get feedback on how our learning is going. We gradually digest and make sense of the information. We test our learning by communicating it – explaining things to others, having a go at teaching it.'
>
> Race, 2014, pp. 47–8

Knowledge, Lave (op. cit.) argues, is not static since 'knowledgeability' is routinely in a state of change. Knowledge always undergoes transformation in use, as learners transform and are transformed by it. How knowledge becomes internalised, providing scholarly structures on which to base practice, requires from learners considerable intellectual effort combined with reframing of perceptions, as she suggests:

> 'Acquisition of knowledge is not a simple matter of taking in knowledge; rather, things assumed to be natural categories such as bodies of knowledge, learners and cultural transmission, require reconceptualisation as cultural, social products.'
>
> Lave, 2009, p. 203

Throughout the remainder of this chapter, I will explore how we as educators can foster learning that is student-centred and dynamic, leading to changes not only to students' grasp of significant amounts of information, but also to the ways in which they are able to use and apply it through scholarship and practice.

▶ Learning to think in the 21st century

Traditional transmissive models of knowledge acquisition placed less emphasis on encouraging students to think about and apply their learning and more on taking as given curriculum content provided by their lecturers with the purpose of getting to grips with it and using it within assessed assignments and exams. Entwistle warns of the danger of such approaches since:

> 'Relying too much on the teacher's understanding may leave the student without a fully functional personal understanding, being able to pass exams by mimicking the lecturer's understanding, but not able to use it in other situations.'
>
> Entwistle, 2009, p. 50

Unsurprisingly, students on occasions adopt what Kneale (1997) and others term 'strategic' approaches to where they place their efforts, making judgements about how much energy to invest in various learning activities, seeking always for high pay-off from what they do. However, being strategic, Race argues, is at times a valid study approach choice:

> 'We could regard [strategic learning] as making informed choices about when to be a deep learner, and when to be a surface learner. It could be viewed as investing more in what is important to learn, and less in what is less important to learn. It could be regarded as setting out towards a chosen level of achievement, and working systematically to become able to demonstrate that level of achievement in each contributing assessment element. It can also be argued that those learners who go far are the strategic ones, rather than the deep ones. It can be argued that they know *when* to adopt a deep approach, and when it is sufficient to adopt a surface approach.'
>
> Race, 2015

Race (2015) argues for learners to be doing and not just receiving, to be active learners who co-create learning through engagement and interaction with content, and particularly through appropriate and fit-for-purpose assessment (see Chapter 7).

Despite what we know, transmissive teaching approaches still remain dominant in many institutions today, often for reasons that have little to do with promoting effective learning, including:

- The existence within most universities' estates of large rooms, designed to accommodate this mode of teaching, which adapt poorly to more discursive modes of learning, particularly when these take the form of raked lecture theatres with fixed rows of teaching in which students are penned immovably for the duration of the lecture. These are normally designed to maximise sight lines for the students looking at the lecturer and to enable students to hear what the lecturer says rather than vice versa.
- Rigidity in the working methods of those who run timetabling within a university and rely on fixed blocks of time (often an hour) and fixed delivery frequencies (e.g. once a week, once a fortnight). Block delivery, immersive learning, blended experiences and so on are all very difficult to timetable and so sometimes get blocked.
- A static and seemingly immovable academic timetable (at least in the UK) that requires students to start their studies at fixed points in the year,

for assessments to take place within examination periods, and that make activities like field trips outside term/semester time problematic.

- The existence within some academics' minds of similarly fixed models of learning, based on how they themselves were taught. Some academics really relish the control a lecture theatre gives them over students who are required to listen to what they are saying, and some don't have the confidence to relinquish this power.
- The existence within some university managers' minds of a risk-averse view of curriculum delivery that enables them to feel confident that, as long as material is covered in lectures, they will not be open to charges of having failed to teach students what they need to know.

These fixed concepts and structures are nowadays counterbalanced by movements that include:

- Desires by academics and others to be more student-centred and to enable students to negotiate their own fluid pathways through learning programmes.
- The changing nature of the relationship between students and the universities in which they study, with students expecting (and requiring) more individual control over what and how they are studying, especially in nations where full-cost fees are paid.
- Movements by senior managers to harness free resources including open educational resources, TED talks and what is offered by Massive Open Online Courses (and variants of these), sometimes for good pedagogic reasons and sometimes for more nefarious ones, including what is often termed 'driving down the unit of resource', i.e. using fewer academics to teach more students more cost effectively.
- A recognition by educational developers and others that what worked in a pre-digital age just isn't enough at a time when accessing content is easier than ever before, but selecting relevant, appropriate and trustworthy content is a much tougher proposition altogether.
- Student expectations that multi-tasking and concurrent activities support learning, so that learning experiences can involve multiple facets, with students using digital and social media while in classrooms, studios and labs, and interacting with academics, externals and one another virtually at the same time as undertaking tasks overseen by their teachers.

So we are looking for ways to encourage an approach to teaching and learning that helps students to:

- Develop the knowledge, skills and values that they are likely to need to be productive, engaged and erudite citizens who make informed choices.

- Be able to make sensible judgements with incomplete information.
- Research reliable, current and useful information just in time to help solve problems and reach conclusions.
- Work in productive teams with fellow citizens without rancour, envy or excessive conflict.

I would argue that this requires a non-traditional approach to curriculum design based on some key principles which could include:

- Active involvement of students in the meaningful co-production of knowledge: this is likely to include, for example, students undertaking research within their undergraduate as well as post-graduate courses, allowing them to work with real data and apply theory to practice rather than being involved in formulaic prescribed laboratory tasks and multiple repetitive essay and report writing.
- Learning activities that involve not just encountering a body of information from a single canonical source, but seeking out, selecting and justifying the use of a range of outputs personally sought and used.
- Providing safe opportunities for open dialogue, debate and questioning (live and virtual) which promote open rather than closed thinking, and disruptive rather than passive learning, which nevertheless make space for multiple voices to be heard, rather than allowing single discourses to dominate.
- A measure of autonomy that might, for example, involve choices about modes of learning (face-to-face, online, blended...), subjects of study (including special interests and closely focused studies...), methods of assessment (by unseen time-constrained examination, oral defences, portfolios...) and choice of pace of learning and accreditation, with flexibility on duration of programmes of learning that permit accelerated or slow-paced accumulation of credit.
- A commitment that, although much learning is undertaken individually and in private, university learning requires an element of peer engagement, peer support and potentially peer assessment.
- Recognition that, in a global age, learning needs to encompass cross-cultural perspectives, with content, contexts and examples derived from multiple nations, rather than tied to a single system.

What counts as a 'traditional' approach' varies from context to context, but a global trend is a movement from perceiving the university teacher as an all-knowing, unchallengeable authority figure. The good practice account that follows describes challenging this concept in what many regard as quite a traditional setting.

Challenging the paradigm of the 'guru' in Bangladesh

Jahirul Haque, University of Liberal Arts Bangladesh (ULAB), Bangladesh, **Carolyn Roberts**, University of Oxford, UK and **Brian Shoesmith**, ULAB, Bangladesh

Background

Traditional teaching in many Bangladeshi higher education institutions is based on a highly respected teacher (the 'guru') imparting their experience to their followers, with only limited acknowledgement of the talents and creativity of the students, or their latent ability to explore for themselves and to offer insights for wider discussion. Over the years, concern has risen that modern Bangladesh is ill-served by an ossified system encouraging rote learning, non-creativity and undue passivity among its students, whereas contemporary challenges require collaboration, proactivity, and communication skills, alongside specialist knowledge of rapidly changing fields of study.

Transition into higher education

Faced with the demands of compulsory attendance for a rapidly growing but overwhelmingly poor population, and only limited numbers of trained teachers, school education has evolved from a system essentially established for a privileged minority during colonial times, into a more modern system where emphasis is placed on examination success for the majority. Although school drop-out rates remain high, particularly for girls, a series of government and NGO-backed support programmes has achieved some remarkable outcomes, and the numbers of successful Higher Secondary School candidates grew exponentially until 2013 when a sudden decline prompted much soul-searching in the local media. Recent debate has focused on whether, in the interests of fairness, there should be a return to questions requiring stronger reliance on recall, rather than more 'creative' questions. Many Bangladeshi students currently enter universities lacking the skills required for more active or exploratory styles of learning, and most institutions continue to utilise traditional, conservative teaching methods of set texts, dictation of notes, and testing. However a minority, mainly Dhaka-based private sector universities, have sought to create an environment in which students discuss ideas, undertake research and manage projects with external stakeholders as they learn.

The University of Liberal Arts Bangladesh (ULAB) is probably unique in Bangladesh in attempting an institutional-level shift in emphasis by developing a set of policies and activities that have enabled staff and students to experiment with their learning methodologies, and to draw on experience of active learning amongst their colleagues and internationally. From the student's perspective, their first challenge is to make the transition from one 'learning' model to another, which some find easy, while others struggle. The University offers an orientation programme in which students are not only introduced to the concept of Liberal Arts and provided with basic information about the course structure and its administration, but crucially are engaged with the institutional expectations of them as learners. Sessions are interspersed with games designed to encourage participation and communication, mingling groups of people from disparate backgrounds, and concluding with a celebratory concert. Most ULAB students live at home, so in future a session for parents and guardians is to be included, since in Bangladesh they remain a major influence on students' learning activities. Orientation includes a number of other university-wide activities designed to engage the student, encourage self-confidence and collaboration, and motivate them to take leadership roles. Particular emphasis is placed on co-curricular 'Club' activities where students can explore their interests beyond the formal curriculum, from adventure, to drama, to social welfare and Bengali culture.

In formal curricula, active learning has been adopted in a planned and systematic way, driven by policies and rewards established by the University's senior management team. Each year, local and overseas experts facilitate workshops designed to foster staff understanding of active learning techniques. Individually the workshops have varied in impact, but cumulatively over six years they have had a major influence on the way staff conceptualise student learning. The active learning concept is now firmly embedded into the ethos of the University and widely practised, with new staff receiving an appropriate induction, and mentoring from active learning practitioners.

Individual schools and departments have tailored their approach to active learning. Media Studies and Journalism, for example, has adopted an integrated curriculum where a theme for the term is agreed and individual courses find ways of exploring it. Different undergraduate classes adopt various aspects of the agreed theme and build it into their syllabus. Thus the Photography classes will take photographs around the theme, Public Relations will develop a campaign to advertise the topic, Journalism students will write related articles and so on. The activities are then drawn together in department-wide exhibitions of students' work.

The General Education Department (GED) has adopted a different approach, with a series of core 'survey courses', such as 'World History Since 1500' or 'Approaches to Sustainability'. Staff teams, again an unusual concept for Bangladeshi universities, design the courses and completed sections are then co-ordinated. Teaching packages including video, sound, stills, written excerpts and poetry, have been shared amongst colleagues. ULAB mandates that all students study GED courses irrespective of their major discipline area. The highly interactive approach taken to teaching is one of the key reasons for its growing popularity. Active learning has become central to the modes of delivery, and tutors include role-playing, field trips, guest speakers, model-making and debates. Engineers and computer scientists sometimes complain, but on the whole students express satisfaction with the courses studied and there is heavy demand for a minor in GED to be included in the programme.

continued overleaf

Challenging the paradigm of the 'guru' in Bangladesh *continued*

The problems for staff and students in working together are compounded by political and civil unrest, in which political parties resort to *hartals* (general strikes), which cause havoc with the timetable and class scheduling, and 75% of classes can be lost. *Hartals* are dangerous times and lives are frequently lost to violent action. ULAB cannot demand that its staff and students attend during *hartals*, as it is deemed too dangerous to be on the streets or to take public transport. Consequently the University has developed a comprehensive rescheduling strategy with catch-up classes conducted on every available free day, including weekends.

It is challenging to undo a national tradition in a short period of time, but ULAB seems to be succeeding. The termly student course evaluations overwhelmingly favour courses that have adopted active learning techniques, whilst those retaining predominantly traditional methods of tuition have declined in popularity. The staff feedback has also been exceptionally positive; most have experienced the active learning workshops and view the new collaborative approach as a practical application of the concept, although recognising that it has required effort and patience across the University. ULAB is committed to developing active learning further, through researching and fashioning the approach in a way specific to the Bangladeshi local and global context.

Conclusions

Enabling students to have a transformative experience of higher education is not a simple matter of applying theoretical approaches to practical contexts (although as some argue, there is nothing more practical than a good theory). However, as Stewart posits, well thought-through theoretical perspectives over the years have provided us with a contested but nevertheless sound scholarly basis on which to make informed choices about how and what we teach, as well as through which media. He suggests:

> 'Theories of learning arise from multiple disciplines: philosophy of education, psychology, pedagogic studies, sociology and more recently neuroscience. This variety of feeder disciplines provides a rich understanding of learning. It also presents us with a complex evidence base and mix of interpretations with contrasting vocabularies and epistemologies that lead to debate and controversy.'
>
> Stewart, 2012, p. 3

This rich mix, together with considerable evidence-informed research over at least four decades across the globe, provides university teachers with good ideas about what kinds of practices can really help university students to learn in a complex and fast-changing pedagogic environment. The good practice accounts in this book exemplify the application of considered thinking to assuring and enhancing the quality of teaching. Throughout the following chapters I aim to demonstrate how flexible and fit-for-purpose approaches can be implemented to maximise the positive impact on student learning.

3 Designing, managing, reviewing and refreshing your curriculum

Introduction

Although in some nations curriculum design is determined at national or state level, in many countries, academic teams working with administrative staff in universities are responsible for all aspects of the curriculum, including:

- choosing what is to be taught, how it is to be delivered;
- how it is to be assessed;
- assuring the quality of the curriculum by ensuring that programmes align with the requirements of professional, subject and regulatory bodies (PSRBs);
- taking programmes through accreditation and validation;
- ensuring the quality assurance and enhancement of the programme, including responding to external scrutiny (by external examiners and others) and internal review (including student evaluations).

This is no small task (or set of tasks) and this chapter offers some suggestions to those charged with doing this well.

Designing the curriculum

Conventionally nowadays, curriculum designers, having chosen the broad area of study, tend to start from deciding what the students need to be able to do and to know by the end of the programme and to constructively align it (Biggs and Tang, 2011). This means that there should be clear links between intended learning outcomes, evidence of achievement, assessment criteria and provision of feedback to students. This alignment is likely to be sought internally and externally in the validation of your programme, and will help it to be recognised as excellent by internal and external scrutineers.

Choosing what is to be taught

When designing the curriculum content, it's worth considering the purposes, the make-up and scope of the material being taught, as discussed below.

The **purposes** of the curriculum content you are delivering can include, for example, raising awareness of particular issues, providing an overview, getting students excited about a topic, prompting deep engagement with the material, putting forward contrasting viewpoints, adding colour to dull detail, explaining difficult concepts, enthusing students with a passion for the subject, giving students data they need to undertake a task and so on, as well as giving them things to learn so they can pass exams.

The **make-up** of the content you are teaching is likely to be a matter of lively debate among curriculum designers, since there may well be differing points of view between teaching staff about the prominence their own specialisms will play in each year of the programme, and the final outcomes may depend as much on internal power plays and institutional politics as on pedagogic concerns. Financial issues may also play a part, with off-the-shelf existing components sometimes included because they are ready-made and cheap to run, as may be the case with some big elements of Business Studies or Liberal Arts degrees.

The **scope** and **extent** of the content you are delivering also need careful consideration, as does the way it is ordered so that students can make sense of disparate elements and recognise the coherence of what they are learning. All are critical to effective learning. Many would argue for a progressive, iterative approach where big ideas and difficult concepts are introduced gradually, although in a poorly aligned curriculum where separate modules or programmes are delivered by separate academics who don't communicate with one another, this is often not the case.

Meyer and Land (2003) describe what they term '**threshold concepts**' as being core elements within subject areas which students need to be able to make sense of and with which they must engage meaningfully if they are ever to be able to really progress in that subject area. They suggest that in certain disciplines there are 'conceptual gateways' or 'portals' that lead to previously inaccessible and, initially perhaps, 'troublesome' ways of thinking about something. A new way of understanding, interpreting, or viewing something may thus emerge leading to a transformed internal view of subject matter, subject landscape, or even world view. In attempting to characterise such conceptual gateways Meyer and Land suggested that they may be transformative (occasioning a significant shift in the perception of a subject), irreversible (unlikely to be forgotten, or unlearned only through considerable effort) and integrative (exposing the previously hidden interrelatedness of something). Effective curriculum designers are likely to want to think through what particular threshold concepts and troublesome ways of thinking need to be incorporated into learning programmes, and how best to make them accessible to students.

Once decisions have been made about what to teach, the logical next step is to think through the rationale for the programme by asking such questions as:

- Is there a novel and really exciting curriculum area that will form the basis of the programme? Are you simply emulating more successful institutions, and if so, what would be the features that will attract students to study this with you?
- Is there a need for you to offer this area of study in your university, and is there market evidence for this? What market gap are you aiming to fill? Have you done the calculations to check that running this programme will be cost effective within a reasonable period (say five years) taking into account any specialist equipment or text purchases needed, staff appointments and adaptations to the physical and virtual campus? Who are your competition, both in your own nation and internationally (who may be offering a similar course online or by distance learning)? Why is your programme potentially better than theirs?
- Is there evidence of student demand in the curriculum area? Are there enough students at this level who are likely to want to study your programme? Have you checked out how attractive courses offered by competitors are and how well they recruit?
- Is there an employer-led need which requires fulfilling to support workforce planning and to help your students become employable graduates?
- Is there a university strategic imperative which you wish to address? Will this programme enhance the university's curriculum offer? What calculations do your university managers use in order to deem the viability or otherwise of programmes?

If there are affirmative answers to most of these questions, it is probably worth proceeding to the planning stage, at which the following checklist may be helpful.

Creative curriculum design: a checklist

1. Check out at a very early stage any PSRB requirements that may impact on your curriculum design. Some, for example, specify that they

will only accredit programmes if students recruited are sufficiently well qualified at entry (for example, engineering bodies in the UK). Others direct the numbers of hours of teaching that must be delivered, or whether a placement is to be included. Commonly the types of assessment to be included are specified (e.g. unseen time-constrained written exams, presentations, computer-based multiple-choice questions and so on), and sometimes the duration or word-counts of assessments. However, don't always assume that PSRBs will put blocks in the way of innovations: it's important to inform them at an early stage of your plans, discuss any controversial issues, negotiate where there are conflicting views and compromise as necessary to develop a curriculum that works well for all stakeholders.

2. Cross-check national quality assurance requirements. For example, in the UK the Quality Assurance Agency (QAA) requires programmes to take into account sector-agreed threshold standards and benchmark statements available on the QAA website. These provide guidance on standards required.
3. In some nations, there is an expectation that students be engaged in discussion of all aspects of curriculum design, delivery and quality assurance. It's worth cherishing students as they can give you perspectives on the curriculum as it is to be experienced from a learner's point of view.
4. It's a good idea to scope out what others are doing before starting as if with a blank sheet of paper. You can perhaps collaborate with fellow designers, both those in other universities in your own country or others in the same subject area, who may be solving very similar issues to those you are addressing, and curriculum designers in other subjects in your own university, who may be more experienced in negotiating institutional requirements than you are. Where it is possible, 'buddying' with someone at the same stage as yourself in curriculum design can be reassuring and helpful.
5. Conserve candidly the best elements of other programmes in similar or identical fields that have been run previously within your university. Are there elements that are worth retaining (without sentimental over-attachment to favourite elements)?
6. Cherry-pick the most appropriate people to act as validators, critical friends and, where used, external examiners for your new programme. It is worth taking your time to pick people who really understand your subject area and context, and talking through complex issues with them in advance of finalising their agreement to work with you.

7. Create virtual spaces to provide a repository and discussion space for the curriculum design process, so you can be sure that you are working with the most recent versions of documents and can check off institutional and PSRB requirements. There are software companies that can supply systems to help you with this, for example Taskstream and LiveText.
8. Charge others with tasks as part of the curriculum design journey: this isn't a task to be undertaken by a lone hero, you need to delegate activities and use critical friends throughout the process.
9. Communicate your plans to your colleagues and institutional managers: it can be heart-breaking to get to an advanced stage of curriculum design only to find that for political or strategic reasons your managers or your university don't want to proceed with them.
10. Capture the comments of people who are giving feedback on the design of your curriculum, particularly, for example, external examiners whose comments welcoming particular developments can be very helpful in leading to the acceptance of your curriculum by PSRBs.

Further guidance is provided in the good practice account opposite.

How will the topic be taught?

The means by which content is delivered is often less discussed than the content itself. The default position in many nations is a series of large group lectures supported by smaller group seminars, tutorials, problem classes, lab classes and studio work. The size of both the large and small classes varies from nation to nation (in some places 60 is considered a large group for a lecture, in others 1,000 is not unusual and seminars can have fewer than ten or more than 40 students in them and still bear the name). Alternatively, commonly nowadays there is an assumption that much content will be delivered online even for campus-based students, reframing the curriculum building blocks into new forms of interaction where plenary sessions are used for discussion, problem-solving, tasks and activities. Whatever decisions are made, it makes sense to map out the student experience over the duration of the programme, asking ourselves about:

- The **pace** of activities students are experiencing: it should be enough to keep students busy and engaged, but not so much as to be overwhelming. It should take into account that some students work faster than others, so differentiated tasks can be provided. For example, directed reading could include texts that must be read by all students, with extra reading offered as extension tasks for those working faster.

Holistic course design at Leeds Metropolitan University

Belinda Cooke, Sue Smith, Pauline Fitzgerald, Catherine Coates, Justine Simpson, Steve Jones, Simon Thomson, Stephanie Jameson and **Ruth Pickford**, Leeds Metropolitan University, UK

This good practice account describes how modular courses are designed holistically in a large UK university to foster integrated, deep learning.

Holistic course design

Undergraduate courses at our university are generally split into modules. However, we are working to ensure that each course is designed as a whole, engendering a strong course identity, and has embedded within it the development of graduate attributes and professional skills. Learning outcomes are designed to support and align learning across and between levels. A course-level assessment strategy ensures that assessments encourage development throughout the course, giving students an opportunity to build on feedback. The curriculum is viewed as a whole and the course team work together to design programme-level outcomes. Courses are, where possible, designed to support synoptic learning and assessment across modules. Teams of academics, administrators and students meet regularly to discuss the student experience, and review meetings are reported formally as part of an integrated quality enhancement and quality assurance process.

Effective practice

The students' learning experiences are progressive and developmental. Courses are purposefully designed to facilitate integrated learning across modules. This is supported by effective team communication, and by individual teachers adopting a genuine interdisciplinary approach to their teaching. This emphasises application in real-world contexts. In addition, our university has three clearly articulated graduate attributes (digital literacy, enterprise, global outlook) which we require our students to develop and which are integrated into each course, and a series of curriculum design principles underpin inter-module coherence, integration and curricular alignment. In parallel, these principles and attributes also have the flexibility to accommodate diverse student needs from enrolment right through to graduation, by which students are able to pursue their lifelong aspirations and identify and work on their learning needs.

Challenges

Competing priorities between the Course Leader and Module Tutor may require debate and negotiation. For example, potential conflicts can arise between time dedicated to learning of subject specific content and that focused on the development of broader transferable skills. Difficulties may also be experienced in mapping graduate attributes and employability

continued overleaf

Holistic course design at Leeds Metropolitan University *continued*

requirements against the course goals, which necessitates consideration of integration and balance.

There may additionally be a challenge in reconciling PSRBs' requirements and QAA expectations together with University regulations and requirements. Introducing student choice into the curriculum can also make the effective coherence of the course challenging.

Addressing challenges

Each module leader needs to see how their module design and content is effectively embedded and isn't repeated and/or contradictory. Course team development meetings and communication at each stage requires strong facilitation (not necessarily leadership). The course teams should agree together how skills and personal development planning (PDP), and development of graduate attributes are embedded throughout the course. It can be useful for a wider consultative team including professional/academic and employers to take an overview and provide feedback/suggested changes.

Our advice to university teachers wishing to share our approach

- Ensure that you have a team agreement to the approach to ensure all colleagues are fully engaged.
- Remember that this is a long-term activity: don't rush into implementation at the start if the change process is set to take several years.
- In order to engage colleagues from the outset, start with very open conversations and don't be afraid to consider radical solutions.
- Consider from the beginning what you want your graduates to be like when they leave and plan the curriculum accordingly to help them achieve these requirements.
- Agree on core course philosophy/identity/principles for the programme of study, since they drive the curriculum in context.
- Work systematically through the process of curriculum design to ensure constructive alignment between learning outcomes and assessment.
- Consider linkages between this and other subjects, planning coherently to integrate the skills that need to be developed across the board.
- Involve students in the process of curriculum design for current and future students, asking them to help identify what they would like to see prioritised within the curriculum.
- Involve colleagues including librarians, careers staff and employability specialists in curriculum design.
- Ensure that those teaching on the course continue to work together throughout the delivery of it to ensure that students perceive and value the links between components.
- Create conditions through which the course team can agree any revisions and enhancements to the curriculum so they can evaluate their impact on course delivery.

- The **sequencing** of content delivery and activities so that competence and knowledge are built cumulatively. In poorly aligned curricula, lab tasks are not sequenced to match lectures, for example, with the theory presented completely separately from practical implementation, making it difficult for students to make sense of their learning and encouraging an unquestioning attitude to simply following set routines in practical tasks.
- The **rationale** of including particular topics within the curriculum needs to be explained, especially early on, so students can see the value of what they are being asked to do and can get practical pay-off in terms of learning gain.
- The **coherence** of various components within the overall curriculum and prescribed content linking to tasks and assignments.

Fostering autonomous learning

In those contexts where student-centred approaches have been applied to curriculum design, this is likely to imply building in more independent learning opportunities and self-management, where we encourage autonomous, independent research-based and shared learning. Some describe this as an almost Copernican shift in the way in which we perceive teaching, with the removal of the teacher as the centre of the learning universe and the foregrounding of the student as the locus of autonomous learning. However, autonomy doesn't mean leaving students to their own devices: instead a steady progression from early support to later independence is required.

The next good practice account (overleaf) describes an approach to fostering independent learning that gives undergraduate students considerable flexibility by undertaking real research that can contribute to scholarship.

Another approach to fostering autonomous learning is exemplified in problem-based learning, which has developed in a number of universities, particularly in Medical and Scientific programmes as a means of encouraging students to move away from reliance on what has been learned in university and towards developing the capacity to seek out information on which to base competent decision making. Tan argues that:

> 'Developing intelligence is about learning to solve problems: problem solving in real-world contexts involves multiple ways of knowing and learning....PBL approaches involve harnessing intelligences from within individuals, from groups of people and from the environment to solve problems that are meaningful, relevant and contextualized.'
>
> Tan, 2003, pp. 1–2

Undergraduate research as a teaching practice in the first two years of university coursework

Laura Guertin, Penn State Brandywine, USA

Introduction

The Council on Undergraduate Research (www.cur.org) defines undergraduate research as an enquiry or investigation conducted by an undergraduate student under the mentorship of a university teacher that makes an original intellectual or creative contribution to the discipline. Undergraduate research typically has been reserved for students in the final year of their undergraduate education and for the students that are the strongest academically. This type of 'senior capstone experience' is conducted as a solo activity for students to pull together their content knowledge and skill sets for one final form of engaged scholarship. However, this practice of waiting until the end of a student's academic schooling is not necessary. Academics can incorporate relevant research topics and approaches into their courses to start students immediately on a successful pathway to an effective undergraduate research experience.

Pedagogical approaches to undergraduate research

Undergraduate research provides an opportunity for students to experience the process of an investigation from its beginnings, from setting up the research question through to the conclusion of the work with some form of dissemination via a presentation or publication. There are several components and approaches to undergraduate research that can be incorporated into courses, including introductory-level courses taught in the first two years at a university. Below are some topics that can be adapted to either classroom discussions and investigations or to take-home assignments:

- **What makes a good research question?** How can students begin to formulate a question to begin an investigation? What are the components of a valid question necessary to serve as the foundation for research?
- **Has this work been completed in the past?** How can students learn, with the assistance of library staff and academics, if a particular research topic has been investigated in the past? What are credible sources in the research literature to reference?
- **What information must be collected to move forward?** What is needed to answer the research question? Can existing data sets be utilised, or must new data be acquired? Is the required information dependent upon location, time, or space?

- **What tools/skills are required to conduct this work?** Are specific computer skills required to collect or analyse data? Are there particular field methods that must be learned, or equipment that must be purchased?
- **Are additional people needed for the success of the research?** Will there be a need to consult with a museum curator or community partner during the research process?

By creating assignments that require students to answer foundation questions involving critical thinking and problem solving skills, students learn how to effectively set up and approach a research project. This can serve as an excellent introduction to the research process. However, if academics wish to continue moving students along a research track, they can ask students to complete original enquiry-based experiences during laboratory sections of science courses, or as creative works for writing/composition courses. Cejda and Hensel (2009) provide several examples of undergraduate research projects and mentoring practices for students in first- and second-year courses.

Benefits and drawbacks

University teachers will cite several reasons to use teaching approaches that encourage undergraduate research experiences for students in the early years of university study, but just as many instructors will list the negatives to developing research skills in students so early. One criticism is that students in the first two years do not have enough content knowledge to be able to frame a research question. Another concern is that students are not likely to have had any experience in formulating original enquiry-based investigations in their disciplines, which could lead to a research result that could not contribute to the discipline knowledge. However, undergraduate research experiences early in a student's studies can provide early training on how to be a scientist, artist and so on, can help a student to identify an academic specialism and career track, and can provide the student with the confidence and foundations to pursue investigative studies in the future.

References

Cejda, B.D. and N. Hensel (2009) *Undergraduate Research at Community Colleges*, USA: Council on Undergraduate Research. Available at www.cur.org/urcc/ (accessed 24 March 2014).

For further information on Undergraduate Research as Teaching Practice, please visit: serc.carleton.edu/NAGTWorkshops/undergraduate_research/index.html

He proposes that PBL emphasises the following facets of learning:

- real-world challenges;
- higher-order thinking skills;
- problem-solving skills;
- interdisciplinary learning;
- independent learning;
- information-mining skills;
- teamwork;
- communication skills. (Tan, op. cit., p. 27)

This approach, rather than offering formal lecture programmes, places the onus on groups of students to identify what they need to know and then seek the support and resources to inform themselves, letting them loose on source material to find their own ways around it and welcoming their findings, while encouraging them appropriately to evaluate what they find. It's important when using PBL, or indeed other approaches, to acknowledge what students bring to class from their prior formal and informal learning and encourage them to use their peers as valuable resources from whom they can learn much.

How will the curriculum be assessed?

Potentially the most crucial component of a well-aligned curriculum is a fit-for-purpose assessment strategy (see Chapter 7). Race argues:

> 'A well-designed set of intended learning outcomes is evidence of good curriculum design, but more importantly should link really strongly to the evidence of achievement which will be developed by successful learners. After all, it is such evidence of achievement which is drawn from learners in assessment contexts, and such achievement can be regarded as the whole point of education and training. The word "attainment" is sometimes used by policy-makers, but I don't think this adds much to our thinking about curriculum design, as attainment is only "real" to the extent that we are able to quantify and accredit achievement.'
>
> Race, 2014, pp. 52–3

Finding ways of assessing authentically evidence of achievement by students of the learning outcomes is a matter of high importance. The kinds of things that currently impede assignment design include:

- A badly-paced diet of assessments so students (and staff) have patches of manic activity with long gaps between.

- Lack of opportunities to learn from formative feedback from one assignment before tackling the next.
- Lack of understanding of the assessment regime (for example, does it matter if I am couple of days late handing in? Why haven't I got a second chance to do it again better?).
- Lack of understanding of the vocabulary of assessment (for example, students not understanding terms like condonement, weighting, compensation, trailing modules and so on).

If we want to improve assessment practices we need to undertake wholesale review, not only to consider our diet of assessment to ensure that we are not over-assessing, repeatedly assessing the same skills, and rewarding risky behaviour like guessing what will come up, but also to review the programme as a whole to make sure assessments don't bunch together, putting unnecessary pressure on students and the staff who are doing the marking. The PASS Project at Bradford University (McDowell, 2012) provides useful guidance on how to design assignments to align with curricula across a whole programme, rather than piecemeal within individual modules or units. The PASS team outline the approach used by programme-focussed assessment as follows:

> 'The first and most critical point is that the assessment is specifically designed to address major programme outcomes rather than very specific or isolated components of the course. It follows then that such assessment is integrative in nature, trying to bring together understandings of subject and skills in ways which represent key programme aims. As a result, the assessment is likely to be more authentic and meaningful to students, staff and external stakeholders.'
>
> PASS, 2012, p. 3

It's helpful to consider how good assessment design can prompt authentic kinds of learning behaviours that we would wish to see, and discourage those we don't, including simple reproduction of text books or lecture notes in exams, plagiarism and other forms of poor academic conduct and uncritical use of internet sources, including cutting and pasting of text without considering its relevance and value.

Effective assessment design implies rethinking what various methods of assessment including exams and essays actually achieve, and choosing those on each occasion that best help students demonstrate their achievements, distinguishing between essentials and optional extras when choosing what to assess. It's important to plan for consistency of standards and inclusive practices from the outset, rather than trying to retrofit these subsequently, and also to communicate assessment requirements clearly to students, since these can impact highly in student success or failure. Before validating your course, it is helpful to do the calculations to work out how many hours you estimate each student's work will take to mark and scale this up over the number of students you are likely to recruit, and work out if what you are planning is feasible. Do you have enough assessors of the right quality and experience to do the job? And do you have enough specialised equipment, learning resources and learning spaces to achieve your assessment aims?

It's also important to consider how and when students will receive feedback on their progress at various stages of their journey through the curriculum you are planning. In particular, it's important to think about when they will really benefit from formative feedback, allowing them to remediate difficulties before getting too deep into the next assignment.

To maximise the impact of effective assessment design, Gibbs (1999) suggests that curriculum designers:

- Increase the use of course requirements that capture and distribute student effort, without student work being marked on each occasion.
- Sample these requirements for marking purposes, increasing the risk to students of not taking all of them seriously.
- Use frequent 'quick and dirty' feedback mechanisms with rapid 'turn-round' and discuss feedback and student work in class.
- Use student marking exercises and exemplars to communicate standards and criteria instead of ever-more detailed specifications.
- Reduce the variety of types of assessment so that students have some chance to come to understand, through practice and feedback, how to tackle each at a reasonably sophisticated level.

These features can valuably be implemented in curriculum design at all levels. I concur with Royce Sadler when he argues that good assessment design is a pivotal feature of good curriculum design:

> 'Assessment is a high-stakes activity for students, and has a major impact on how they approach learning. Regardless of innovations in assessment techniques, developments in interpretive frameworks and increased adaptability made possible by new and forthcoming technologies, the core activities that cover the design and production of appropriate assessment tasks, the emphasis on higher order cognitive outcomes, the criteria for appraisal, the assignment and interpretation of marks and grades, and the overall maintenance of academic standards clearly remain ongoing responsibilities for the higher education enterprise as whole.'
>
> Sadler, 2010a, p. 254

Reviewing the quality of the curriculum

Once a curriculum has been designed, students have been recruited and enrolled, and teaching has commenced, it's important to be continually aware of the need for ongoing scrutiny of its effectiveness by undertaking periodic internal and external reviews to assure and enhance the quality of the programme. In some nations, periodic review is mandated: for example, in the UK quinquennial review is a regular requirement of programmes accredited by PSRBs and the national quality bodies – the Quality Assurance Agencies for England, Wales and Northern Ireland and Scotland (which, though all parts of the UK, have different systems) – similarly look closely during quality audit visits to institutions. Where it is not a requirement, it is nevertheless good practice to establish a regular timetable of evaluation to ensure programmes remain current and relevant.

The good practice account that follows demonstrates how curriculum review can lead to significant and powerful changes in the student experience.

Integrated and inclusive learning

Kalyan Banerjee, Centurion University of Technology and Management, India

Introduction

Traditional education programmes in India are syllabus-bound and examination-driven. Examinations are necessary, but the drive towards standardisation of the examination system has led to predictable questions with unambiguous answers. When the quality of education is measured primarily by marks or grades, it could lead students, teaching staff and education administrators to single-mindedly focus on good grades. This is likely to result in students acquiring enough nuggets of information on the subject, but not necessarily with much wisdom or fundamental understanding, since concentrating on metrics alone risks missing critical insights.

The challenges

When such risks engage the mind, impact-oriented educators design courses focused on creating inspiration, curiosity, and a lifelong desire to learn. A preferred route is to offer hands-on learning, ensuring students learn through the process, irrespective of the grade. In teaching computer programming, for example, one needs to focus not just on the number of original programs written, but also on the complexity, on the problems

continued overleaf

Integrated and inclusive learning *continued*

encountered, and how defects were corrected by students after feedback. Since elegant programming is an art, there is much value in learning in groups or finding a buddy whose code students can critique. Students can thus learn there are different ways to reach the goal, and even different ways to code the same solution. They learn also from mistakes made by others, and how to avoid them. Another problem in teaching programming is that students come with varying degrees of skill, thinking ability, and even motivation. Teachers strive to do justice to the entire spectrum. Students of computer programming and a software engineering practitioner often learn best through making mistakes. Arguably, writing code that works right first time is evidence of genius but may not offer a predictable and reusable learning process. When the code does not work as desired, students struggle to find the errors, and hence some much-cherished 'Aha' moments emerge, thus building the foundations for confident programming. Our challenge as teachers is to create such an environment, aiming to ensure students struggle, fail, think, and learn.

Creating achievable challenges, nurturing initiative and peer learning

The approach we tried was as follows:

1. The course curriculum requires 50 programs of varying complexity to be written, which is announced in the beginning of the semester. Students write programs and collect points based on complexity of programs they have written.
2. A 10-point scale is created to assess and objectively find students' levels at the start of the course.
3. Based on this, they are assigned customised challenge levels.
4. The students at the highest levels are designated captains, and other students choose their captains. Thus teams are formed. Teams are given their targets and incentives.

This can lead to interesting results, with the most motivated students cutting across groups and sharing experiences, while the least motivated are not sufficiently confident to interact. Most students, however, do learn questioning, taking initiative, and discovering the thrill of writing code that works.

Creating an inspiring ambience

Another course element involves creating an off-site learning excursion centred around multiple technical challenges, to be solved over a 3–4 week period in a 'stretch' routine, starting at 8am every morning and going on till midnight. Since doing technical work all day can be boring, the programme is filled with variety of other useful activities, including mini-excursions with industry leaders who focus on a chosen theme, psychometric instruments for self-assessment, outbound learning, debates, selected movies, and competitions that widen their exposure. The presence of academics right through the technical grind and the structured fun takes the students through a holistic experience, aiming to create a lifelong love for programming challenges which subsumes the lesser objective of teaching programming skills. When the student is infected by the joy of doing something, she will discover the rest on her own, and the teacher's presence will only accelerate the discovery. A single teacher provides continuity throughout the programme, from design to evaluation and this is critical to success.

The off-site holistic activities engaging industry leaders, with diverse exercises, games and competitions together create an inspiring and memorable experience, offering a warm ambience where that programming habit is born. However, many question why all this is necessary, and parents of daughters (in the Indian context) with all good intentions may not allow their children to be part of this. Education thus needs to involve the parents as critical stakeholders.

Assessing this intense engagement is complex; students may copy, so we have to create problems that are new every time. And students will make mistakes or fail in different ways, so the teacher has to monitor every error and show students the path from ***that*** error forward, careful not to simply reveal the right answer. This customised effort is necessary – depending on standard questions and uniform approach has proved ineffective.

Similar methods, another context

Centurion University also aims to create employability for young people from under-privileged sections of society, offering not just training for skills but on cultural aspects of living in an unknown society; these students study free, alongside students from privileged backgrounds pursuing sought-after professions. We take a holistic view of education, exploring, for example, big-city living, coping with long commutes, working in corporate environments with potentially impatient and sometimes insensitive managers, dealing with unfamiliar food issues and even getting acquainted with urban toilets. These lessons in inclusion are critical enablers to their success as professionals and in building responsible citizenship.

Our rationale for change

We are today in a knowledge era, with free access to information, deluged by choices that can cause disconnection between learning systems and expectations from the real world. The challenges of education have moved beyond knowledge transfer as we witness an exponential increase in content. Our approach offers an integrated and inclusive education involving critical stakeholders like parents and peers. Ethics, curiosity and motivation are critical to our foundation. If the purpose of education is to build the next generation of nation builders, to bring in equitable opportunities to all sections of society, or to create responsible, happy citizens in a sustainable environment, we need to change, aligning ourselves to the needs of 2020 rather than looking back to structures that worked well in 1920.

Refreshing and revalidating programmes

When reviewing or revising a curriculum, it's worth taking stock of experiences to date and reviewing what has worked well and what has not in order to help you decide whether to carry on as before, modify the programme, change the programme radically or stop offering it altogether. Here are some questions to prompt your thoughts:

- Are there contextual or political changes that you need to take into account in order to improve the programme?
- Is your programme helping students gain graduate-level employment on graduation? Are students developing the knowledge, skills, behaviours and attributes that are attractive to employers? Are they learning to be autonomous and flexible, so they can change fields if necessary? Are they developing a good set of graduate attributes?
- Are there advances in knowledge in the field that need to be integrated within a revised curriculum? Are there tired or outdated elements that should be dropped?
- Are you happy that your content delivery approaches are fit-for-purpose? Do you need to use more technology-enhanced delivery? Are you offering sufficient personalised support to your students through, for example, live or virtual tutorials? Would a problem-based learning approach be more suitable? Could you be using more Open Educational Resources for curriculum delivery?
- Are the learning activities that students are being asked to undertake relevant and sufficient in quantity and scope to engage and challenge them fully? Are your students working hard enough at the right kinds of things? Is the programme sufficiently intellectually demanding?
- Is the pacing of student activities appropriate, or are there periods of over-intense activity interspersed with times when too few demands are being made on them?
- Is there a continuing and buoyant market for the programme? Or are you struggling to recruit? Are your competitors (in your own nation or globally) offering better programmes than you, that are more attractive to students?
- Does your programme retain students in sufficient numbers to match institutional and national benchmarks?
- Do the sums add up? Do the costs exceed the income generated, and if so, is there a mitigating case to be made for keeping the programme?

- To what extent can you demonstrate that the students are satisfied? Are there aspects of the student experience that have been unsatisfactory and in need of improvement? Are such improvements viable within the resource envelope of the programme?

External examiners

In nations where the higher education system has developed from UK practice and elsewhere, external examiners feature strongly in regular review. These are normally peers recruited from benchmarked higher education institutions, that is ones with similar status and prestige, who have a role in assuring equivalence of standards between institutions by attending exam boards, scrutinising the range of marks awarded, looking at assessed student work and the comments given on it and, sometimes, meeting students to gauge the impact of the course and the student experience. The best universities offer training and updating for their external examiners, and there is usually a role for them in the processes of validation and review. There is an overall expectation that external examiners are appointed to make sure that the curriculum is designed, delivered and assessed appropriately. Their annual reports are often read by a senior manager within the university, and programme/course leaders are normally expected to formulate an action plan to take account of any criticisms of the programme or course, as well as celebrating external examiners' positive comments. External examiners usually receive only token remuneration for their work, although they can claim expenses incurred as part of a collegiate system of reciprocality across the sector, but there are significant benefits to being an external examiner, including gaining a wider perspective about practice in other universities and demonstrating professional status by being asked to undertake the role.

The role of student evaluations within 21st-century universities is more prominent than ever before: it is common practice in many nations to ask students not only to evaluate their teachers' teaching, but also to evaluate *inter alia* the learning context, learning resources, the effectiveness and value of assessment and feedback, the organisation and management of programmes, extra-curricular opportunities and overall satisfaction with the course. Evaluations can take the form of 'happy sheets' used in classes, hard copy or virtual questionnaires, student- or staff-convened focus groups, open forums and a variety of other methods.

In a number of nations, including the UK and Australia, national student surveys are used, enabling universities to compare satisfaction rates using the same questions and delivery mechanisms across departments within universities and between universities nationally, resulting, on occasions, in league tables. There are mixed views on the efficacy of national student surveys and the extent to which they can really measure good curriculum design, delivery and assessment (or conversely, whether they privilege approaches principally concerned with keeping students happy, like marking generously and making few demands on students, rather than good, challenging teaching and assessment). Nevertheless, they have become important performance indicators in many nations and cannot be ignored. For me, the most important thing is not to focus on how to improve scores, but on how to enhance the student experience and hence bring about meaningful and positive change (Brown, 2011, 2012). It is important to review student evaluations objectively and use both the data summaries and free response comments, and address them positively to improve areas in need of remediation, as well as sharing and celebrating areas of identified good practice.

Learning from student evaluations

As Peter Knight and I remarked in 1994, you don't fatten pigs by weighing them and all the information we derive from student evaluations is without value unless it is put to work to improve matters. The following questions could be helpful if you are engaged with the process of reviewing student feedback on your course, as part of a quality enhancement process:

- **What evidence around student satisfaction do you have**? Do you have both qualitative and quantitative data? Do you have free comments as well as numbers and percentages? Do such free responses add to your understanding of key issues, or merely reinforce them?
- **What is the timing of feedback from students?** Is it mostly gathered immediately after they've experienced individual modules, or is there useful ongoing feedback throughout their studies? Are requests for student feedback paced or spaced out? Are students continuously bombarded with evaluation requests so they get 'questionnaire fatigue'?
- **How do students give feedback?** Is it all by questionnaire, or is there a healthy balance including face-to-face feedback, focus groups, and online feedback? Are there ways in which students can give unsolicited feedback easily?

- **What is the history of feedback, in your students' previous experience in your institution?** Are they coming to you from programmes which have attracted really positive (or negative) feedback? If so, is this having a 'halo' effect on this year's feedback, and if so, what caused this? Or is your programme their first experience of learning at your institution, and if so, how well are they inducted into how your institution works, and can you improve this if necessary?
- **What can you discern from the feedback data?** What does it tell you about students' perceptions? Can you see any themes within this year's data and any trends over the years about whether your course/module is improving or deteriorating? Are there outliers or blips that should not be taken too seriously? Can you track down the causes of particular positive changes, or deteriorations?
- **How confident are you of the data?** Is it representative? Where are the gaps? How important is it? What impact will it have on, for example, recruitment and league tables? Does it reinforce your gut reactions about how courses are going or are there any real surprises in what your data is saying about the student experience?
- **Who needs to have access to this data**? Does it need to be made widely available through websites, or is it just shared with the people delivering the programmes? Are students (and prospective students) entitled to see it, for example in nations where there is a statutory requirement for open data?
- **How can this data best be used for quality enhancement purposes**? What steps might this involve? For example, if your data tells you, as it does in most student surveys, that students are unhappy with the promptness and quality of the feedback they receive on assessed work, what can you do about it? What would be the milestones and performance indicators for improvement?
- **Who is responsible at a local and macro level for making consequent improvements?** Who needs to be informed about enhancements and on what timescale?
- **What else is going on in your institution?** Are there other programmes which have shown dramatic improvements in student feedback, and can you track down what made the difference? Can you benchmark your evaluations against others leading similar courses? Are there programmes which have climbed or slipped in terms of student feedback, and what in particular have the students there found to praise or criticise?
- **Can you learn from similar programmes at the top of league tables?** Why are they so successful – is it the staff, the resources, the student

profile, or the institutional ethos? What can you do to address the differences between these programmes and your own?

- **What else needs to be done to make your curriculum viable, attractive and useful to students?** Are you making good use of critical friends to offer advice and support to enhance your curriculum offer? Are there issues on the upcoming agenda you need to keep in mind? Do you know what your strengths, weaknesses, opportunities and threats (SWOT) are? Is it possible for you to take a day away from the normal routine for you and your team to undertake a 'spring clean' of your curriculum to make sure your programme is as good as it could be?

The next good practice account describes how a review of practice in a national system of training for tertiary teachers has prompted a recognition of the need to change assessment to ensure it is more fit-for-purpose (see also Chapter 7).

Training for higher education teachers in China

Danqing Liu, Tianjin University of Commerce, Tianjin, China

Introduction

There have been significant achievements in the reform of higher education in China since the implementation of economic reforms. A two-level educational provision system has been developed, in which central and local governments take different responsibilities for educational provision and the former undertakes the overall planning and management. According to the Ministry of Education of People's Republic of China (PRC) (2012), in 2010, there were altogether 2305 higher education institutions, of which 1090 were universities, 322 were independent colleges and 1215 were other non-university higher institutions. There were also 384 higher education institutions for adult learners. In order to ensure the quality of teachers who work at higher education institutions in China, since 1990s, the government has adopted a range of policies. Several relevant laws and regulations cover higher education, including the Teachers Law (1993) which requires that the administrative departments of education under the People's governments at various levels have responsibility to design teachers' training programmes at all levels including higher education, as well as to conduct various forms of ideological, political and professional training among teachers. Additionally, Regulations for Training Teachers working in Higher Education (1996) emphasise the importance of teacher training and state that pre-employment training for HE teachers is compulsory. In January 1997, Interim Guidelines for Pre-job training for HE Teachers were adopted to guide new teachers training and in 1998, the PRC Higher Education Law was adopted which emphasises teachers in HEIs must meet the following basic requirements:

- to be qualified as a teacher in a higher education institution;
- to have a systematic mastery of the basic theories of his/her branch of learning;
- to have the necessary competence in education, teaching and research as required by the title held;
- to shoulder/deliver the curriculum commensurate with the title and the teaching assignments in required class hours.

Pre-employment training for university teachers plays a very important role in the process of helping the transition of students into university teachers. New HE teachers in PRC receive generic training on teaching and then they are expected to adapt such knowledge to the higher education context, largely adopting an intensive model including lectures and case presentations.

Although having regulatory requirements, pre-employment for HE teachers emphasises the importance of teaching capability, and such training has achieved incredible impacts in improving the quality of teachers. Some issues concerning training programmes remain:

- Organisation and assessment of such training tends to be simplistic; most universities offer intensive training for new teachers from different disciplines through several lectures in June or July, with the assessment being by open- and closed-book exams, so many new teachers are more interested in learning material to pass exams rather than other aspects.
- The content of this training prescribed by the Ministry of Education includes Higher Education Regulations, Pedagogy, Psychology and Professional Ethics. Although some universities update and to some extent customise required contents to their own universities' contexts, they all tend to focus on a purely theoretical discussion model. Teaching practice and observation are discussed but not undertaken.
- In this way, new HE teachers' attitudes to pre-employment training are compromised because, as it is compulsory, many new teachers feel pressure to undertake training to gain formal teacher qualifications and to work towards promotion, so lack enthusiasm for the training itself.

Human resources managers with extensive experience in such training and lecturers in a number of Chinese universities would suggest the following proposals:

1. University senior managers need to support such training by providing funding and time allowances for new teachers to develop.
2. The curriculum for such programmes shouldn't simply cover elements required by government but should also integrate real teaching case studies. Furthermore, each university's own regulations and rules should be emphasised.

continued overleaf

Training for higher education teachers in China *continued*

3. Curriculum delivery should include more practical teaching observation and discussion, with discussion of best practice.
4. Pre-employment training should be integrated with on-the-job training to help new teachers achieve their lifelong learning objectives and have successful HE careers.

Reference

Ministry of Education of People's Republic China (2012) *Current Situation of Higher Education Institutions in China.* Available on www.chinaeducenter.com/en/cedu/hedu.php (accessed 31 March 2014).

Conclusions

It's all too easy when designing and delivering curricula to fall back on old certainties and to go for safe options, relying on what has worked well in the past and playing safe with familiar and 'tried and tested' approaches. Universities have moved a long way from expecting that providing a reading list and offering access to formal lectures was enough to foster learning leading to exam success and hence graduation. Working in a global environment, in which students can choose where and how to study, it is necessary to be more strategic and thoughtful to ensure not only that students are attracted to study at our university, but also that we provide them with meaningful and relevant programmes of learning that enable them to move on to fulfilling lives, and in many cases, fruitful employment. If we don't do it, plenty of other providers will.

4 Delivering the curriculum

In Chapter 2, I discussed a conceptual shift from thinking about higher education teaching being a matter of a tutor-centred process, where 'instruction' is the central paradigm, to one where curriculum designers see learning as the process through which students construct learning for themselves. The term 'curriculum delivery' for me is not so much about content being *delivered* as a postman delivers a parcel, but more like the process by which a midwife *delivers* a baby, sometimes referred to as 'maieutics', where the student (like the labouring woman) can be supported, advised and offered interventions when things go wrong, but in fact only the student can bring forth learning in an active rather than a passive process. Student-centred learning has implications both for curriculum delivery and assessment, with the process seen as a partnership rather than a Gradgrindian experience, where students are seen like pupils of Charles Dickens's Gradgrind, who wanted to fill young minds with facts like little vessels being filled from a jug. Many of us in a post-modern world are uncomfortable with the concept of immutable facts in any case, since much 'knowledge' is subject to change as advances in understanding are made.

High quality teaching, Ramsden suggests:

> 'implies recognising that students must be engaged with the content of learning tasks in a way that is likely to enable them to reach understanding … Sharp engagement, imaginative inquiry and finding of a suitable level and style are all more likely to occur if teaching methods that necessitate student energy, problem solving and cooperative learning are employed.'
>
> Ramsden, 2003, p. 97

The implications of this for university teachers is substantial, undermining as it does many of the precepts many hold dear about how curriculum delivery should be effected, in particular, the role of the traditional lecture, originally conceived of as an opportunity for experts in possession of rare and valuable books (sometimes chained to lecterns) to read them to large numbers of students, whose job was to listen to and write down the content. The next section discusses lectures, and later in the chapter, considers ways in which to teach large numbers of students.

Lecturing: is the lecture dead?

Many argue that the era of lectures has passed, that it is archaic to expect students to sit physically present in the same room as the lecturer, passively listening to and noting what is said, and thereby absorbing content. If you sit at the back of the lecture theatre and watch what students are actually doing on their laptops and mobile devices, it is evident that few students nowadays simply sit and make traditional lecture notes with pens and paper. But look again and see that as well as updating their Facebook pages, students are making mind-maps of what they are hearing, following the structure of the lecture based on previously-pasted up presentations, Googling unfamiliar words or Tweeting about the subject of the lecture (although there are still students who are absent in all but body from the lecture as there always have been). But again, this is nothing new. Look at medieval and 18th century paintings, for example Hogarth's famous image of scholars at a lecture, and it as apparent that totally attentive behaviour has never been the norm, since he portrays students chatting, sleeping, daydreaming and exhibiting other common in-lecture behaviours: it was ever thus!

Making better use of traditional lectures

Lectures look as if they are here to stay, if only because university systems in most nations still use the lecture timetable as the building blocks not only of the student experience but also of academic staff deployment models and this is likely to remain the case for the next decade or two at least. For example, in much of continental Europe, traditional lectures remain the principal means of teaching in most subjects.

Most of us can recall lectures where we have listened enthralled when a great practitioner of the art of lecturing has held an audience's attention for a full hour or more, conveying erudition and passion for a subject that leaves no room for inattention. Nevertheless, most of us can't ourselves reliably and dependably call up that level of performance week in and week out. Many of us can also remember sessions of stultifying boredom when we sat through poorly-delivered recitals of information with which we were already acquainted through reading. This means that planning for lectures for the average lecturer requires not just very thorough preparation of the content, but equally rigorous preparation for the processes involved in retaining students' attention.

Discussions of student attention spans vary from the deeply pessimistic three minutes to the more reassuring twenty minutes (Brown and Race, 2002), but this inevitably implies that we will need to use some tricks of the trade (often called 'attention recall points'), varying the activity around every fifteen to twenty minutes to keep students with us throughout the timetabled period. These might include:

- Giving students short tasks, either individually, in pairs or in threes (but not larger groups in a tiered lecture theatre), for example to answer or propose a question, to solve a problem on the board, to discuss an issue, to decide on a strategy or to resolve a dilemma.
- Using audio or video clips to illustrate a point you are using, either self-prepared, borrowed from expert colleagues or sourced from Open Educational Resources (OERs) available copyright free online. These should be kept brief (no more than a few minutes at a time) and care needs to be taken not to waste too much in-class time locating them on shaky internet connections, which tends to have the immediate effect of diverting students' attention beyond the topic in hand.
- Giving students a quick in-class test or quiz which they can answer either using interactive devices ('clickers'), a show of hands, or by asking them to hold up different coloured cards or pages from their course handbooks, so you can get an immediate visual idea of what students are thinking.
- Inviting guest inputs, for example from colleagues, visiting scholars, your own top research professors, practical specialists in the field and indeed your own students who may have particular expertise gleaned from the work environment. These don't need to be full lectures: although the best guest speakers can be truly inspirational, matters often go wrong when a poorly briefed or wilfully self-indulgent guest speaker rambles on at length off the topic they were invited to illuminate. Valuable instead can be short inputs within your own lectures of say 20 minutes, where guests can enliven a lecture and contextualise current thinking. If the guest is willing, you can video such episodes and turn them into podcasts or other reusable learning objects for use with subsequent or parallel cohorts. Whole guest lectures can usefully also be edited into usable segments to be similarly used.
- Reading tasks: students can read about three times faster than you can speak, so intervals of silent reading can be productive so long as you are confident that students can see what they are being asked to read either on screen or within a handout, and you have made appropriate provision for students with visual impairments. Reading tasks can provide

an alternative perspective from yours, can provide real immediacy if focused on current events and can give you and your students a break from your voice.

- Reflective silences in lectures can be very powerful: 30 or 60 seconds can provide students with a chance to think about what they've heard and seen so far and can provide a breathing space for students who've been concentrating hard to zone out for a short while. However, expecting silence to be maintained for anything much longer than a minute might be over optimistic. It helps if students are given a task for their reflection such as 'Think back about what we've been discussing so far in this lecture and work out what for you are the most surprising/perplexing issues', 'Check you are clear in your mind how this theory can be applied in practice, and be ready with your questions in a minute's time when I ask you for issues about which you need further clarification'.

Some things it's best to avoid

- Using the whole allotted time talking at the students without making space for interaction.
- Making jokes that don't translate into other cultures (British humour for example relies heavily on puns, which often require a highly sophisticated understanding of synonyms) or that could be regarded as offensive, sexist, racist, ageist and so on.
- Picking on individuals to answer questions, particularly if their personal or cultural circumstances make it difficult for them to speak in front of peers.
- Overreliance on your written lecture notes, meaning you can't look at your students frequently enough to gauge what's going on.
- Using screen shots from websites where the text is too tiny to be visible.
- Expecting students to read from the screen material that is only flashed up for seconds.

The lecture room itself may be a source of difficulties with effective delivery. Table 4.1 (pages 60–61) lists common problems and suggests solutions or avoidance tactics.

Flipping classrooms

The term 'flipping' (which is a jokey inoffensive expletive in colloquial English, hence punning titles) is the term used to describe the practice of swapping round the activities normally undertaken in-class and as individual tasks. Typically a lecturer will create short (5–10 minute) videos or podcasts delivering curriculum content which students can watch independently prior to classes. Class time in lectures and seminars then can concentrate on making sense of what has been viewed, with the time used for group or collective workshops, exercises, tasks, projects and discussions which can test understanding, foster skills development and help students apply theory to practice.

This isn't so different conceptually from the old idea of 'reading for a degree', when curriculum information comprised a reading list and the principal learning resources were set texts and other books that students were expected to read alongside tutorials and seminars. Lectures were used to inspire and help students make connections between elements of what they had been reading. This worked well (and still does in some elite institutions) where staff–student ratios were favourable, students highly motivated and staff passionate about their subjects.

During the 20th century, an expectation evolved as part of a risk-averse managerialist approach, that the material required to pass exams, outlined in a syllabus, would be 'delivered' within lecture periods and teaching staff became over-concerned with full 'coverage' of material in class-time, potentially to avoid student complaints about teaching. This sometimes resulted in 'quick fire' delivery of content, with little interaction in class, and largely passive student behaviour, often described in the cliché of information being passed from the lecturer's notes to the students' notes without passing through the brains of either.

In the current period in many nations the curriculum is described in terms of learning outcomes, that is, a specification of what students are expected to know and be able to do by the end of a programme of learning. Flipped classrooms help to keep a focus on the student experience of 'doing, verbalising and making judgements' thereby helping them to engage fully with learning materials, make sense of them and be able to use them, which Phil Race describes as 'learning by doing' (Race, 2014).

▶ Some tips on flipping classrooms

- ▶ The pedagogic rationale for flipping classrooms is to enhance the student experience, not to deliver curriculum as cheaply as possible, and it must be recognised that design and creation of good materials takes time and resources.

Table 4.1 Lecture rooms: what's the problem?

What's the problem with the room?	What does this feel like for you and the students? What's the problem?	What can you do about it (apart from try to get a different room, which should be your first resort)?	*In extremis*, you can:
The room is too big for the class.	Students often spread themselves out in places where it is hard for them to see and hear you and vice versa. It's hard for them to get into little groups for tasks.	Ask students (nicely) to sit close together in the centre of the room near the front. Work on your voice projection. Use a radio microphone.	Obtain some 'do not cross' tape and block off all but a central section of the lecture room.
The room is too small to hold the students.	Students have to sit on steps or stand at the back and sides and are, unsurprisingly, unhappy about this.	Repeat the lecture. Split the class into two groups and teach for half the time (or alternate weeks) with independent learning tasks set for students not in class.	Video the lecture, and make it available online so students who have been too uncomfortable to concentrate can choose to see it online.
You are teaching a cohort that is too large to fit in one room, so the timetablers have allocated you an additional lecture room to which the audio and visuals are streamed.	The students in the 'other' room aren't getting as good an experience as those in the room where you present. Behaviour in the overflow room is sub-optimal(!).	Abandon the streaming and adopt suggestions above. If the rooms are close enough together for you to move between rooms, share out your presence. Use course-reps to collect questions from students in the room where you are not and text or Tweet them to you (make sure you respond!).	Use a flipped approach, with students attending and working on tasks you set on alternate weeks.
The lecture theatre has fixed tiered seating.	It's hard to get students to work in small groups. Sight lines for screens can be very difficult.	Use pair tasks, or threes with two behind and one in front, or vice versa. Make sure all materials on the screen are in sufficiently large font to be visible even at the back.	Don't try to use the room for group tasks.
The fixed seating is 'bleachers' which can be rolled back.	This makes getting into and out of seating very noisy and it's disruptive if any students arrive late or need to leave early.	Encourage students to fill seats in blocks, leaving the seats nearest the doors and at ends of rows for late arrivals. Include plenty of noisy tasks at regular intervals so disruptions can be managed.	Have a rule (that will be unpopular) that late arrivals will not be admitted until a suitable interval in the lecture, as at the theatre.

Students have nothing but their laps to write on.	They have to balance their laptops, pens, paper, text books etc. on their knees.	Minimise the amount that they need to write, using handouts (or web files), and concentrate on talking and dialogue. Record the lecture, or encourage students to do so themselves so they can make notes later.	Suggest they 'don't even try to make comprehensive written notes at this lecture' and advise instead that they make their own summaries from chosen reference materials.
The room is very hot or very cold.	Students and lecturer get very uncomfortable and potentially faint.	Open doors and windows unless noise becomes distracting. If too cold, have the odd 'warm-up' minute, where students vote on questions you ask by standing up, sitting down, and waving arms around.	Shorten the lecture considerably, and explain that other resources will be provided online between lectures.
The audio-visuals are poor or unreliable.	Sightlines to screens are poor, for example, in wide or narrow rooms.	Use handouts on paper. Ask Estates Services to fit additional screens. Minimise the use of materials on-screen, and make supplementary materials reliably available online very shortly after the lecture, for a week or so.	Give up on using screens altogether and work just using your voice and student interaction.
The acoustics are very poor. There's a lot of noise from outside the room.	Students get fed up if they can't hear you. Lecturers get voice strain trying to be heard.	Investigate whether radio mikes are available. Take classes on voice projection to avoid voice strain. Speak from different parts of the lecture theatre so that the same students aren't always being disadvantaged. Experiment with a colleague to give feedback regarding where is the best place to stand so that you can be heard.	Audio-record the lecture and make the recordings available to anyone who wants them after the lecture.
Actually it's a lab rather than a lecture theatre, or indeed a draughty old assembly hall not designed for lectures or a corridor (all of these are real examples!).	It's really hard to make a productive learning environment and manage appropriate learning activities.	See if there are any features you can work with, for example, an old assembly hall is only really workable as a lecture room if you can use sound amplification, and don't try to use visual presentations too much. They can actually work quite well for group activities with the lecturer in the centre of the room as a help desk.	Abandon working in the room altogether other than for briefings and set resource-based learning tasks, using the library and other places on the campus, with you continuing to be available in the ghastly room at timetabled hours for drop-in question sessions.

- Don't just video lectures one year and then expect students to watch them in subsequent years: few students will watch an hour's live recording (let alone one from last year), as HEIs find when they try to cope with large cohorts by having students being taught by a lecturer in one lecture theatre, with a second overflow room used to live stream to students with no lecturer present. Behaviour in the two parallel rooms tends to be very different.
- Extracts from recorded live videos can make really good reusable learning objects but they will need careful editing to make them usable and attractive to students.
- You can use a program such as Camtasia® to cut in presentation materials such as Prezi or Microsoft® PowerPoint with the 'talking head' elements of curriculum delivery, so that text is interspersed with image.
- It can be helpful to embed some questions and exercise prompts within the video and follow them up in the shared plenary sessions.
- The live class sessions need to balance structured elements, so students feel there is value in being there, with flexibility to allow follow-up of student queries, misapprehensions and uncertainties.
- Open resources such as YouTube videos and TED talks can helpfully form part of the mixed diet of multimedia elements of flipped classrooms.
- When using commercial resources, such as extracts from film and TV programmes, copyright issues need to be borne in mind.

What do students do in lectures?

Formerly, when students were asked what they most wanted from lectures, many would say "a good set of notes". Nowadays in many nations students expect to get these automatically, either in the form of a photocopied handout or in terms of downloads of slides and other material from the web. Whereas in the past students would commonly spend most of class time attempting to write down material put on the blackboard, whiteboard, overhead projector or Microsoft® PowerPoint screen, this activity is much less in evidence nowadays. In earlier times, assiduous students would read back their notes straight after classes, check they were legible, highlight key points and summarise information. Not all students did this and there were then, as there are now, many students (including me on occasions) who did nothing much in lectures and even slept through some. Advice to students in study skills guides tended to assume that students were hand-writing notes within lectures, attempting to capture what was being said, but nowadays students increasingly rely on lecturer-provided materials together with their own audio recordings, often made on their phones, photos of screen shots, using mind mapping software and taking notes directly onto laptops, tablets and, again, phones. The still and moving visuals used in lectures nowadays are often highly sophisticated and can't really be recorded in written words, so attempting to do so may distract from learning.

Theoretically these innovative approaches give students much more time to listen attentively and think in classes. Anecdotally, however, many are worried that students can instead be distracted by other activities including texting, messaging, Tweeting, using Facebook and so on, possibly on curriculum-related matters but possibly not. At least when students were rapidly writing down content, they were engaging on at least a superficial level with the text, even though the very act of scribbling potentially hampered deep thought. Today many students question the value and relevance of attending lectures, especially where the dominant curriculum delivery model fails to take account of changing circumstances.

Lecturers who want to help students could advise them to:

- Maintain clarity about what lectures are for: help them understand that this is not a straightforward knowledge transfer process but rather an opportunity to be inspired, gain current contextual perspectives and review what could be learned from books through the lens of an educated and committed practitioner.
- Engage actively with handouts and downloaded material immediately before, during and after lectures, rather than just relying on the material being there at revision time. This might involve setting formative tasks associated with the material so students can be confident they have taken on board key concepts and relevant information.
- Be strict with themselves about using personal devices and electronic media, focusing only on the lecture topic.
- Use electronic media productively to join in Twitter conversations about the lecture, Google unfamiliar terms, expressions and references.
- Keep focused on the lecture topic, even if all around them people are losing concentration. Jotting and doodling may help, and making quick summaries is likely to be more helpful than attempting to reproduce every word you say.
- Keep notes not so much of the content of the lecture, if this is provided elsewhere, but of their own thoughts, ideas, questions, challenges, anomalies, gaps in understanding, comparisons, and so on that occur to them during the lecture for checking later.

- Be proactive in lectures, constantly asking questions to themselves including 'How does this link to material I've learned earlier?', 'What am I expected to be able to do with this material?' and 'How does this connect with the learning outcomes of the course?'.
- Use constructively the opportunities for question and answer that you provide by noting queries and being ready to propose them when you solicit questions, and to forward them to you outside class if there isn't time to answer them all within the allotted time. It makes sense for you to answer such questions collectively through a course web page or the virtual learning environment (VLE), where many more students can benefit, rather than responding privately at length to individual students.
- Take responsibility to make up any missed lectures by reviewing and interrogating materials provided as soon as possible after the event, and checking understandings with peers and tutors.

The following good practice account describes how colleagues in South Africa use case study teaching in larger classrooms to help students learn and keep them engaged, without overrelying on traditionally-delivered lectures.

Using case teaching in teacher education with large class groups

Sarah Gravett, Josef de Beer and **Nadine Petersen**, Faculty of Education, University of Johannesburg, South Africa

Introduction

This account describes using case study approaches with large cohorts (400+) in Teacher Education in South Africa. Teacher education is often criticised for being too 'theoretical in many nations including ours'. Smagorinsky et al. say university teacher educators are often viewed as 'aloof within the ivory tower, espousing ideals and the principles that govern them' (2003, p. 1400). In contrast 'school-based teachers engage in practice in the teeming world of the classroom' (ibid.).

We have been using case-based teaching successfully to examine the practice of teaching. Good cases are designed to encourage discussion and debate about the dilemma(s) central to the case (Merseth and Lacey, 1993). We agree with Shulman (2004), citing Spiro, Coulson, Feltovich and Anderson (1988), that cases are powerful because the complexity, contextuality and richness of cases afford students the opportunities to 'criss-cross the landscape of theory and practice'. He adds that 'principles are powerful but cases are memorable. Only in the continued interaction between principles and cases can practitioners and their mentors avoid the inherent limitations of theory-without-practice or the equally serious restrictions of vivid practice without the mirror of principle' (p. 467).

Using case studies with large groups

We concur with Mulryan-Kyne (2010) that large university classes are often characterised by student passivity, high absenteeism and low motivation. We have adapted the classical case teaching method, often used with small groups, for our large-group teaching, resulting in engaged students and lively discussions.

1. Students are required to read the case prior to the class. To prompt class discussion we provide a short summary of the case narrative. Students then discuss it in small groups (3–4 students), guided by a few questions to direct the discussion.
2. Next we elicit feedback from some of the groups, using a roaming microphone, to ensure that all students can hear the feedback. Students are generally keen to provide feedback. The group reports are enlightening because they reflect students' assumptions and experiences about pertinent education issues captured in the case.
3. The lecturer summarises the general trends in the feedback.
4. The students' feedback is then used as a springboard to introduce theoretical notions related to the planned curriculum themes. Sometimes students come with valid but unexpected inputs, and the lecturer then has to be creative to incorporate these aspects in the theoretical input that follows. Sometimes we use more than one theoretical lens when exploring the case.
5. Students then discuss the case again in their small groups, but this time they have to use the theoretical lens to examine the practice captured in the case.
6. This is followed by large-group feedback.
7. The class is concluded by summarising the main practice points explored.
8. After class students write personal reflections, which they post on the university's Blackboard system online. The discussions therefore continue in a virtual space.

From a qualitative inquiry with teacher educators and student-teachers on their experience of using cases we found that case teaching stimulates active engagement in large class groups and proves to be a powerful springboard for introducing conceptual knowledge. Cases elicit student-teachers' preconceptions about teaching and learning, built through the 'apprenticeship of observation' (Lortie, 1975) in schools. Their agreement or disagreement with the stance of a case character is often based on their own role models or experiences. Understanding and challenging students' preconceptions is crucial because they filter how students make sense of conceptual knowledge. We also found that starting with the concrete, practical dilemmas of teaching in cases and then introducing theoretical lenses, makes the theoretical notions more accessible. The debates that

continued overleaf

Using case teaching in teacher education with large class groups *continued*

ensue also foster analytical and reflective thinking. Another strong advantage of case teaching is that it brings the complexity of teaching, through the dilemmas in the cases, into the university classroom.

Students comments on this pedagogy

"I got a lot more respect for the complexity of the career and … insights into their [teachers'] actions."

"You get that real experience, where you have to think … if I'm the teacher in this case what would I have done?"

"I can also say that the theory part alone is not enough. School experience alone is not enough. You need other people's experiences to learn."

References

Lortie, D.C. (1975) *Schoolteacher: A sociological study*, Chicago: University of Chicago Press.

Merseth, K. and Lacey, C.A. (1993) Weaving stronger fabric: the pedagogical promise of hypermedia and case methods in teacher education, *Teacher and Teacher Education*, 9(3), pp. 283–99.

Mulryan-Kyne, C. (2010) Teaching large classes at college and university level: challenges and opportunities, *Teaching in Higher Education*, 15(2), pp. 175–85.

Shulman, L. (2004) 'Just in case. Reflections on learning from experience', in S.M. Wilson, *The Wisdom of Practice. Essays on teaching, learning and learning to teach*, San Francisco: Jossey-Bass.

Smagorinsky, P., Cook L.S. and Johnson T.S. (2003) The twisting path of concept development in learning to teach, *Teachers College Record*, 105 (8), pp. 1399–436. Available on www.tcrecord.org/content.asp?contentid=11552 (accessed: 9 August 2012).

What is a large group?

Much has been written in the three decades since the emergence of the massification of higher education (Gibbs and Jenkins, 1992) as a global trend, where higher education became less the domain of a privileged elite, and where nations including Ireland, Australia and the UK provided a tertiary education experience for close to 50% of the age cohort leaving school. For some institutions, this shift meant moving from regarding groups of, say, 60 students as a large group, to offering classes to hundreds or even thousands of students at the same time, constrained only by the size of lecture theatres available. Nowadays, of course, lectures can be delivered to even vaster groups using technologies to deliver synchronously and asynchronously to practically unlimited numbers, while not, of course, offering the same kind of experience as being physically present in the same room as the lecturer delivering the lecture. The next good practice account describes how really big classes in Egypt are encouraged to learn.

Learning and teaching in Egypt

Hala F. Mansour, Keele University, UK

Overview of the Egyptian higher education sector

Although Egypt recently has launched important reforms in the higher education sector, there are still many challenges facing the change of the sector. In Egypt there are 35 universities (17 public, 17 private and Al-Azhar), 8 public technical colleges and 121 private higher institutes, and its university sector is the largest in the Middle East and North Africa region (ETF, 2011). The public sector is still the main source of funding to the higher education sector. Teaching and learning in the Egyptian higher education sector is very traditional: for economic reasons, lectures remain the main way to teach students and the onus is on the lecturer to make teaching very large cohorts work well through effective lecturing and subsequent smaller seminars. This good practice account offers a review of lecturing in Egypt where I worked for more than fifteen years.

Teaching and marking for large groups

Some schools in the Egyptian universities have very high enrolments, for example Business, Art and Law. In each undergraduate year, there are around 8000 to 10,000 students across each university in Egypt. Teaching large groups is considered efficient in terms of transmitting information to large numbers of students in one sitting. Egyptian universities provide good learning environments in terms of teaching staff, student support and large lecture theatres. To cover the substantial teaching load, each year the graduates with the highest marks in every discipline are recruited as Graduate Teaching Assistants. Lecturing is the most popular teaching style. Each subject is taught by a team of teachers who together teach very large groups of students (around 2000 students in each group). The syllabus is common among groups but each teacher is free to teach using different materials and using his/her own style. There are also the tutorial sessions which are more flexible due to smaller number of students in each group and in these there are better opportunities for students to ask clarifying questions of their tutors.

continued overleaf

Learning and teaching in Egypt *continued*

Classroom management is important in teaching big groups. The lecturer is responsible for managing the classroom well, providing learning resources including handouts and allowing enough time for note-taking. Such teaching requires high energy and motivation on the part of the lecturers and it can be exciting to gain the attention of so many students. Teaching more than 1000 students at a time requires special skills in managing student contributions and interactions, alongside the presentation elements where students need to pay attention and listen. It's important to establish an appropriate teaching style from the very first day. To keep the interest of so many students and keep them focused on learning, Egyptian lecturers explain particular issues exclusively in the lecture and they do not include them in the handouts. They then inform students that the final exam will include some questions from the information just explained in the lecture. For students in such large groups, there can be challenges, particularly around asking questions so these are largely resolved within tutorial groups where students can participate fully. With so many students in lectures, written questions are normally passed forward to the front so the lecturer can respond to the whole group.

There is a clear process for dealing with students coming late for lectures whereby students are notified of the policy on the first day of classes and they are required to abide by it. Not allowing students to enter the room more than ten minutes after the start of the lecture puts the responsibility on students to be punctual or catch up in their own time.

References

ETF (European Training Foundation) (2011) *Building a Competitiveness Framework for Education and Training In Egypt*, Working paper.

Traditional lectures rely heavily on the spoken word, often accompanied by textual or visual stimuli in the form of handouts, notes on the web and Microsoft® PowerPoint, WordPerfect, Prezi and other electronic forms of presentations. Incidentally, it's interesting that people still talk about 'slides' to describe what they show on screen, whereas glass mounted or cellophane slides have not been in regular use in most nations since the 1960s. Lectures where the presenter is charismatic, energised, articulate and relaxed in front of the student audience are a pleasure to behold, and can be some of the most inspiring learning experiences we can experience, but this tends to be the exception rather than the rule. Nevertheless, curriculum delivery doesn't have to take the form of a classic talked-through presentation of text and images, sometimes described as 'talking in other people's sleep', as this next good practice account shows.

Cabaret as academic discourse

Geoff Hill, University of Queensland, Australia

Introduction

The pedagogic practice of academic cabaret (Hill, 2001) is not so much a national practice strength, but knowing that its originator is Australian links this initiative to what is often seen as the Australian pastime of challenging authority. Some think of this challenging disposition as being linked to the earliest migration to Australia that involved convict transportation.

While there is potential to position this initiative as cultural, my impetus for 'academic cabaret' arose out of researching non-verbal communication (NVC) and discovering that one form is music. This occurred to me in the early days of my lecturing career and, as I had a parallel passion for musical theatre, I demonstrated this aspect of the theory in my lecture on NVC to undergraduate Early Childhood students by adapting the words of Stephen Sondheim's *Sunday in the Park with George* song 'Bit by bit putting it together' to summarise all the non-verbal issues that students needed to consider when they were putting together their classroom assessment presentation. This lecturing approach appeared to embed the summary of the lecture. At the students' graduation, three years after I had presented this lecture, several students reminded me of that one particular lecture.

My first academic cabaret was written in collaboration with musical theatre colleagues as an after-dinner presentation for the Australian Consortium of Experiential Education annual conference in 1993. The following year I presented my first one-man, two-act, cabaret on reflective practice. A second cabaret, written in the context of my doctoral degree, investigated 'doing a doctorate' and was presented as one of the publications within my doctoral dissertation. I took this research publication approach to an international conference with a cabaret on 'Research Supervision' for the International Quality in Postgraduate Research Conference in Adelaide in 2006.

Original features

What makes this form of research publication and higher degree education innovative is that most conference participants or students are not prepared for a sung presentation. The novelty of the approach often puts the audience in a favourable mood for some of the more challenging aspects of the paper/cabaret which may confront them about their own practices. An example of such confrontation is the song used in the cabaret on research supervision which explores the issue of supervisors losing students through inept supervision. The lyrics of the song suggest 'maybe this time I'll be lucky, maybe this time they'll stay.' The subsequent discussion opens up the possibility that luck has nothing to do with retaining students, rather it requires honed pedagogy and if a research supervisor is constantly losing students then they need to look to the quality of their research supervision for explanations.

continued overleaf

Cabaret as academic discourse *continued*

The uniqueness of this approach also brings with it challenges. Few if any conference convenors have any experience of accepting cabaret as a conference input or output. Sometimes when I offered one I was offered a poster session instead, and had to write back to decline and explain why this genre of conference presentation does not fit into a poster format. As the time commitment for a two-act cabaret is often challenging to include in a conference schedule, I have recently adapted the model into a 30-minute version. The first of these was presented at the Inaugural Storytelling Conference in Prague in 2013 and subsequently toured internationally. A cabaret works best in a conference setting when convenors have heard about my presentation approach and invite me to develop and present in this format.

As a teaching strategy, whether in higher education lecturing or in the conference setting, presenting in cabaret creates an edge of difference. It positions the content differently from other content and this adds to the educational impact. I see my approach not so much advocating cabaret *per se*, but encouraging the educator to bring to their topic skills that reveal their passion for a topic. Revelation of the passion one has for one's topic brings an emotional understanding to the topic. In my using cabaret I can demonstrate both passion and mastery and embrace that into my pedagogy. Others may have different skills which they desire to include in their mainstream work. In the light of the shifted recognition for what counts as research, both from the OECD *Frascati Manual* (2002) guidelines and in the Australian context (ERA, 2010), there is room to consider creative works as research in their own right and thus to consider their creative publication as research publication. In the case on lecturing on research publication, delivering in cabaret models the very issue on which I am lecturing.

References

ERA (Excellence for Research in Australia) (2010) *Submission Guidelines*, Commonwealth of Australia.

Hill, G. (2001) Educational Cabaret, *Action Learning and Action Research Journal*, 6(1).

OECD (2002) *Frascati Manual: Proposed standard practice for surveys on research and experimental development*, 6th edn, OECD.

A maieutic approach to curriculum delivery implies education being a matter of 'drawing out' (as the Greek term implies) knowledge that is latent within the unconscious mind, in a dialectical approach where the role of the philosopher, according to Plato, is like that of a midwife. Much in this chapter has focused on delivery in large class settings, but as illustrated elsewhere in this volume, there are myriad different contexts in which learning can be fostered rather than information being simply delivered in a unidirectional manner. These approaches can be apparent at all levels in higher education where there are opportunities for students to interact closely with academics, and none more so than at post-graduate level where traditional didactic approaches are less relevant. The next good practice account describes offering doctoral supervision using appropriate models of educational practice across two very different nations, the UK and Malaysia.

Doctoral supervision in the cross-cultural arena

Christopher Hill, Research Training and Academic Development, and **Ganakumaran Subramaniam**, School of Education, University of Nottingham Malaysia Campus, Malaysia

Introduction

Malaysia is rapidly becoming known as a hub for tertiary education and is seeking to attract up to 200,000 international students by 2020. As the presence of international universities increases and, with it, the numbers of international academics working in private and public universities, issues of cross-cultural supervision become more and more prevalent. The Malaysian government aims to dramatically increase the number of PhD holders within the nation and this means up-skilling existing academics, developing professional doctorates with industry and attracting international staff and students to the system, both residentially and also through distance and joint PhD programmes. All of these factors lead to the reality that issues around competing pressures, different agendas, educational systems and understandings all come to a head in an environment where high-quality interaction and supervision are critical to the success rate, experience and quality of PhDs produced.

The key issues that arise, as a result of these competing pressures, are both cultural and procedural in nature. The diversity of educational approaches, the nature of dissemination of information, fundamental pedagogical approaches and the hidden hierarchy of power, both in terms of gender as described by Leonard (1997) and culture outlined by Gundara (1997), often hinder the supervision process. Student's understanding of what is expected of them during their PhD can, at times, differ greatly from the understanding of the supervisor and the institution and, when coupled with cultural and contextual methods of communication and question raising, this can lead to a breakdown of the system and a loss of confidence on the part of the student. Ultimately of course, this can lead to increased levels of failure and impact upon recruitment, research development and capacity building.

continued overleaf

Doctoral supervision in the cross-cultural arena *continued*

The University of Nottingham Malaysia Campus ensures that training is provided for both staff and students to encourage discussion and sharing of expectations. As Deem and Brehony (2000) outline, 'research training courses may provide a bridge between research student cultures and research cultures for international students, as well as affording academic benefits.' We provide orientation for our new PhD students and a series of training courses that develop key skills alongside a fundamental awareness of the nature of a Nottingham PhD. This training is mirrored for our supervisors and we use project management techniques and cross-cultural discussion sessions to ensure the institutional quality framework supports, informs and guides the wealth of international experience amongst our staff and students.

Success factors

It is critical to build up a relationship of trust whereby students feel free to raise concerns and issues with their supervisors and do not follow blindly along a path they do not fully understand. This trust takes time to build but can be achieved through consistency of message and transparency of purpose. We provide training sessions on cross-cultural teaching and interacting with a diverse audience that introduce staff and students to differing expectations and learning styles and promotes interaction and awareness through a series of workshops, teamwork activities and reflection. In addition to these training sessions, that are embedded at the start of each academic cycle, we provide opportunities for students to develop confidence and negotiation skills throughout their degree experience through a series of planned activities, such as International Young Entrepreneurs Scheme, that encourage and support cross-cultural engagement.

We encourage our students to plan for the year ahead and then discuss their plans with their supervisors, and we run a series of training workshops that discuss assigning involvement and responsibility for various elements of the PhD process, such as setting meetings, developing research topics, providing feedback and reporting on progress. These workshops are delivered for staff and students independently and then the results are compared and discussed during individual supervisory sessions. This process facilitates discussion and provides an opportunity for agreement to be reached through dialogue and consensus. Once the student has 'bought into' the project and process the rates of success are much higher and a relationship of mutual trust and co-operation can begin.

The University of Nottingham Malaysia Campus recognises the value of diversity within higher education and works to incorporate this within the teaching experience, while at the same time, ensuring that agenda setting, open discussion and consistency of delivery exist to support our PhD students as they navigate the difficult journey ahead.

'The training and feedback sessions were of great assistance in this matter, and very encouraging. We also had the chance of meeting our peers from different backgrounds and hearing their feedback and ideas as well. This training was also very pivotal in developing our research projects.'

UNMC PhD Student

'Diversity and internationalisation are at the heart of everything we do at the Malaysia Campus and the training provided by the Graduate School and other departments provides a fantastic platform for reflective discussion and interaction. On a daily basis our research staff and doctoral students navigate a multi-cultural environment and the support we provide helps to both prepare them for this and allows the university to further learn from the plethora of international experiences and perspectives on offer.'

UNMC PhD Supervisor

References

Deem, R. and Brehony, K.J. (2000) Doctoral students' access to research cultures – are some more unequal than others?, *Studies in Higher Education*, 25(2), p. 157.

Gundara, J. (1997) 'Intercultural issues and doctoral studies', in N. Graves and V. Varma (eds) *Working for a Doctorate*, Abingdon: Routledge.

Leonard, D. (1997) 'Gender issues in doctoral studies', in N. Graves and V. Varma (eds) *Working for a Doctorate*, Abingdon: Routledge.

Conclusions

At the heart of good curriculum delivery is a productive working relationship between university teachers and students, with each playing their part, whether this is in large face-to-face classes, smaller teaching contexts, one-to-one supervisions or virtual learning environments. So what is required to be effective in curriculum delivery? Refuting the view that all those in possession of a higher degree can make good university teachers, McKeachie (1951/1994) argues that:

> 'Effective lecturers combine the talents of a scholar, writer, producer, comedian, showman and teacher in ways that contribute to student learning.'
>
> McKeachie, 1994, p. 53

Among the characteristics of excellent curriculum deliverers, Bain suggests they are those who:

- '[A]re willing to spend time with students, to nurture their learning.
- Do not foster a feeling of power over, but investment in, students.
- [Ensure their] practices stem from a concern for learning.
- Make the class user-friendly by fostering trust.
- Employ various pedagogical tools in a search for the best way to help each student.
- Have the attitude that, "There is no such thing as a stupid question."
- [Ensure that] everyone can contribute and each contribution is unique.
- [Do not behave as a] "high priest of arcane mysteries"...
- Foster the feeling that teachers are fellow students/human beings struggling with mysteries of the universe.'

Bain, 2004, p. 49

This is quite a tall order, since as well as being knowledgeable about one's subject material, those who deliver the curriculum well in whatever context tend to be scholarly, systematic, consistent, well-prepared and highly committed to student learning. They can usually work well at different levels and in diverse contexts, having developed their own styles and approaches that suit the context and their learners appropriately. In the next chapter, the focus moves to the other partners in the working relationship, the students, and the ways in which university teachers can help them develop the skills and capacities they need to be effective learners.

5 Making spaces for learning work: learning in diverse settings

Introduction

In much of this book I have written about learning that is largely done sitting down, in lectures, seminars and at computers. Here I want to consider how we can help university learning happen in all kinds of other places: in laboratories, in performance venues, in fieldwork, on the playing field, in the studio, on hospital wards, in law courts and in other professional contexts where this kind of learning is usually learning by doing (Race, 2014). In this chapter I will explore just a few of these contexts, but the expectation is that ideas may well be transferable into other contexts.

In terms of Boyer's four scholarships (Boyer, 1990), learning in diverse settings may involve the scholarship of discovery of new ideas and interrelationships (in undergraduate student-led research projects and in masters and doctoral research) but also the scholarship of application where, as Boyer suggests, 'the scholar asks, "How can knowledge be responsibly applied to consequential problems? How can it be helpful to individuals as well as institutions?"' (1990, p. 21). More particularly, this kind of learning involves what he terms the scholarship of integration whereby scholars give meaning to isolated facts, putting them in perspective:

> 'By integration we mean making connections across the disciplines, placing the specialties in [a] larger context, illuminating data in a revealing way, often educating non-specialists too. ... What we mean is serious disciplined work that seeks to interpret, draw together and bring new insight to bear on original research.'
>
> Boyer, 1990, p. 19

Students learning beyond the lecture room are likely to develop over the course of a programme all of these kinds of scholarship. Managing and assessing students working in diverse settings requires different models of context-dependent teaching which will include the places in which learning happens, different kinds of interactions and different modes of assessment.

As discussed earlier in the book, the **places** in which learning takes place are hugely variable according not only to what is being taught, but also to the local and national context and the economic environment in which the university is placed. One can be stunned by the astonishingly lavishly-appointed and technologically-enhanced learning environments provided in universities in Singapore and disconcerted by the paint-splashed scruffiness of many places where art is made, but the crucial factor is in the focus on learning and the ways in which it is enabled.

The nature of **interactions** in diverse learning spaces is very different from traditional teaching in lectures where for the most part students listen to and watch lecturers speak (for alternative lecture models, see Chapter 4). It is possible to adopt lecturing approaches to use in acoustic labs, theatres and IT labs, but this rarely works well, and instead the nature of the transaction between lecturer and student tends to be more dialogic, often with a focus on fostering practical skills and relating them to theoretical elements of the course delivered elsewhere live or virtually.

Assessment of learning that is undertaken in diverse contexts can also be highly traditional, in the form of unseen time-constrained exams or multiple-choice questions, but this rarely does justice to the transformative experiences that can take place in live learning environments at their best.

In this chapter, recognising that it is not possible to cover every available learning context, I aim to explore how we can really make learning work in labs, in studios, on field trips and in employment contexts.

Laboratories as active learning spaces

A range of subjects including medicine, traditional sciences, engineering, food technology and sports science make use of laboratory settings where students can experiment and explore how theory can be applied to practice. Such experiences can be exciting and transformative for students in helping them really get to grips with the subjects they are studying. All too often though, students and staff describe the lab experience as dreary, formulaic and unproductive, sometimes resulting in students mindlessly following methodological 'recipe books' and resulting in lots of repetitive marking of lab books for staff. There are obvious issues around safeguarding students in complex and sometimes dangerous environments, but this can result in highly constrained safe working practices which can hamper real experimentation. Resource-based learning materials can help make learning science practically a more meaningful experience (Exley and Gibbs, 1994), but this alone is insufficient.

Davidowitz and Rollnick (2001, p. 18) describe what can go wrong when students view laboratory practicals as simply an exercise in task completion, where students can suffer from information overload in complex, information rich environments and neither students nor staff really benefit from the experience. They found their students, many of whom came from disadvantaged backgrounds, arrived badly prepared at their practicals and just went through the motions in order just to get the job done and have the associated marks awarded. Just as the meticulous following of recipes helps cooks make specific meals, but may not give them the confidence to branch out into devising their own original culinary creations, so also students working in labs who unthinkingly follow specified routines may never really understand the science behind the practicals.

Their alternative approach focused on changing the nature of the interaction between staff and students by modifying practices and assessment. They enforced preparation in advance by requiring students, before setting foot in the lab, to construct flow diagrams (which included images and text) for each experiment, thereby helping students to achieve a detailed understanding of the both the underlying chemistry and the experimental steps to be carried out during the experiment. (op. cit., pp. 18–19).

The good practice account that follows describes an innovative and coherent way of using the space available for learning by using lab spaces differently, so that students working on different topics and at different study levels can productively work alongside one another.

Using large, flexible and multidisciplinary Biomedical Science labs

Biddy Unsworth, Leeds Metropolitan University, UK

Introduction

Leeds Metropolitan University has an estate which has been extensively modernised and developed in recent years. A significant development for the Faculty of Health and Social Sciences was the Biomedical Sciences laboratory opened in January 2011. This lab enabled us to bring together science lab provision which had previously been delivered in six separate locations across three separate buildings. From the outset, the lab was designed to be flexible and multidisciplinary, with students on different programmes at different levels working alongside one another. Our brief to the developers was informed by visits to other recently completed laboratories and by consultation with academic and technical staff. We wanted to provide a space that would facilitate active learning, stimulate innovation in teaching and increase student satisfaction.

continued overleaf

Using large, flexible and multidisciplinary Biomedical Science labs *continued*

The lab can accommodate several different activities at the same time, with four separate teaching stations, each linked to a large screen and to repeater screens. It can also function as a space for delivery for one large group of 106 students. The ancillary support areas were also crucial to the design. We brought together two teams of learning-officer staff, who now work together in a single team to provide all the materials and equipment for the students and offer technical support for teaching, research and consultancy. The learning-officer team is now much better able to work efficiently across a number of disciplines. The lab functions as a Class 2 microbiology containment area, enabling us to run a full range of biosciences practicals and carry out research and consultancy work.

Evaluation

Staff and students have responded very positively to the new lab and we have seen a significant rise (c. 30%) in applications and enrolments on our biosciences courses since the lab was opened. Staff particularly welcomed the audio-visual facilities in the labs and quickly developed new PowerPoint slide sets, with animations and images, for introducing practicals for students. The flexible set-up enables each repeater screen to be linked to the lead teaching station, ensuring all students have a clear view of the slides. We also have a video camera that can be linked to the screens for real-time demonstration of techniques. The presentations can be left running during the practical so students are able to remind themselves of key points as they work; they can also be uploaded onto our virtual learning environment for students to use for revision at a later point.

The student response continues to be positive, with many students citing working in the lab as the thing they are most looking forward to when they arrive. The concurrent running of activities also enables students to get a feel for practicals they might do later on in their studies and when the final-year project students are working, students can see the sort of thing they might do themselves. This enhances the continuity of the course and student satisfaction scores as measured in the National Student Survey have risen to around 90% overall satisfaction in the last two years. The larger space has also enabled us to offer a much wider range and larger number of laboratory-based final-year projects, with more new areas being introduced every year. We are able to link our undergraduate students to our active research scientists, both for their project work and for an innovative Undergraduate Researcher Scheme which was introduced in 2013. In this scheme, students work with a researcher over an eight-week period. This differs from the final-year project as they are part of a research team and carry out parts of ongoing research, rather than undertaking a discrete piece of work. This gives them additional research experience and laboratory skills, which are key to many of the jobs our students aspire to on graduation.

Staff have developed a better understanding of the modules on the courses as a result of working alongside one another in the lab and there is more cross-disciplinary working, as we run larger classes and so utilise a larger staff team. This provides increased opportunities for peer-observation of teaching and we have also enabled new or part-time staff to deliver introductions to practicals and receive instant feedback from the staff team.

Overall, the new Biosciences laboratory has had a major impact on both student and staff satisfaction, which clearly provides major benefits for the £1.1 million investment the University made.

Reference

Sharp, D. and Fitzgerald, P. (2014) *Students as Researchers: Improving collaborating research output*, HEASTEM conference paper (HEASTEM2014), April 2014, Edinburgh, UK.

Art and design studios

In traditional *atelier* models at their best, students work alongside 'master' practitioners (not always men, but people who have gained mastery of their subjects) and learn from them in the studio by watching their practices, emulating and modifying them, and finding inspiration from being in the company of acknowledged experts. Interaction with experts can provide opportunities for informal guidance and feedback, leading to personal advancement in capabilities and understanding. However, at their worst, in studios students commonly complain that they are left to their own devices, feeling ignored by their tutors and receiving scathing, negative and damaging feedback (if any) on their own practical efforts.

Good practice in studio teaching can involve making the most of available space, carefully considering the nature of interactions and using appropriate assessment by:

- Emulating the kinds of contexts graduates will encounter when they leave university and providing well-equipped and state-of-the-art facilities where students can hone their capabilities.
- Fostering interaction between students and staff, and students with one another, so that a community of learners is established in the studio.
- Fairly sharing time between students as far as is possible, so that each student feels capable of seeking guidance as necessary and there is no perceived favouritism among the cohort.
- Balancing offers of support and guidance with enabling students to work uninterrupted with high levels of concentration on their own practice.

- Working one-to-one and with the whole group as appropriate to share practical techniques and critical perspectives.
- Discussing terms such as 'creativity', 'criticality', 'originality' so that students develop their own understandings of what these mean for them in practice.
- Offering feedback during the production of artefacts rather than just at the end, to help students shape their individual practices.
- Commenting within feedback on the work produced and the behaviours demonstrated rather than the personality of the individual student working in the studio, and using language which enables development rather than what David Boud (1995) describes as 'final language' which gives students nowhere to go: ('hopeless', 'useless', 'awful', 'inadequate').
- Recording informal and formal feedback so that it doesn't get lost or ignored in the heat of the moment. It is possible to provide audio or video records of in-studio conversations or to ask students to provide paper or electronic write-ups of the guidance they have received for checking against the tutor's recall of the key points of discussions.
- Providing a wide diversity of examples of artefacts that have received good marks, so students can get a clear picture of the standard of work required, without suggesting that these comprise the full range of potential creative responses.
- Enabling students to interrogate what assessment criteria really mean through discussion and rehearsal, ideally including some guided peer review.

See Martinez, Raven and Trees' good practice account in Chapter 7 (pp. 123–5) for an example of how studio teaching can work at its best to build partnerships with and between students.

Fieldwork

For some students fieldwork is the pivot for transformative learning in their university studies. Boyle et al. (2007) argue in their study around Geography, Earth Sciences and Environmental Science field experience that it can be a really powerful energiser for learning. Their research focuses on the effects of fieldwork in the affective domain, which they argue is strongly linked to the adoption of effective approaches to learning. However, many of us have unhappy memories of fieldwork where we were cold (or too hot), wet (or parched), frustrated at our own lack of fitness (or the lack of fitness of our peers), lost (intellectually and geographically), confused and uncertain (or unconvinced) of the value of learning in the field (or up a mountain or at the foot of a valley). Fieldwork doesn't always have a strong reputation for inclusive practices either: Hall, Healey and Harrison (2002) have highlighted the sexist and ableist assumptions that can underpin the lived experiences of fieldwork for both staff and students. Nevertheless, higher education field experience doesn't have to be like that, and in the next good practice account the authors describe ways of making fieldwork relevant, useful and accessible.

Technology-enhanced learning on an international fieldtrip

Alice Mauchline and **Rob Jackson**, University of Reading, and **Derek France**, University of Chester, UK

Microbiology is a key biology discipline, however students often work with a microbial culture in the laboratory without any real appreciation for the environment from which it was taken. This lack of environmental understanding and the need to develop students' field sampling skills led to the development of a joint field-based module for students from the University of Reading, UK and the University of Akureyri, Iceland.

The fieldtrip, led by Dr Rob Jackson, is held in Iceland and aims to teach undergraduates a variety of skills in microbiology research and to provide the opportunity to study microbes that inhabit extreme environments such as glacial rivers and areas of geothermal activity. The students spend several days sampling different environments and then spend ten days culturing and characterising the microbes in the laboratory. The students from both institutions are paired off to work together and are taught and supported in their learning by staff members from the UK and Iceland alongside guest lecturers/demonstrators from other countries. Students from each institute can advise each other on techniques they are taught. Staff members have been able to benefit from this collaborative teaching experience through funding from the ERASMUS Lifelong Learning programme of the European Union.

In 2013, these fieldwork research activities were supported through the use of mobile technologies and social media to engage students in their learning and to facilitate communication between the students and staff in the large multi-national team in three distinct phases:

Pre-fieldwork: an enterprise social networking site (Yammer) was used: to facilitate communication within a closed network; for collation of literature and lecture materials; and for disseminating preparatory material prior to the trip.

In the field: the students were paired up and provided with a ruggedised iPad. They were asked to capture field data using a variety of fieldwork-related apps. They were encouraged to collect geo-referenced, real-time data at each sample position (using GPS Log), which included photos, videos and field notes of environmental conditions. These data were captured offline while in the field and stored.

continued overleaf

Technology-enhanced learning on an international fieldtrip *continued*

Post-fieldwork: once back from the field and connected to the internet, the students shared their field data using cloud storage (Dropbox) and a 'live' database of results (using Google Drive) to link to their lab experiments. The geo-referenced sampling positions were shared using a social travel log website/app (Geospike) for long-term data retrieval. The photos and videos were used in their assessed presentations and to make short reflective videos of the sampling environments (using Splice, iMovie and others). Social media was used extensively for informal communication (Facebook) and reflection (Twitter); see this Storify for a summary, http://tinyurl.com/ovksh9f.

Many of the students further explored the use of the iPads and apps for their learning and found them useful in ways they weren't expecting, e.g. to display lab protocols, for recording lecture notes, as prompts for presentations.

Benefits: the feedback was very positive from the students. Some examples of the benefits they identified were:

> "the iPad was exceptionally useful for the fieldwork; recording data and geographical info together"

> "brings together several useful applications in one place e.g. GPS, photo/video/internet, so we don't need 3–4 pieces of equipment"

> "instant note-taking, no faffing about with pens and paper. All pictures, recordings etc. in one place, can use and manipulate data instantly"

Drawbacks: there were concerns over breaking the iPads (which didn't happen!) and there were some drawbacks as identified by the students:

> "hard to share as you potentially lose some data"

> "not enough time to acquaint ourselves with the iPads – would have been helpful to have a brief introduction"

The concerns of the students from this initial trial have been taken into account and will hopefully be resolved by better preparation and organisation next time. However, the students were overwhelmingly positive about their experiences of technology-enhanced learning in the field and we hope to build on this in the future.

In conclusion, mobile technology provided a more efficient and accurate way to capture, store, analyse and share data during fieldwork. Moreover, it provided a means to establish good working relationships between the students and helped team cohesion between both nationalities.

Further information

The Enhancing Fieldwork Learning project: www.enhancingfieldwork.org.uk

'Heading to the Arctic to teach students about the wonderful world of "extreme" microbes': http://tinyurl.com/pvkgac2

Simulations: for fieldwork when you can't get out in the field

Nowadays it can be difficult for academics to organise site visits to live learning environments because Health and Safety regulations or resource constraints make it a highly complex matter to get permission to take students into remote or dangerous environments. Ellis et al. (2006) were faced with exactly this problem when they wanted to give surveying students real-world learning experiences and so developed a multimedia application which virtually allowed students to crawl all over a building site when it wasn't possible for them to do so in reality. Ellis arranged to have equipment sited high on a building site in Leeds, allowing images to be recorded and built them into an interactive multimedia levelling resource, which comprised text-based guides, video instruction, photo-realistic panoramic scenes and multi-row object movies. Students could explore 360 degree images of building sites, using traditional computer input devices, and click on hot spots to gather detailed information about the position of the optical level and staff. Readings could be taken directly by staff and students and the approach really worked in maintaining student interest and bringing learning to life.

Computer simulations are very widely used for learning in a number of undergraduate and post-graduate areas nowadays, including hospitality and tourism students modelling costings for package holidays, trainee surgeons learning to use complex surgical techniques involving cameras and lasers before being let loose on live patents, and airline pilots working in simulated cockpits and managing simulated environments as training for the real thing.

In the good practice account overleaf, colleagues describe using role play to simulate foreign language teaching companies where real-life opportunities are difficult to offer to students. They learn a wide range of intellectual and practical skills, not just language proficiency but also about business practices, including tendering for bids and dealing with HR issues.

Reviewing teaching in diverse learning settings

Evaluating the effectiveness of teaching and learning outside the standard classroom is potentially not as straightforward as watching a conventional presentation and making judgements about its quality using criteria such as audibility, use of audio-visual aids, ability to engage an audience, delivery and pace and taking questions. Much that is written about teaching observations concentrates particularly on lectures (with honourable exceptions, including Race et al., 2009), and some of the proformas proposed for

Simulations as a teaching method in Belarus

Maya Bogova, Minsk State Linguistic University, Belarus, and **Nadya Yakovchuk**, University of Surrey/The Open University, UK

Background

The *Common European Framework of Reference for Languages: Learning, Teaching, Assessment* (CEFR), which provides a 'basis for the elaboration of language syllabuses and curriculum guidelines, the design of teaching and learning materials, and the assessment of foreign language proficiency' (Council of Europe, 2012), is used by foreign language teachers in Belarus in their professional activity. The document identifies three components of communicative language competences that every student is expected to master in the course of study: linguistic, sociolinguistic and pragmatic competences. It is not sufficient for learners to acquire the pronunciation skills, vocabulary and grammar of the target language: they have to learn how to use the target language in different social contexts, in distinct social and professional environments. They have to master different registers, politeness rules and linguistic markers of social relations. One of the teaching methods which we found extremely useful to this end is simulation.

Simulations for learning

By simulation we mean a prolonged role play, an interactive model of real-life situations which the speakers of the target language are likely to encounter. We have found that this practice can be an answer to one of the main challenges of foreign language teaching in Belarus: a shortage of opportunities to use the target language in real-life situations and to have language practice with native speakers of the target language.

At Minsk State Linguistic University, the interactive character of simulations gives second-year students of the Faculty of Cross-Cultural Communication the opportunity to attain the CEFR level of Independent User (B2), alongside developing their skills and competences in running a business company. These students major in linguistic support for cross-cultural communication and minor in IT/PR/International Tourism/Political Relations/Economic Relations and thus need basic skills in Business English. The simulation lasts throughout the academic year and can be roughly divided into three stages:

1. Setting up a virtual company and hiring personnel.
2. Everyday life of staff members and their interactions.
3. Dealing with extreme situations which can cause a collapse of the company.

In the process, students develop a whole range of skills of communicating in a target language: *reading skills* (e.g. while looking through job applications), *speaking skills* (e.g. when making telephone calls or attending interviews), *writing skills* (e.g. while dealing with business correspondence or creating a company portfolio) and *listening skills* (e.g. when taking part in meetings or watching a video on ergonomic furniture and equipment). They also develop their *critical thinking* skills and the ability to make *tactical and operational decisions*.

Throughout the simulation, students are immersed in the new language of their future profession. The process is facilitated by staff who make necessary adaptations depending on the requirements of particular contexts and tasks, and who monitor and provide feedback on students' language choices and communicative behaviours. Staff also develop assessment strategies and actively involve students in self and peer assessment. For example, students fill in evaluation forms and discuss how their performance can be improved after each new stage in the simulation. Occasionally, their companies get the task to participate in a tender offer. Afterwards each company analyses why they failed or what made them win, and how they can do better next time.

Benefits and disadvantages

A distinctive feature that makes simulations an effective teaching method is their potential to create meaningful communicative situations where students use a target language to interact with others and to co-ordinate their actions in order to achieve a purpose, which reflects some of the main functions that language fulfils. It keeps students motivated in their studies and helps them become more aware of how to 'do things with words'.

However, as effective and motivating as they are, simulations require a lot of time on the teacher's part to plan them in detail, design tasks and materials, and give learners regular feedback throughout the process. Teachers need to be very specific in their instructions to maintain learners' interest and to make everybody involved; they also need to be able to foresee possible snags and develop strategies to mitigate against them.

One of the issues sometimes encountered is the learners' lack of subject knowledge in the field around which a simulation is built (for example, differentiating between different forms of company ownership), which may distract students from focusing on developing their language skills. An enthusiastic teacher, however, can always find a way of turning these disadvantages into the strengths of the course and using them as learning opportunities for language development. We suggest letting the 'virtual company employees' attend a series of in-house professional development workshops focused on the areas they are struggling with.

Reference

Council of Europe (2012) *Common European Framework of Reference for Languages: Learning, Teaching, Assessment.* Available at: http://www.coe.int/t/dg4/linguistic/cadre1_en.asp (accessed 1 December 2013).

review in lectures are inappropriate for other settings. Contexts including laboratories, studios, sports halls and so on require an observation that is concentrating more on dialogue and facilitation rather than traditional-style delivery or formal class-based activities. Criteria to be used in these settings might include:

- The extent of the teachers' ability to build a rapport face-to-face with students using empathy and emotional intelligence to bring out the best in them.
- How well the teacher is able to ensure all students can participate equivalently in learning sessions (since it is rarely possible to provide identical experiences in a living context).
- How much students are motivated to engage in the activities provided.
- How well students are guided to develop a wide range of practical and intellectual skills, and bring them together to become capable practitioners.
- How they are helped to learn by their mistakes, and to learn that the process of achieving an outcome is often as important (or more so) than achieving the outcome itself, so long as reflection on practice takes place.
- The extent to which a safe environment is assured, where risk is managed and students learn to be safe-to-practise in the outside world.
- The extent to which students with disabilities are supported in an inclusive environment, so all can achieve to their maximum potential.
- How effectively students are given feedback that is meaningful (and isn't allowed to be ephemeral and readily forgotten) about how to develop their practices.
- To what extent students become able to work autonomously and to judge their own performance in ways that will stand them in good stead in practice after graduation.

To achieve all of these things may call for a radical review of how learning can be engendered in diverse learning settings, and this will rarely be either easy or popular. Focusing particularly on students' needs to develop appropriate and discipline-relevant capabilities is likely to be the best route to achieving this.

Conclusions

University teaching is often characterised, and its sometimes high cost justified, by the specialist facilities and equipment made available for higher-level learning, with an expectation not just that students will listen and watch, but more often participate and do, in the interests of being transformed into experts and specialists who can work alongside their teachers. Boyer (op. cit., p. 80) argues that the discovery of knowledge, the integration of knowledge, and the application of knowledge should be equally honoured in the academy (alongside the scholarship of teaching to which he accords great value also). Providing learning opportunities in diverse settings can offer authentic experiences of these three types of scholarship, which at their best are the ultimate student-centred engine houses for learning.

6 Helping students develop appropriate literacies for effective learning

Introduction

At first sight some might think helping students to develop appropriate literacies for higher education study is a strange thing to attempt: surely students arriving to study in higher education, having 'matriculated', that is demonstrated having been admitted to university, will be literate? Of course we can assume a level of literacy of undergraduates and postgraduates, due to the rigours of the university application process. Many would argue that they are not as literate as in previous years (and others would dispute this), but that is not the focus of this chapter. Here instead I want to discuss the specific capabilities that many believe are necessary 'literacies' for effective tertiary study in the 21st century. These include academic literacy, information literacy, assessment literacy, digital literacy, social and interpersonal literacy.

Academic literacy

Academic literacy is usually taken to mean understanding how higher education works. It includes a range of abilities including knowing how to negotiate university systems, for example, to apply for late submission of work when ill or indisposed and what comprise 'extenuating circumstances' (which can be used to trigger compensation of marks for example, or penalty-free re-sits). Students with high cultural capital, perhaps those with many family members who've been through higher education, are likely to know who to turn to when things go wrong, but those from less advantaged backgrounds are less likely to 'know the ropes'. Such implicit knowledge can be made explicit through good induction and effective personal tutoring to encourage the behaviours that indicate that students have good academic literacy. These include good self- and time-management, getting assignments in on time, managing competing deadlines without becoming over-stressed, effective record keeping, particularly in relation to reference sources, and working at the right level for the programme being studied. Importantly they also include writing and reading for academic purposes.

Writing for academic purposes

A key element of academic literacy is knowing what kinds of writing are needed in specific contexts. Students, particularly those from disadvantaged backgrounds, may need help to understand the various academic discourses that are employed within the subject/institution. Northedge proposes that:

> 'An academic discipline is a discourse community of a particularly systematic and committed kind (or, more accurately, a constellation of overlapping communities, with somewhat blurred boundaries). It is a community that discourses primarily through writing, giving its discourse a very distinctive style.'
>
> Northedge, 2003b, p. 19

He suggests that:

> 'students need an insider's expertise to support them in gaining access to the academic discourses they seek to become conversant with. The teacher, as subject expert, has three key roles to play in enabling learning: lending the capacity to participate in meaning, designing well planned excursions into unfamiliar discursive terrain [and acting as a sherpa working through the foothills of the discourse] and coaching students in speaking the academic discourse.'
>
> Northedge, 2003a, p. 169

For a student who has joined a degree course from a Foundation preparation course perhaps in a feeder college, it can be hard moving from a reflective style of writing in the first person, as is often encouraged on such courses, to writing in a more formal, third-person mode, using the passive rather than the active voice and adopting a suitable register for academic essays. It is important to help students understand when writing needs to be personal and based on individual experience, such as within a reflective practice account, and when it needs to use academic conventions and specialist vocabulary.

The right words?

Students need familiarity with generic key terms, core academic vocabulary and discipline-specific vocabulary, as suggested by Godfrey (2013a) in her

'Students Phrase Book Vocabulary for Writing at University', designed to help students use words precisely and powerfully, to give students a 'way in' to core academic vocabulary via writing functions, to raise awareness of common errors and provide practice in error correction and most particularly to help students use words and phrases precisely in their writing. 'Critique', 'critical analysis', 'reflection' and so forth are likely to be terms with which students are familiar at some level, but they may not have the expertise to use them appropriately in disciplinary and academic contexts.

Godfrey (2013b) suggests students are likely to have problems with specific issues including:

- Lack of/only partial familiarity with core academic vocabulary.
- Inability to control and clearly communicate their ideas.
- Lack of confidence in developing their own written voice.
- Tutors giving help with technical language but expecting the students to be familiar with the sub-technical lexis. Core vocabulary is therefore less marked and given less attention by students also.
- Dictionaries, since students need to know which word they want to look up and dictionaries don't give adequate contextualisation within real academic writing.
- Thesauruses, again since students need to know which word to look up, compounded by the fact that synonyms are grouped and that there is no indication of differences in meaning and context, nuance, connotation or register.
- 'Confusable words' and 'key words' books, where students need to know which word to look up with the potential that they have got a word wrong. (After Godfrey, 2013b, slide 2.)

Godfrey suggests that academic writing should be uncomplicated, clear and precise and controlled by the student to communicate ideas effectively. They should be encouraged not to seek out 'high-fallutin' words and phrases, but instead understand the purpose of 'good words' and use them purposefully. She argues that successful and powerful writing is mainly a product of sound research, thinking and ideas combined with the ability to communicate these to the reader.

Reading right?

Arguably there is a crisis in terms of students' reading at university. In the past we talked about students 'reading for a degree', with the implication that the curriculum was not so much 'delivered' like a postman delivering a parcel, but that students themselves bore the responsibility for their learning. We spoke of students on Humanities and other degrees being expected to 'read around' a topic, that is, undertaking independent rather than directed reading.

Students have always been selective about what they actually do with reading lists, which is probably sensible because not all academics have been meticulous in keeping them current and clarifying their status as core texts, required reading, useful options or relating to specialist sub-topics. Although it is now, with ready electronic access, much easier for students to locate and use texts than when packs of students would run to the library after lectures to seek out rare copies of recommended texts, hide reference books in unexpected places to ensure other students wouldn't have access to them, or rip out pages of journals because they couldn't or wouldn't pay for photocopying, there are often still issues about students being prepared to hunt for texts they need.

In recent years, there has been a higher expectation among many students at all types of universities that significant guidance will be given on exactly what to read, and many HEIs nowadays provide electronic or hard-copy course readers, particularly for first-year students, which contain the core readings, including for example, chapters from different books and relevant journal articles and 'grey material' like newspaper cuttings.

Students don't seem to have an expectation of putting in numerous hours poring over books within their independent study time and some consider it an imposition when their teachers expect them to read material prior to class activities, as is often the case with a 'flipped classroom' approach, where the focus in the classroom is primarily on interaction, and content is gleaned largely from students' own text and web-based reading.

Certainly attitudes to book buying are changing. Through my informal discussions in university book shops in a dozen countries I have been advised that students today tend to buy fewer books and are more strategic in their purchases, choosing course texts and 'readers' including extracts from other texts recommended by their lecturers over more general reading. Anecdotally, students also regard book purchases as being temporary events, since online suppliers regularly contact students asking if they want to re-sell or part-exchange previous purchases within months of selling them. University libraries nowadays often replace hard-copy text purchases with electronic licences that allow several students simultaneously to use them, and journal articles are widely available electronically at home. It is possible nowadays to undertake a degree and only rarely visit a library in person, since electronic access to core readings in some nations is ubiquitous. And students (as well as staff) demonstrate limited patience in seeking and locating texts: if it's not available within four clicks, many will give up the search.

Reading on screen is a qualitatively different experience to reading on a page. Publisher Colin Robinson argues that nowadays so many books are being published that readers paradoxically may be reading less, perhaps outfaced by so many choices. He suggests that:

> 'The literary equivalent of channel surfing replaces the prolonged concentration required to tackle a book. Condensed capsules of digital communication are infecting all forms of reading.'
>
> Robinson, 2013, p. 17

Traditionally we have exhorted students to become active readers, with a pen and Post-its™ in hand, rather than passive ones, just looking at pages or screens. We don't yet know the extent to which comprehension and absorption of information is different in the different modes. What we do know is that fitting in the task alongside television and other noisy distractions doesn't help, and it seems likely that multiple interruptions associated with a continuous online presence (the siren call of Twitter, texts, Facebook updates and so on) changes the nature of interactions with academic texts.

It can be really helpful to work during induction to help students understand that different kinds of approaches are needed for reading depending on whether they are reading for pleasure, for information, for understanding or reading around a topic. We can helpfully give students clear guidance in the early stages of a programme about how much they need to read and what kinds of materials they need to focus on, so they establish good academic literacy habits early on. We can also talk to them about the value of re-reading, deliberately reading slowly, reading material aloud with the intention of focusing on the sounds or the sense of the words, intense reading, reading to reinforce their own scholarly thinking, reading to and with others and reading just for fun.

▶ Information literacy

As implied in Emma Coonan's good practice account opposite, the capacity to find, sift and use information well is a key academic skill. A complaint of many academics is that students fail to reference texts and other sources appropriately and effective induction provides an opportunity to help all students understand what is required of them, although it doesn't help if different tutors in the same faculty have different referencing requirements (as I have recently found to be the case in a prestigious UK university). An

Helping students to read effectively in ways that support learning

Emma Coonan, Information Skills Librarian, University of East Anglia, UK

The issue

'Reading' can mean many things, including the demanding process of studying for a degree or one of the activities that students engage in during that study. Yet a connotation of passivity still hangs about our notion of reading, interfering with a recognition that reading scholarly material is very far from being merely receptive or absorptive: rather, it's an active, interrogative dialogue with a work and its argument. However, the active nature of academic reading is not generally well-signposted or explained to learners. Many students I encounter, most of whom are postgraduate, have never before encountered the idea of 'active reading' with its attendant practices of questioning, challenging and synthesising, rather than merely absorbing, information.

The often-invoked shift in information availability from scarcity to abundance, which is associated with (or blamed on) the rise of the internet, has produced some interesting myths about reading in the digital age. One is the belief, apparently dear to many academics, that there was a pre-internet Golden Age in which learners attentively and conscientiously read every word of an academic work, all in the right order. When CIBER's (2008) deep-log analyses of online information resource use revealed that much online interaction involves skimming, bouncing and power-browsing through web pages, this bolstered the pessimistic belief that, since the advent of the internet, nobody reads anything at all in any depth.

Those who hold this view are rarely willing to acknowledge either that reading behaviour in the digital context might be more nuanced – for instance, that many researchers print out material in order to engage with it intensively – or, indeed, that students *have always approached reading in these ways*. In the tangible world we also skimmed indexes, flicked and bounced through tables of contents, chapter titles, graphs and subheadings, and power-browsed printed works – all of which are perfectly acceptable modes of active reading. Indeed, these selective or strategic reading activities are approaches that I actively encourage researchers to use as a means of evaluating whether a work is relevant and useful to their topic, and how much time they wish to devote to it. They are also strategies that many academics themselves often employ to help stay on top of new work in their field.

A related issue is the concept of *disintermediation*, a term used by librarians to describe the ability of individuals to access information directly via the internet, whereas before they would have had to negotiate with a gatekeeper (a government entity, school, university or library, for example). There is much debate around whether disintermediation and the associated rise of more intuitive library interfaces have made it 'too easy' for students to access bibliographic information. Many librarians feel that electronic access

continued overleaf

Helping students to read effectively in ways that support learning *continued*

generally, and click-through online reading lists in particular, give a false picture of how easy it is to access information: they worry that students will be inadequately equipped for information-finding in the real world beyond library-subscribed resources.

This belief correlates ease of access to information with a lack of criticality about its use. Library colleagues who embrace this view often perceive Google as a competitor or threat rather than an information source, and speak often about how rarely searchers look beyond the first page of results. They infer that, as *using* information (critically) is hard, it follows that *finding* information should be equally hard – or, if necessary, made to be so.

I would argue that Biggs's (2003) concept of constructive alignment is crucial to this debate. Without contextualising the information-finding task within the wider educational mission – that is, the task with which the student is engaged – we cannot make a judgement on its value at that particular point of the learning journey. Directed learning, which occurs in at least the early stages of many undergraduate courses, relies heavily on core or mandated reading selected by the course tutor. This is often supported by faceted reading lists (with entries grouped thematically as opposed to merely alphabetically) and correspondingly easy click-through access from those reading lists, and remains an effective and appropriate mode of scaffolding learning, even in higher education.

In 'gateway' subjects, for example, where a significant body of factual learning or a firm grasp of threshold concepts is required before the student can progress (for example, in some Science, Technology, Engineering and Maths (STEM) subjects), it would be inappropriate for us as librarians to erect access barriers between the learner and the information for the sake of introducing well-meant artificial difficulty. When a supervisor or tutor has decided that directed reading/learning is the appropriate mode to help students gain confidence, we need to recognise and support this decision. Equally, where more independent learning or self-directed exploratory reading is required – for instance in Arts/Humanities disciplines, for a dissertation or major final-year project, or in later stages of STEM study – it's incumbent on us all, educators as well as librarians, to model teaching modes that support the independent learning with which we're asking our students to engage – and on which they will be assessed.

Some suggestions for helping students read to good effect:

- Introduce the concept of reading as an active dialogue.
- Offer strategic reading techniques like skim reading and scanning.
- Scaffold students' development of strategies for understanding and navigating the structure of an academic work.
- Give advice to university teachers on working with information specialists to support effective reading.
- Recognise that reading involves a complex cluster of activities.

- ▶ Recognise that a reading list is a learning tool for developing critical selectivity.
- ▶ Consider whether the appropriate mode of study for each course is directive, independent, or a composite of both.

References

Biggs, J. (2003) *Aligning Teaching for Constructive Learning*, Higher Education Academy. Available at www.heacademy.ac.uk/resources/detail/resource_database/id477_aligning_teaching_for_constructing_learning (accessed 22 August 2013).

CIBER (2008) *Information Behaviour of the Researcher of the Future*. Available at www.jisc.ac.uk/media/documents/programmes/reppres/gg_final_keynote_11012008.pdf (accessed 22 August 2013).

early assignment on undergraduate courses could usefully include requiring students to complete (ideally before their first written assignment) an appropriately-referenced annotated bibliography, including books, journal articles, electronic and other sources, with a gloss indicating how the sources were found and prioritised, and commentary on how useful they were to the student. These can then be shared and compared in groups, with an opportunity to clear up any confusion and impress on students what the locally required referencing conventions are. If students are shown the rules of the game from the outset, the chances are that they will establish referencing patterns that will live with them throughout their studies.

Whereas in the past it was hard sometimes to find reference sources, nowadays a key task is selecting the most relevant ones from the vast number of sources available. Students may need guidance on understanding how the quality of information they wish to use has been assured and, for those new to academia, a discussion about the importance of independent review of texts, that is, what differentiates a peer-reviewed journal article from, for example, a vanity publication can be very useful.

Sadly many schools and colleges do not encourage discrimination in locating and selecting source materials. It is here that partnerships with university librarians and information management specialists can be invaluable. Students may need encouragement to use trusted web systems, rather than turning immediately to Google and Wikipedia as they may have always done in the past. Showing them in class (or in briefings) how Google Scholar can take them to rather better academic sources may be a key step. Similarly, getting students to create and post made-up Wikipedia entries, then waiting to see how long it is until they are re-edited, can demonstrate the limits to its trustworthiness as an academic source. It is also worth asking students to interrogate the value of personal postings on websites, and the extent to which Twitter postings can include fake information (as is well-documented in the press from time to time).

Nevertheless, students can use digital and social media in their academic studies to good effect. They can create, share and discuss a topic, interact with their peers on their own web-spaces using blogs, Twitter feeds and Facebook groups, and outputs can be collated for assessment and other purposes via a course blog which can also post resources and activity prompts, to structure the learning experience. Students can thereby draw on a hugely diverse range of fellow learners with shared interests, provide peer support in answering each other's queries, and also provide moral support and motivation for those faltering. The next good practice account provides examples of how staff as well as students can be helped to do so sensibly and safely.

Using social media to enhance teaching

Helen Webster, Anglia Ruskin University, UK

Background

Social media such as Twitter and Linked-In have been embraced by many teaching and learning staff and students in many nations as a way to deliver and participate in open education courses, build a personal learning network to share resources and information, create a backchannel for the classroom, present their professional portfolio and manage their online identity. However, it cannot be assumed that all students, even if young, are 'digital natives', nor that staff teaching in the classroom or engaging in professional development online are comfortable with either the relevant technologies or their uses. A tutor-centred instructional training approach to getting acquainted with new technologies, whether it is offered in the computer lab or via self-guided manuals, doesn't necessarily help build either the confidence needed to get to grips with the more intuitive approach to software user interfaces in the future or the digital literacy needed to illustrate benefits or integrate the tools effectively in the context of their work.

Helping staff and students use social media to promote learning

One approach to teaching social media in the context of higher education is by providing an open online course which uses a scaffolded approach to teaching uses of social media through the social media platform itself and in the context of a network of other learners. An example is the '23 Things' programmes which developed in the context of libraries for the professional development of their staff and use a network of facilitator and participant blogs to explore various social media tools and share tips and practice in a structured way. A variant of this approach is my Ten Days of Twitter or #10DoT, which uses a central blog to publish a post every day for ten days, each outlining a small feature of Twitter with instructions for use, and examples and a task embedded in the professional context of its participants. Participants learn to use Twitter and also learn about its potential as a networking tool for their studies or professional development by completing the tasks and thereby building an authentic social network amongst and beyond themselves.

When encouraging the use of social media among those who either haven't had the confidence to explore it independently, or who don't yet perceive the relevance, overcoming these barriers is itself a significant stumbling block. As there is no formal accreditation for learning to use social media, it is hard to anticipate the real level of experience of participants and pitch the materials appropriately. It may also be the case that potential facilitators feel they aren't sufficiently qualified to support colleagues or students – on what basis can anyone call themselves an 'expert' in social media? There is also the issue of time – if learning to use such tools and behaviours is an additional task on top of either the subject learning or the demands of professional practice, then retention on such training courses can become problematic.

The 'Ten Days of Twitter' overcomes these barriers using a bite-sized, scaffolded approach which offers reassurance for complete beginners while also involving detailed tips and contextualised suggestions for those who have a little more experience. Through facilitation and moderation, it also encourages interaction between course participants (and those who had done previous iterations of the programme). This facilitates the building of a learning community in which the more experienced participants can support those with less confidence, experience or conviction, answer questions and model practice in more authentic ways than can interactions purely between the facilitator and participants. The community developed by participation in the programme also provides an authentic and lasting outcome.

If running a similar open education programme on social media, it is sensible to re-use creative common licensed materials such as '10DoT' or the '23 Things' resources, embedding instructional videos from YouTube and linking to articles in the professional press (including blogs) to illustrate issues of professional practice (checking to see that they are up to date). Don't feel that you are not enough of an expert – the facilitator can be as much a participant as the others, and the role is largely that of creating a structured experience and encouraging participation. It also helps to build a network of your own of experienced users who can advise you, and engage with and encourage participants.

References

There are various iterations of 23things; for example, Cambridge's http://cam23things.blogspot.co.uk/ or more recent versions from Oxford, http://blogs.bodleian.ox.ac.uk/23things/all-about-23-things/ and Minnesota, http://23mobilethingsmn.org/.

Assessment literacy

This implies understanding how assessment systems work in universities. Sambell (2013) makes a strong case for enabling students to have a sophisticated and articulated understanding of what goes on inside the 'black hole' that assessment is sometimes perceived to be. She and colleagues, including me (Sambell et al., 1997), propose that students often have little idea of what happens to work once it is submitted, and give little thought to the agency of marking or how grades link to criteria. Working on a course on Early Childhood Studies at the University of Northumbria which had very high attrition rates, she devised a module that required students to engage deeply with issues like criteria, weightings and level, and enabled them to encounter and review a variety of assessment methods (see Chapter 7) so they could see how performance needs to match to practice.

Boud and associates argue:

> 'Students need confidence and competence in making informed judgements about what they produce. They need to develop the ability to evaluate the quality, completeness and/or accuracy of work with respect to appropriate standards, and have the confidence to express their judgements with conviction. This requires deliberately managed assessment processes and practice that relates to judgements required in professional practice and mature community engagement.'
>
> Boud and associates, 2010, p. 2

Fostering assessment literacy can include getting practice using diverse assessment methods through un-graded rehearsal and practice opportunities, and helping students gain clarity on how assessment regulations work in their own university. In a global context, the issue of what a pass mark comprises can be a fruitful topic for discussion, with students from some nations having experienced pass marks in the 80s and others more used to only having to obtain 40% or less. Grades similarly can cause confusion: whereas students in the US may commonly encounter the grade A+, this is not normally used in the UK for example, where A tends to be the top grade. A C grade may mean adequate but not brilliant work to some students, but when counted towards a grade-point average in other nations spells disaster. Making all this kind of information explicit can really help students understand the localised context. Students possessing assessment literacy capabilities can be more strategic in their behaviours, thereby putting more work into aspects of an assignment with high weightings and interrogating criteria to find out what is really required and so on.

The following good practice account describes a specific three-year research and development initiative to enhance first-year assessment through encouraging and enabling staff to foster assessment literacy in their students.

Designing first-year assessment and feedback

Ruth Pickford, Leeds Metropolitan University, UK

Introduction

The first few weeks at university can be emotionally traumatising and lonely. Many students drop out of university in this period and for many this is a personal disaster. How successful students are depends very much on their peer support networks and the extent to which they feel they belong to a cohort. In those early days, we are encouraged by Mantz Yorke (1999) to believe that assessment that helps students get the feel of what is required of them without allowing them to feel overwhelmed or discouraged can help. Royce Sadler argues that:

> 'Students need to be exposed to, and gain experience in making judgements about, a variety of works of different quality…They need planned rather than random exposure to exemplars, and experience in making judgements about quality. They need to create verbalised rationales and accounts of how various works could have been done better. Finally, they need to engage in evaluative conversations with teachers and other students. Together, these three provide the means by which students can develop a concept of quality that is similar in essence to that which the teacher possesses, and in particular to understand what makes for high quality.'
>
> Sadler, 2010, p. 544

The 'Fe, Fi, Fo, Fun' approach to assessment and feedback

For this reason, using a National Teaching Fellowship project award, a team at Leeds Metropolitan University developed a project to personalise the first year of study through promoting effective feedback and assessment, based on a 'Fe, Fi, Fo, Fun' approach (in a reference to the daunting utterances of the giant in the European fairytale Jack and the Beanstalk), focusing on students' **Fe**elings, **Fi**tting in, **Fo**rmative activity and **Fun**. Academic staff working with us on the project:

1. Designed assignments that provided opportunities for students to work together and build peer-to-peer and student-tutor working relationships.
2. Used assessment and feedback to empower students to develop a sense of control over their own learning.

continued overleaf

Designing first-year assessment and feedback *continued*

3. Ensured that teaching was shaped by diagnostic assessment.
4. Ensured that students regularly gave and received formative feedback so they could gauge what good performance looked like.
5. Worked in partnership with students to design assessments with an element of choice of topic, method and criteria and with some flexibility in timings.
6. Built in opportunities for students to use feedback shortly after receiving it, to reflect on learning and to close the gap between current and desired performance.
7. Designed assessments that develop underpinning skills for lifelong learning.
8. Created assignments that weren't excessively onerous to mark and manage.
9. Focused on engaging students through enjoyable assessment tasks.
10. Designed challenging assignments that enabled learning though experimentation in a non-threatening environment.

As Diane Nutt (2008) argues: 'By introducing real relevance at the beginning of their studies, you can engage students. Once they are involved, they are more likely to stay.'

Colleagues across the university provided 50 suggestions in a Staff Guide to help them consider how to change the design of first level assessment and feedback to help students thrive, succeed and stay, and these are detailed at http://repository-intralibrary.leedsmet.ac.uk/IntraLibrary?command=open-preview&learning_object_key=i782n732249t.

These include:

- Offering immersive early experiences, enabling students at the start of courses to spend a significant proportion of time together as a group.
- Using group projects and tasks to encourage co-learning.
- Building in time to share oral feedback to students collectively.
- In a supportive environment, asking students to comment on each other's work and give positive feedback to their peers.
- Involving students from previous cohorts to mentor first-year students.
- Designing authentic tasks so students can visualise themselves in professional roles.
- Using simulations based on real-life scenarios.
- Creating assignments that stretch students early on and progressively become more difficult so students at all levels are challenged.
- Providing online tests where students can practise and assess their understanding in private.
- Focusing feedback in early tasks on students' successes rather than their mistakes.

We also provided a student guide which helped students understand how assessment at university level works, and developed in students what Sambell and Hubbard (2004) term 'assessment literacy' whereby students gain a fuller understanding of assessment systems and practices, thereby becoming more successful in their studies. Throughout the project we were keen to use assessment and feedback to empower students to develop confidence and competence in a supportive and developmental climate.

References

Nutt, D. (2008) Student retention: if you don't want to lose students, recruit honestly, and be sure freshers know what to expect, and what support is available right from the start, *Times Higher Educational Supplement*, 21 February 2008.

Pickford, R. (2009) *Designing First-Year Assessment and Feedback: A guide to university staff*, Leeds: Leeds Metropolitan University Press

Sadler, D.R. (2010) Beyond feedback: developing student capability in complex appraisal, *Assessment and Evaluation in Higher Education*, 35(5), pp. 535–50.

Sambell, K. and Hubbard, A. (2004) The role of formative 'low-stakes' assessment in supporting non-traditional students' retention and progression in higher education: student perspectives, *Widening Participation and Lifelong Learning*, 6(2), pp. 25–36.

Yorke, M. (1999) *Leaving Early: Undergraduate non-completion in higher education*, Abingdon: Routledge.

Social and interpersonal literacy

There are high expectations in the 21st century that students will be capable of learning in social contexts: in virtual contexts this is becoming as important as in face-to-face environments, since group tasks, peer support and peer evaluation are increasingly expected of all students in all environments. The ability to work productively as a member of a group is highly prized by employers and fellow citizens alike, and a goal of good higher education is to produce students who can relate to others and demonstrate what Salovey and Mayer (1990) describe as emotional intelligence. Such students, they suggest, can perceive accurately what others are thinking and doing, appraise and express their own emotions appropriately, access and/or generate feelings when they facilitate thought, understand emotions and emotional thought and regulate their own emotions to promote emotional and intellectual growth.

In the UK, Alan Mortiboys has led much of the thinking about how emotional intelligence can help students be more effective learners by:

- Being better at understanding and working with others.
- Employing empathy to achieve the ends they are seeking.
- Noticing and using non-verbal cues from others.
- Productively considering how their own non-verbal cues are being perceived.
- Understanding, expressing and regulating their own emotions.
- Improving their own capacities for flexible planning and creative thinking. (After Mortiboys, 2005)

What this implies in practice is that students may need coaching and support to enable them, for example, to:

- Develop autonomy and independence in their academic lives, rather than always expecting reading and other learning tasks to be directed.
- Practise good leadership and good 'followership' in group work, participating collegially and in a mutually supportive fashion, rather than acting in domineering or passive aggressive ways.
- Recognise when it is acceptable to interrupt to ask questions and voice opinions in classroom sessions, and when it is best to hold back.
- Give positive and developmental feedback during peer assessment, avoiding excessive negativity and what David Boud terms 'final language' (Boud, 1995), that can be damaging to fellow students and make them feel as if they have nowhere to go.
- Recognise when to seek personal and/or academic support, and when it is best to go it alone.
- Be socially and culturally inclusive towards fellow students very different from themselves (inclusivity specialists indicate that much discrimination in higher education stems from fellow students rather than other sources).
- Behave responsibly in relation to other students in social media contexts, without scape-goating, excessively embarrassing or bullying others.
- Develop the resilience necessary to cope with setbacks and problems within the academic context, and the intellectual stamina to complete tough and lengthy tasks.

We recognise today that being single-minded and highly focused on one's own achievement might well achieve high scores, but may not be enough to help a graduate have a fulfilling and productive life. Universities and colleges have always been social communities, but this is an increasingly important aspect of their purposes. If we can encourage social and interpersonal literacy among our students, this is likely to be conducive to collaborative learning and collegial behaviour, helping students work together well beyond face-to-face classroom time.

The good practice account that follows demonstrates how students are supported in transition from schools into higher education, from one mode of thinking about learning and assessment to another, and in the course of this, are challenged to become more active and reflective learners.

Fostering self-efficacy and interpersonal competences: Linking what we are learning to the real world

Junxia Hou, College of Humanities and Social Sciences, National University of Defence Technology, Changsha, China

Introduction

English is an important module for Chinese students. They start to learn the language in primary school. However, in order to get a desirable mark in the National Higher Education Entrance Examination, they have to do thousands of test papers during middle school. Thus, the prevalent teaching and learning practices in use in an English as a Second Language (ESL) class then are focused on grammar and vocabulary, paying great attention to mechanical memorisation. When students move on to tertiary education, a great number of them continue their previous learning strategies with the aim of passing College English Tests. Therefore, at university level, new practices are encouraged to change their orientation.

My personal 6-year learning experience in the UK as a Masters and Doctoral student has offered me valuable opportunities to reflect on the aims of ESL modules. Apart from language competence, ESL modules offer an important platform to promote students' critical thinking and intercultural competence, which are tools to enable students to explore the globalised world and solve real-world problems.

I conducted an action research in my teaching for an 18-month module, College English, for first-year undergraduate students ($n = 81$, 3 cohorts). Collaborative research-based learning is encouraged throughout the module. Features include:

- **Round-table working**. Instead of sitting in rows, students form groups and sit at round tables in class, which encourages them to discuss and debate more extensively. Their participation in class is very active.
- **Regular meeting outside class**. Students conduct two group research projects, involving secondary research in semester 1 and a primary research in semesters 2 and 3. During the process, they meet regularly and meetings are recorded in research logbook, some elements of which are videoed.

continued overleaf

Fostering self-efficacy and interpersonal competences *continued*

- **Weekly reflection** in research diaries. Students are encouraged to reflect on their learning processes. They share their ideas, joy and confusion in their diaries which have become a channel for us to communicate with each other individually and privately.
- **Rigorous research processes**. The whole process follows a rigorous research journey, identifying research questions, writing brief proposals with oral presentations, making outlines, conducting literature reviews, entering the research field with ethical concerns, analysing data, writing up reports and making the final group presentation.
- **Formative feedback** in and outside the class. I also set up a small Centre for Enhancing Teaching and Learning on campus providing formative feedback to students, which they use at weekends.

Review

I fully embed language teaching requirements in practice. As a result, students' listening, speaking, reading and writing skills are improved. Their motivation to learn English has changed from being about just passing examinations to using it as a tool to solve real-world problems. The secondary research projects are on topics they choose from the English text book, with implications relating to our current society, while the topics for their primary research projects are those problems puzzling them every day on campus. My research has shown that their critical thinking and intercultural competence have been enhanced.

Additionally, I find that this collaborative research-based approach can provide ways to facilitate students' transition from high school to university through improving their communication skills, management skills and team-working skills. It also reduces their anxiety in ESL classes. My practices and the findings strongly imply that academics, especially those from Western countries, should abandon their stereotypical views of Chinese ways of teaching and learning enforced by Hofstede's individualism and collectivism theories (Hofstede, 1991). It is current practice rather than the dominant culture that influences students' learning strategies and encourages desirable outcome.

In those wishing to emulate these practices, an understanding of social science research methodologies is required, to enable giving students suggestions and delivering training. There also needs to be an awareness of ethical issues. Students' benefit must be the top priority. Timely formative feedback is essential during the process. Although such approaches are quite time-consuming, it is very rewarding in terms of students' ultimate achievements.

Reference

Hofstede, G. (1991) *Cultures and Organizations: Software of the mind*. New York: McGraw-Hill.

Conclusions

Helping students develop appropriate literacies for higher education study has never been more important. The concept of 'literacies' as a range of capabilities to which all seek to aspire is a helpful one in encouraging students and academic staff to take them seriously. As Geisler argues:

> 'Not being an expert in our society is seen as the default value, something of which no one is ashamed and some are even proud. Being illiterate is another matter ... Literacy is expected to be a competency, not an expertise.'
>
> Geisler, 2013, p. xi

In a student-centred learning environment, we recognise that content-delivery is not the only, or even the main, task in hand, and that fostering students' expertise, skills and behaviours is crucial to success and fulfilment both in their lives and in their academic careers. The next chapter reviews how we can integrate assessments that go beyond simply requiring the regurgitation of memorised curriculum content, and instead offer opportunities for students to make sense of learning and use it in their lives as graduates.

7 Making assessment and feedback fit-for-purpose

▶ Assessment in context

Why does assessment matter so much?

> 'Assessment methods and requirements probably have a greater influence on how and what students learn than any other single factor. This influence may well be of greater importance than the impact of teaching materials.'
>
> Boud, 1988

Assessment is a complex, nuanced and highly important process. If we want to improve students' engagement with learning, a key locus of enhancement can be refreshing our approaches to assessment and sometimes we need to take a fresh look at our current practice to make sure assessment is *for* rather than just *of* learning. This chapter has been informed not only by my own work on assessment and feedback over three decades but also by three key initiatives which have impacted significantly on how assessment is regarded and practised in recent years: propositions for assessment reform, assessment *for* learning, quality assurance and enhancement initiatives.

▶ Propositions for assessment reform

The seminal evidence-based *Assessment 2020: Seven propositions for assessment reform* was produced in 2010 by senior staff representing all Australian universities (together with some international assessments experts). This proposes basic principles of good assessment practice, arguing that:

> 'Assessment has most effect when:
>
> - [It] is used to engage students in learning that is productive.
> - Feedback is used to actively improve student learning.
> - Students and teachers become responsible partners in learning and assessment.
> - Students are inducted into the assessment practices and cultures of higher education.

- Assessment for learning is placed at the centre of subject and program design.
- Assessment for learning is a focus for staff and institutional development.
- Assessment provides inclusive and trustworthy representation of student achievement.'

Boud and associates, 2010

Assessment *for* learning

The Assessment *for* Learning movement, originally arising from discussion in the schools sector, has been extensively developed within the higher education context, most particularly through the work of the Assessment for Learning (A4L) Centre for Excellence in Teaching and Learning at the University of Northumbria. Their approach, building on more than a decade of research, proposes that A4L:

- Emphasises authenticity and complexity in the content and methods of assessment rather than reproduction of knowledge and reductive measurement.
- Uses high-stakes summative assessment rigorously but sparingly rather than as the main driver for learning.
- Offers students extensive opportunities to engage in the kinds of tasks that develop and demonstrate their learning, thus building their confidence and capabilities before they are summatively assessed.
- Is rich in feedback derived from formal mechanisms, e.g. tutor comments on assignments, student self-review logs.
- Is rich in informal feedback, e.g. peer review of draft writing, collaborative project work, which provides students with a continuous flow of feedback on 'how they are doing'.
- Develops students' abilities to direct their own learning, evaluate their own progress and attainments and support the learning of others as illustrated in Figure 7.1 overleaf.

Sue Bloxham, whose own work with Pete Boyd (2007) complements that of the Northumbria team, argues that assessment for learning implies that:

- Tasks should be challenging, demanding higher-order learning and integration of knowledge learned in both the university and other contexts.
- Learning and assessment should be integrated, assessment should not come at the end of learning but should be part of the learning process.
- Students are involved in self-assessment and reflection on their learning, they are involved in judging performance.

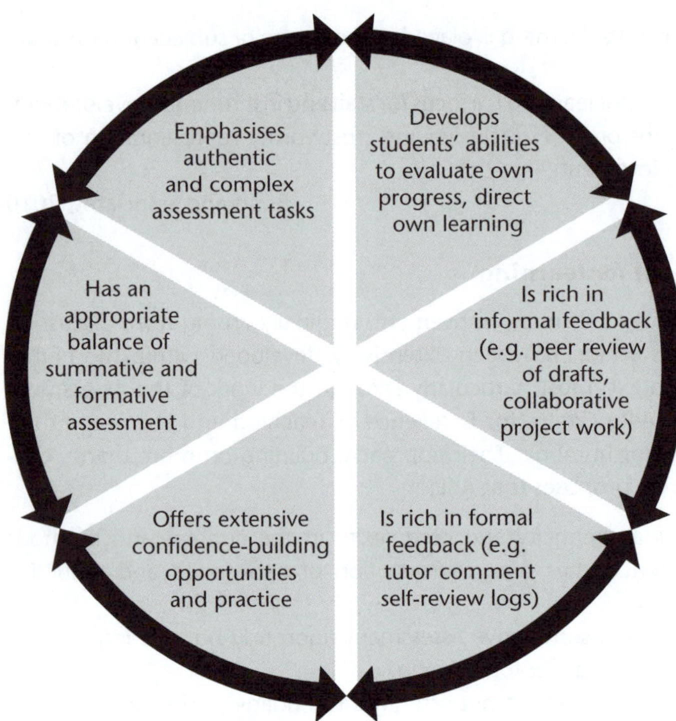

Figure 7.1 Assessment for learning

Source: Reproduced with the permission of Northumbria Assessment for Learning CETL.

- Assessment should encourage metacognition, promoting thinking about the learning process not just the learning outcomes.
- Assessment should have a formative function, providing 'feedforward' for future learning which can be acted upon. There is opportunity and a safe context for students to expose problems with their study and get help; there should be an opportunity for dialogue about students' work.
- Assessment expectations should be made visible to students as far as possible.
- Tasks should involve the active engagement of students developing the capacity to find things out for themselves and learn independently.
- Tasks should be authentic; worthwhile, relevant and offering students some level of control over their work.
- Tasks should be fit-for-purpose and align with important learning outcomes.
- Assessment should be used to evaluate teaching as well as student learning.

Quality assurance and enhancement initiatives

Quality assurance and enhancement programmes in the UK are led by the Higher Education Academy (HEA) and the Quality Assurance Agency (QAA). The HEA's 'Transforming Assessment' project, with the linked publication *A Marked Improvement* (2012a) explores how assessment can be enhanced through strategic approaches. This proposes six tenets or principles for good practice, with templates enabling institutions to review their institutional and local assessment practices. Building on the Weston Manor Group's *Assessment Standards: A manifesto for change* (www.brookes.ac.uk/aske/documents/ASKe_Manifesto.pdf, accessed 5 June 2014), developed by the Assessment Knowledge exchange Centre for Excellence in Teaching and Learning (ASKe CETL), the HEA guide proposes that:

> 'Assessment of student learning is a fundamental function of higher education. It is the means by which we assure and express academic standards and has a vital impact on student behaviour, staff time, university reputations, league tables and, most of all, students' future lives. The [UK] National Student Survey, despite its limitations, has made more visible what researchers in the field have known for many years: assessment in our universities is far from perfect.'
>
> HEA, 2012a, p. 7

The guide further suggests that:

> 'Assessment practices in most universities have not kept pace with the vast changes in the context, aims and structure of higher education. They can no longer do justice to the outcomes we expect from a university education in relation to wide-ranging knowledge, skills and employability. In a massified higher education sector where tutor-student ratios have gradually been eroded, students can remain confused about what is expected of them in assessment. Efforts to make this transparent through learning outcomes, assessment criteria and written feedback have proved no substitute for tutor-student interaction and newer groups of students are particularly likely to need this contact.'
>
> HEA, op. cit., p. 7

This work in the UK aligns with the QAA's redrafting of their Code of Practice on assessment, which took place in parallel with the HEA initiative and whose steering group membership overlapped with the *Marked Improvement* design team. Intended to help universities in the UK demonstrate both assurance and enhancement of assessment quality, the Code is the definitive reference point for all UK higher education providers, making clear what higher education providers are required to do, what they can expect of each other, and what the general public can expect of them. It provides eighteen indicators of good practice, and usefully provides a benchmark against which institutions can review their own assessment practices (QAA, 2013).

A strategy for making assessment 'fit-for-purpose'

Having learned much from the first initiative and contributed to both of the last two, my own particular approach to effective assessment, refined over twenty years and drawing on my joint work with Peter Knight, is a fit-for-purpose one (Brown and Knight, 1994). My model collects together a series of quite penetrating questions with which to interrogate any particular assessment element. There are five broad headings under which these questions are located: purposes, methodologies, agency, timing and orientation. At the outset of assessment design I would argue we need to ask about five dimensions of assessment – purposes, methodologies, agency, timing and orientation – using the questions as a checklist to review fitness-for-purpose.

Purposes

- Why is assessment being undertaken at this point in time?
- Is it to help students know how they are doing?
- Can it enable students to get the measure of their achievement or help them consolidate their learning?
- Is it to offer students formative guidance on the remediation of errors while they still have time to improve matters?
- Is it perhaps a summative assignment, designed to make a judgement about whether a student is fit to practise in a clinical setting, or to determine whether professional requirements have been satisfied sufficiently to achieve professional accreditation?
- Is it to determine with what grade or classification students will graduate?
- Can this particular assignment help to motivate students so they better engage with their learning?
- Does it provide them with opportunities to relate theory and practice?
- Does it help students make sensible choices about option alternatives and directions for further study?
- Are there opportunities through this assignment for students to demonstrate their employability?
- Can this assignment provide statistics for internal and external agencies?
- Can it give us as teachers feedback on our own effectiveness?

Once the rationale for assessing on a particular occasion with a particular cohort of students at a particular level in a particular subject area has been determined, the next stage is to determine which methods and approaches are best for the task in hand.

Methodologies

Is the best method an essay, a practical task, a viva or oral defence, an e-portfolio, an assessed blog, a performance, the production of an artefact, an exhibition or poster, a critique, the final show, a project, an assessed seminar, an annotated bibliography, a diary, a reflective journal, a critical incident account, a case study, a field study, a thesis and so on?

When exams are called for, should these be time-constrained, unseen questions in an exam hall, multiple-choice questions (MCQs) on a computer, a take-away exam completed at home, an open-book exam where reference sources are permitted and the emphasis is on the use of information, not its recall, an Objective Structured Clinical Examination (where students are set under exam conditions a series of short timed practical and intellectual tasks), an in-tray exercise, where students deal in real time with an unseen folio of data and answer complex and changing questions about it, a live, paper-based or computer-based simulation or an assignment relating to real-world scenarios, for example a contemporary court case?

For a detailed review of how best to choose methods of assessment, see Brown and Race, 2012, pp. 79–84. Having decided on methodologies, the next three sets of questions to ask are about agency, timing and orientation.

Agency

Who should be undertaking assessment? Should this be:

- Tutors?
- Peers in the same group?
- Peers in other groups?
- Students themselves?
- Employers?
- Practice supervisors?
- Service users?
- Clients?
- A combination of these?

All can participate in student assessment to good effect, but which is right for particular assessment activities? Should this particular assignment be individual or collective? Has everyone undertaking assessment had relevant rehearsal and training so they know what they're doing when they assess?

Timing

When should we assess students to maximise impact on student learning? Should this be:

- End point?
- Incrementally?
- When it suits our systems?
- When it is manageable for students, avoiding multiple submissions on the same date?
- When the students themselves are ready?
- When students have finished learning?
- When there is still time for improvement?

Orientation

To what extent in each task would we wish to focus particularly on process or outcomes, theory or practice, subject knowledge or its application or both?

What kinds of learning are we assessing?

- Deep learning?
- Surface learning?
- Strategic learning?

What kinds of learners are best served (or most disadvantaged) by this assessment?

- Cue-conscious learners?
- Cue-seeking learners?
- Cue-oblivious learners?

Eight principles underpinning fit-for-purpose assessment

1. Justice

Students need confidence that they will be assessed fairly and justly. This includes both the confidence that all students will when submitting equivalent work be judged on a fair and equal basis whoever marks their work.

Students should not be advantaged or disadvantaged by issues related to their persons such as gender, sexual orientation, disability, race, ethnicity or religion. Nor should students who get on well with assessors have a better chance of getting higher marks than students who are less familiar or distanced from their academic teachers.

Where students normally submit work electronically, this can potentially offer students just assessment, whether it is by multiple-choice tests, which are 'objectively' marked (although the questions may not be objectively designed, for example, privileging Western students) or by tutor-marked submissions (although techniques may need to be used to ensure anonymous marking, if for example, students just email work to tutors without going through an assignment submission system). Tutors need to ensure that students get equitable support, so for example rather than play e-mail tennis answering questions from an individual student, it may be better to acknowledge each query then post it and the response onto a course VLE where others can join in the conversation.

Assessment needs to be undertaken reliably, with good inter-tutor reliability, with multiple markers on a programme assessing to the same standards and with appropriately equal marks being given to work of an equivalent standard. This inevitably requires that everyone marking the same assignment needs to have a shared understanding of the criteria and marking scheme in use and apply them fairly. The best assessment systems require moderation of marks by expert assessors (as is undertaken by the Open University in the UK) and in many nations a system of external examiners provide an extra-institutional perspective on cohort marks, in the best cases sampling perhaps the square root of the total number of scripts (20 scripts out of 400, for example) and looking in detail at the feedback given and the marks awarded against criteria.

Assessors also need to ensure there is good intra-tutor reliability, so that whether the script is one of the first twenty in a batch of five hundred or the last, whether the tutors are marking late at night or first thing in the morning, and whether they are fired up for their marking or just not in the mood to do it, but working against time pressures, the grades they give match the criteria for the assignment and are fairly awarded.

It also includes assurance that scripts are being justly assessed on what was set out in the course documentation as being the subject matter and skills set out in the programme through the learning outcomes or other means. Students regard it as unfair practice when they are assessed on content that has not been 'covered' in the course or mentioned in the course documentation and where a tiny sub-set of course content is examined rather than a representative sample of material. Of course, in an era where students are increasingly working independently using open, online or distance learning materials, what it means to have *covered* the material within the course is less easy to define than in the days when everything the students were expected to know for the exam was *delivered* within the lecture programme (although of course good students were always expected to *read around* the subject too).

2. Veracity

We need to be confident that the work submitted is the students' own. A chilling anonymous article in the *Times Higher Education Supplement* of 1 August 2013 describes the work of a 'freelance ghost writer' who writes essays and dissertations to order, with little risk of discovery. All writers are carefully vetted by the agency (they must be Oxbridge or elite UK Russell group graduates and submit sample assignments before being accepted for work) and rely mainly on Wikipedia and Google Books to write assignments for a pre-specified grade, as outstanding work submitted by a mediocre student would raise suspicion. The ghost writer is well-versed in avoiding plagiarism detection services, which in any case, since these assignments are personalised for each client, are unlikely to show up through Turnitin or other software. Some clients are lazy, others are desperate and yet others know their written English isn't up to scratch to get good marks. From time to time spelling errors or short poorly written sections are added in, just as a cabinet maker faking antiques will rough up the edges of a piece of furniture to age it.

So what kinds of actions can assessors take to ensure the veracity of authorship of assignments? This is particularly an issue with distance and online learning, where impersonation is a recognised phenomenon (although impersonation happens in every kind of assessment context, including famously parents attempting to sit exams for their adult children).

While there are no proven means to be certain of veracity, since clever but unscrupulous students can often outwit us, particularly with large cohorts, precautions taken can include:

- Requiring students in face-to-face contexts like computer-based exams in PC labs to log on to computers with their student ID numbers and show the invigilator their photo ID cards (although this won't prevent identical twins helping each other out!).
- Requiring students to submit with their work statements confirming that the assignment represents entirely the student's own work, clarifying penalties for cheating, and enforcing them publicly when cases of poor academic conduct come to light.

The most successful means of ensuring veracity include:

- Requiring students to submit work incrementally, for example for a dissertation, with regular conversations between the tutor and the student to discuss the work and suggest future directions.
- Undertaking live, in-class assignments and tests where the tutor can identify the student.
- Using assessment design to make cheating difficult.
- Fostering a culture of student engagement, where there is an ethical climate that makes cheating out of the question. This is particularly important in some programmes leading to professional qualifications with high ethical requirements such as medicine, social work, nursing, childhood/early years training, police studies, law and so on, but can be very valuable across the subject range.

3. *Clarity*

Good assessment systems don't play games with students of 'Guess what I want you to do?'. Students need to be really clear about what is required of them and what standards of work are expected. This means that the criteria in use should be available to students at the assignment briefing stage, so they know where to direct their energies to get good marks. This doesn't just mean making the text of the course handbook containing assessment criteria available on the programme website (although this helps) but, particularly in the early weeks of students' time at university, giving them opportunities to discuss, interrogate and practise using the criteria so they really internalise them and can see that there is a genuine relationship between them and the grades awarded. A very good way to ensure clarity of goals and expected outcomes is to show students a range of completed outputs (not just model answers, but outstanding examples, satisfactory ones and weak ones) during an in-class or online opportunity to discuss *why* one piece of work is deemed better than another and how nuances of expression, organisation or practice can make an assignment clearly outstanding rather than merely satisfactory. Such endeavours to improve students' assessment literacy can pay high dividends in terms of reducing drop-out and maximising success.

4. *Professionalism of assessors*

Many would argue that if we want a just and equitable assessment system, all who undertake assessment in universities should be trained to do so and mentored/monitored through early assignments. It is not sufficient, as happens in some universities, to say to a graduate teaching assistant, "Take this pile of lab reports/essays/exam scripts and mark them. You should know what to do as you've been through the system yourself". Such an approach risks merely replicating past poor practice and is unfair both to the teaching assistant and the students being assessed by an inexperienced and potentially clumsy assessor. So much knowledge about how to assess is tacit, which implies the need not just for guidance on how to use particular university systems and technologies like Moodle, but also practical training for new assessors giving them the chance to practise rehearsing assessment before going 'live' with real students. It also implies high levels of monitoring and scrutiny by experienced colleagues for novice assessors, to help them both gauge standards and also to develop an awareness of what kinds of feedback are supportive and developmental.

Boud and associates propose that such support be codified and rewarded:

> 'Academics need particular support in developing expertise required for subject and program assessment responsibilities. Such support could include mentoring, dialogue with peers in informal and formal moderation activities or formal courses. However, while enhanced assessment skills are essential, their acquisition is not sufficient to ensure good assessment practice. Institutions should have explicit requirements that professional and scholarly proficiency in assessment is necessary for satisfactory teaching performance. Further, leadership and exemplary performance in assessment matters should be recognised for promotion, awards and grants.'
>
> Boud and associates, 2010, p. 3

In e-assessment, this also implies not just guidance on how to use particular systems like Moodle, but also practical training for assessors on the kinds of issues discussed in this chapter. It also implies high levels of supportive monitoring and scrutiny by experienced colleagues for novice assessors, to help them both gauge standards and also to develop an awareness of what kinds of feedback are supportive and developmental. Quality assurance practices common in conventional assessment such as moderation need to be equally practised in e-assessment. A key feature of high quality e-assessment is rapid turnaround of assignments with high quality and quantity of developmental feedback, and this is where e-assessment can be a very powerful tool, for example though the use of rubrics in Moodle. Students will also benefit from legibly written comments (rather than handwritten scrawl) which can be provided in various formats.

5. Inclusivity

Since 2000 in the UK and elsewhere globally, legislative drivers, moral imperatives and pressures from disabled staff and students have driven HEIs to make assessment inclusive. Recent advances in technologies have improved the accessibility of curriculum materials. HEIs are not good at advanced planning when arranging alternative assessments. Disabled students want an equivalent experience, fair assessment and the maintenance of standards of achievement.

This needs to be carefully thought through when designing assessments, from initial consideration through to the implementation stage, ensuring that no student is unfairly disadvantaged by virtue of background, disability or orientation. Because planning reasonable adjustments for students with special needs is so time consuming, it is often best to design in some options at the outset for those who don't see, hear or write easily, and potentially making these available for all students to choose. TechDis (www.jisctechdis.ac.uk) offers superb practical advice on alternative formats and understanding user needs.

Boud and associates propose that:

> 'Students come to higher education with great diversity in preparedness and understanding of what it involves. To ensure that all can engage equitably with assessment tasks, the implicit rules and expectations around what is required for success in any discipline need to be made accessible to students and opportunities provided for them to develop the academic skills they require to perform those tasks.'
>
> Boud and associates, 2010, p. 2

When aiming for wider inclusivity, we need to take into account a range of other diversities including:

- Diverse cultural, faith and social backgrounds both for home and international students. Setting multiple exams on the same day in Ramadan, for example, when some students will be observing a day-long fast is likely to disadvantage them. Similarly expecting students to pay for expensive materials for design projects or to go on costly field trips not covered by course fees can disadvantage students without family or other means to support them.
- Diverse capabilities, for example, with understandings of learning, information literacies and language, since students come to study with divergent experiences of learning environments.

- Diverse experience and backgrounds: mature students often bring a wealth of life experiences with them and we ignore this breadth of capability at our peril.
- Differing expectations about higher education since some students will have high cultural and social capital, while others, perhaps first in family, will have fewer resources to draw on when navigating higher education assessment practices.

This implies that we need to design an assessment strategy that involves a diverse range of methods of assessment (since all forms of assessment disadvantage some students) and to consider when designing assessment tasks how any students might be disadvantaged so we can make reasonable adjustments as appropriate. The intention should be in all cases to maximise opportunities for each student to achieve at the highest possible level while at the same time ensuring that we maintain appropriate standards of achievement for all.

6. *Manageability/Practicality*

Problems can arise in badly-paced assessment programmes when students are presented with competing deadlines, causing them stress, and their tutors with workload issues concerning marking. At the same time, there is often over-assessment within programmes, particularly when innovative assignments are added to rather than replacing original ones. Mapping out assignments against the lived student experience week-on-week can help greatly, as can a radical review of the number of assignments, asking whether each is actually serving a purpose. Sometimes things go wrong when well-meaning tutors design excessively complex assignments with different weightings and then try to fit them into university/college/school arrangements for gathering marks. Multiple, separately assessed elements can be an administrative nightmare, but this is another area where e-assessment comes into its own, particularly if a system like Livetext is used, since number-crunching needs no longer be a matter of a lecturer working with a calculator and a self-designed spreadsheet which is then transferred, with potential for many errors, to the institutional system.

7. *Authenticity*

It is often the case that we assess what is easy to assess, or proxies of what has been learned, rather than the learning itself. A valid assessment is one that has close relevance to the criteria, which are in turn constructively aligned to the stated learning outcomes of a programme. Effective assessment is highly relevant to ensuring that graduates can demonstrate the knowledge, behaviours, qualities and attributes that were described in the course outline or programme specification. Assignments that require students to write about something rather than *be* or *do* something may not be fit-for-purpose. Over-use of multiple-choice questions in e-assessment can be problematic; for example, when what is being tested are things like team work, creativity, leadership, without these being authentically tested out in practice. Therefore in our excitement about the potential of e-assessment to save tutor drudgery, provide rapid and detailed feedback, and to provide equivalent and inclusive assessments, curriculum designers should not use it inappropriately, just because we can.

8. Constructive alignment

Biggs and Tang propose that since the intended learning outcomes, expressed with verbs, specify activities that students need to engage in so as to demonstrate that they have achieved those outcomes, unless we match up the assessment tasks and criteria with the outcomes, the assessment is likely to be misaligned (Biggs and Tang, 2007, p. 52). This has significant implications for assessment design and the capacity for assessment to be an integral part of learning. As Boud and associates say:

> 'To improve student engagement in learning, and to support better quality learning outcomes, it is necessary that assessment tasks are designed to direct student attention to what needs to be learned and to the activities that best lead to this. Effective learning can be hampered by assessment tasks that focus student attention on grades and marks or reproductive thinking.'
>
> Boud and associates, 2010, p. 2

The corollary of this is that we need to use strategic and evidence-informed approaches to design the assessment elements of the curriculum, drawing on the expertise cited above. As assessors we provide explicit and implicit messages by how we assess, since the marks and relative weightings imply a judgement by us on how much students should value the tasks we set them. Students will often put less energy and effort into work which is minimally recognised through the marks we give, and we can prompt particular behaviours by loading marks differentially according to what is important at that stage of the learning process. Clever course developers utilise students' tendency to be strategic (Kneale, 1997) and design assessment tools that foster the behaviours we would wish to see (for example, logical sequencing, fluent writing, effective referencing and good time management in essay and report writing) and discourage others ('jumble-sale' data sourcing, aimless cutting and pasting and plagiarism). We might, for example, when assessing first-year students on their first essays, give a high proportion of marks for clear and accurate referencing, to help students get in the habit of always referencing accurately. Later in the programme, we might load more marks onto critical thinking or the ability to offer a personal perspective on a particular issue, but in the early stages we may wish to retain a focus on the basics.

Ensuring assessment is fit-for-purpose also requires us to critique the assignment questions/tasks themselves, the briefings we give students on paper, live and virtually about what we expect of them, the marking criteria in operation, the moderation process by which we assure consistency and reliability and the amount, quality and scope of feedback we give to students. We also need to scrutinise how the assignments align with one another, whether we are over- or under-assessing, whether we are creating log-jams for students and markers, whether we are assessing authentically, and whether our processes are fair and sensible.

Illustrating the application of my fit-for-purpose model and the principles that follow, the next two good practice accounts provide examples of good assignment design in rather different contexts. In the first, the nature of the assignment chosen has been determined to align fully with the intentions of the assessment team, to ensure that the national context is fully represented in the process. In the second, academics working in the design studio redesigned their assessment because they were concerned that students were producing lesser work than they were capable of originating, because they were working towards the perceived agenda of the people who were marking them, rather than to achieve their best creative potential.

On occasions in academic pedagogy, we talk about the values underpinning learning or assessment as if these were universal and readily agreed. As this account shows, priorities vary from nation to nation, but we can all learn from making ourselves aware of the key tenets of cultures other than our own. For example, in some societies, as discussed earlier, reaching consensus and acting collegially is much more important than achieving individual prominence. Achieving agreement may be problematic, and assessment criteria, for example within group work, can be unexpectedly troublesome if expectations of student behaviours are implicit rather than explicit.

Assessment design can therefore require some flexibility on both sides, with outcomes that are not always foreseen. In the next good practice account, it's notable that when the course team started to reframe their assignments to ensure that students engaged more fully in learning, they found many additional unexpected benefits for both staff and students.

Negotiated assignments on a Graduate Diploma in Higher Education

Melanie Miller, UNITEC, New Zealand

Background

Academics have to complete (within two years at the start of their contract) a tertiary teaching qualification, if they have not graduated with one recently. Many will have been teaching for some time, and have achieved competence teaching and learning. Three negotiated courses at 15, 30 and 60 credit points were developed with this in mind at UNITEC and participants undertake an assessed developmental activity project as an alternative way of achieving the graduate profile other than through course work, potentially including evidence of student understanding of how they engage effectively in the bi-cultural context of a multicultural New Zealand and demonstrating their personal growth. They are expected to:

- Design a project that involves a development activity that aims to improve the effectiveness of learning and has outcomes that accord with identified aspects of the graduate profile, and is appropriate for the assigned level and credit rating.
- Develop and negotiate a learning contract for the project, including resource, timeline and supervision arrangements.
- Implement and complete the project, reflect regularly on progress, and renegotiate the contract whenever required.

This requires them to be able to demonstrate a command of wide-ranging highly specialised technical or scholastic and basic research skills across a major discipline, involving the full range of procedures in a major discipline and apply them in complex variable and specialised contexts. To do this they need to demonstrate knowledge, the capability to analyse, transform and evaluate abstract data and concepts and create appropriate responses to resolve given or contextual abstract problems. It is the student's responsibility to plan, resource and manage processes within broad parameters and functions with complete accountability for determining, achieving and evaluating personal and/or group outcomes.

Assessment

Submission of work is negotiated but can be a single package of evidence of achievement for assessment, which includes a critical self-reflection. An oral examination is used to ensure that each student considers issues arising in the assessment of the package including clarifying ownership and achievement issues related to collaborative work.

continued overleaf

Negotiated assignments on a Graduate Diploma in Higher Education *continued*

The projects are negotiated individually and once they have agreed scheduled meetings with the supervisor, the student is responsible for ensuringthat there is appropriate rigour in the work undertaken. Projects may be individual or collaborative or a hybrid. Where they are collaborative, candidates must submit their own evidence and where evidence is shared, the oral examination is used to resolve ownership and achievement issues. Mātauranga Maori teaching philosophy throughout the above teaching and learning approaches will be embedded.

Maori values from the Mātauranga Maori

Aroha: Care, love and respect.

Whanaungatanga: Working together, sense of family.

Iwitanga: Those qualities and characteristics that make aniwi or hapu unique and underpin a shared whakapapa, history and identity.

Whakapapa: Genealogical descent – the descendency from the universe, through autua, to land, air, water and people.

Tino Rangatiratanga: Acts of authority, self-determination and power.

Manaakitanga: Reciprocal and unqualified acts of giving, caring and hospitality.

Awhinatanga: Assist, help, care for, give assistance and help to others.

Koha: acts of giving.

Whakapono: Act of believing or having faith and trust in others.

To fulfil either of the two negotiated courses (120 credits), students can use, for example, evidence of a new course they have developed, reflecting on their personal experience in the teaching field and making use of and evidencing their often extensive experience. These courses aim to be as flexible as possible enabling a variety of self-directed means to demonstrate they have met the required outcomes. They can complete one of two different learning contracts, either submitting what has been achieved to date or a plan of what they intend to do to cover the graduate profile. These means include critical reflection, an enquiring, flexible and critical attitude encompassing adult education and research, appropriate attitudes, values and skills for competent practice, use of current theoretical knowledge relevant to their field, an awareness of diversity issues and an ability to function positively in a multicultural society, an understanding of the relationship between technology and learning, the ability effectively to use appropriate methodologies for open, flexible and online learning situations and an understanding of the practices underpinning self and peer assessment.

Making the most of opportunities

The principal problematic area lies in getting full-time academics to complete in time for submission, hence the requirement to complete a learning contract with timelines and have this approved by programme committee, with progress monitored by the Programme Leader. The handbook provides guidance on required elements that must be achieved. A negotiated approach is an excellent way to fast-track competent academics to gain a qualification they are required to complete, but needs consistent mentoring and supervising and the programmes at first had low completion rates.

Negotiation on a one-to-one basis is time-consuming but, while there are no set face-to-face classes, encouraging several course participants to enrol together can be helpful. Face-to-face time, email conversations, CISCO jabber/Skype are all used, and timetabling these collectively can be time-efficient. A range of resources, including examples of presentations, portfolios, videos, poems, PowerPoint presentations, and online innovative tools have been devised by our most creative students, which fellow course participants can view to help them design their own assessment submissions. As is common in the Maori /New Zealand context, students may use oral presentations in a public context as part of their evidencing of achievement.

Authentic assessment using think-tanks in assessing Design

Yvan Martinez, Darren Raven and **Joshua Trees**, London College of Communication, University of the Arts, London, UK

Introduction

Working on undergraduate group graphic design projects at London College of Communication, we conceived a practical framework for an authentic assessment task called 'Thought Experiments in Graphic Design Education'. The initial task led to a series of candid discussions amongst students and tutors about design education in the UK.

The problem we were aiming to solve

Students reported performance anxiety from trying to make work that pleases tutors, indicating a debilitating preoccupation with grades complicated by a lack of confidence in directing their learning and analysing their accomplishments, especially as it pertains to knowing when to stop researching and start actually designing. They also demonstrated a general lack of interest in attending group critiques (Crits) due to a perceived lack of community and productivity. Tutors reported a concern with rising

continued overleaf

Authentic assessment using think-tanks in assessing Design *continued*

enrolment and unmanageable student/tutor ratios, a growing trend for students to feign learning to satisfy assessment criteria, and they really wanted to foster a climate where students and tutors become equal participants in the delivery of the curriculum.

To address such insights, a project was designed devoted to Inquiry, involving the formation of student 'think-tanks', where they could share ideas with experts, to heighten students' cognitive and collaborative capabilities. The project was structured around three foci: Systems, Processes and Actions. The first two were interpreted and prompted in relation to the participating tutors' affiliated communities of practice. Actions were interpreted and prompted by the think-tanks. Typical prompts to student inquiry included:

- When does noise become information?
- Does practice make perfect?
- Does 1 + 1 = 2 or 11?
- Who needs autonomy?

At the outset, students signed up to groups, having read the Design tutors' practitioner statements. Tutors worked in pairs, meeting 40 students twice-weekly over 7 weeks (120 students total), with each inquiry lasting 2–3 weeks. In this context, the role of tutors was not to 'teach' but rather to collaborate and facilitate, resembling something closer to Vygotsky's concept of a 'more competent peer' (quoted in Harland, 2003). Tutors approached this role in divergent ways while striving to foster a learning culture that sought to be autodidactic, non-hierarchical, non-prescriptive and reflexive.

Throughout the process, think-tanks agreed, applied and revised their own assessment criteria, and tutors examined each think-tank's ability to examine itself. Think-tankers initiated, negotiated and evaluated each other's progress and outcomes responding to prompts.

The tutors subsequently reflected on the experience of leading inquiry-based learning for potential future use. A feedback questionnaire confirmed an attitudinal shift among students regarding assessment, as well as increased engagement, reinforced by better attendance records. Unlike much group work, students didn't complain about the grades they earned, probably because how well they performed was largely in their own hands.

Learning points

The project provided challenges to students and tutors about their practices and perceptions of teaching and assessing design projects. Unlike traditional studio crits which typically occur after a student has been working in isolation, the formation of think-tanks provided a support system defined by continuous feedback, exchange and exposure to design work and the working methods of others. In turn, students demonstrated higher levels of initiative, resourcefulness and solidarity.

The think-tanks exhibited the term's work publicly, which was something we wouldn't have done previously. Students and staff feel we are learning, creating and achieving and have more ownership of the process. We also encountered some ambivalence and resistance as we gradually broke down conventional learning habits, particularly students' high dependency on instruction from tutors, despite receiving hours of feedback from both peers and tutors. Most eventually learned to compare input from multiple sources and trust their own analysis.

Involving students in the setting of assessment criteria also required some coaxing: initially think-tanks struggled to imagine what might be missing from their work before looking outwards to see how other fields assess performance. Some rewrote the university's official 'marking matrix' in friendlier language, others introduced new criteria such as 'authenticity', 'hack value' and 'unintentional meaning' and some chose not to assign grades at all, focusing instead on the quality of oral and written feedback. Assessing the think-tanks' ability to assess themselves also proved tricky at times because students tended to regress towards self-conscious performance if they sensed they were being observed.

Positive side-effects included learning to share research, balancing the time devoted to researching and making, and avoiding the tendency to fall into 'research holes'. In contrast to what is expected from inquiry-based learning in a science education, within our design setting, we noted a tendency for some students at first to treat the inquiries as themes rather than opportunities for critical thinking. Perhaps the most important by-product of this approach was the emergence of a 'meta playground' where students actively participated in assessment and taught themselves to transform examination anxiety into a strategy for taking control of their learning, and articulating their accomplishments rather than falsifying them. One of our students said:

> 'I used to look at a mark-sheet about half-way through a project, and check that I was ticking boxes. Now I've learnt that a mark-scheme should be used as a more integral part of the decision making process, right from the very beginning of the project. It should inform the work, not the other way round.'

References

Martinez, Y. and Trees, J. (2013) *Thought Experiments in Graphic Design Education*, Books from the future.

Harland, T. (2003) Vygotsky's zone of proximal development and problem-based learning: linking a theoretical concept with practice through action research, *Teaching in Higher Education*, 8(2), pp. 263–72.

Conclusions

Effective assessment can significantly and positively impact on student learning, but only if it is designed and implemented well, with the students being active partners in the process, rather than just being acted upon by assessors. Boud argues that:

> 'The fundamental problem of the dominant view for assessment is that it constructs learners as passive subjects. That is, students are seen to have no role other than to subject themselves to the assessment acts of others, to be measured and classified. They conform to the rules and procedures of others to satisfy the needs of an assessment bureaucracy: they present themselves at set times for examinations over which they have little or no influence and they complete assignments that are, by and large, determined with little or no input from those being assessed.'
>
> Boud, 2007, p. 17

Students are more likely to take assessment tasks seriously if assessors engage students in assessment dialogues and provide realistic tasks that safely challenge them beyond their comfort zones. Furthermore, they are likely to put more energy into assignments they see as authentic and worth bothering with. For this reason, in the next chapter I will explore how we can use these principles to underpin good assessment design and practice.

8 Designing and implementing assessment and feedback for learning

In the last chapter, I explored how we can make assessment fit-for-purpose by applying evidence-based principles and pragmatic approaches to underpin good assessment design and practice. In this chapter, I will consider how we can organise assessment so that it really works in the students' interests.

Designing good assessment

There are many reasons for designing and implementing a good assessment strategy which include the recognition that:

- Good assessment can act as a positive lever for learning where it is fully integrated within the teaching process: treating it as an add-on at the end of the curriculum design process is a wasted opportunity to shape student behaviour and skills development.
- In national student surveys in the UK, Australia and elsewhere, the highest levels of student dissatisfaction tend to be around assessment and feedback.
- The majority of student complaints and grievances, which take up much academic and management time, so are therefore expensive to resolve, are concerned with perceived poor practice and misjudgements, particularly associated with perceived unfairness.
- Where students have disabilities, (for example, visual or aural impairments, dyslexia, mental health problems, mobility issues, all of which are covered by disability legislation in many countries, thereby leading to a statutory requirement to remediate potential disadvantage during assessment), good inclusive practice suggests that appropriate arrangements should be designed in from the outset, rather than added hastily at a later stage.

For these reasons, next I will concentrate on how designing assessment that is manageable, particularly designing the ways in which we can give feedback efficiently and effectively, designing fair and equitable assessment that promotes good academic conduct, and designing an organised, holistic and systematic approach to assessment, by thinking about it at a programme rather than at a module level.

The importance of giving good feedback

Concentrating on giving students detailed and developmental feedback is the single most useful thing we can do for our students, particularly those from disadvantaged backgrounds who may not understand the rules of the higher education game. The time we spend on giving detailed and developmental formative and summative feedback should not be skimped: this is crucial to foster student learning and is the most time-consuming aspect of assessment but arguably the most important thing we do for learners.

Formative and summative assessment perform different functions and work in different ways. I suggest that formative assessment forms and informs, and is primarily concerned with giving feedback that is aimed at prompting improvement in student work. It is often continuous and usually involves plenty of words. Summative assessment is concerned with summing up and making evaluative judgements, is often end-point and involves numbers and grades rather than words. Purists argue that they work best without overlap, but in my view there can be an element of hybridity. For example, a poor exam mark is principally summative in nature, but a poor grade can give students some formative information, by implying whether this is an area of study with which to continue (either because the mark is so poor there is little merit in continuing, or by showing an area of weakness where improvement is essential for success in other areas, like statistics for psychologists or live drawing for sculptors).

Sadler, the most cited author on formative assessment suggests that we need to:

> 'provide the means by which students can develop a concept of quality that is similar in essence to that which the teacher possesses, and in particular to understand what makes for high quality ... Students need to be exposed to, and gain experience in making judgements about, a variety of works of different quality ... They need planned rather than random exposure to exemplars, and experience in making judgements

> about quality. They need to create verbalised rationales and accounts of how various works could have been done better. Finally, they need to engage in evaluative conversations with teachers and other students.'
>
> Sadler, 2010b, p. 544

To have best effect, he argues, this understanding should develop during the production of the work, rather than much later, once the work has been handed in and the grade awarded. In an ideal world, what many students would like best would be for us to sit alongside them and talk them through their assessed work over an extended period of time so that they can gauge whether their work is of the right standard and comprehend what they need to do to improve it. However, this is only really possible within an elite, highly resourced higher education system, and only a tiny minority of academics work in one of these. Where this is not possible, it is incumbent upon us, I would suggest, to give as much feedback as we can, which is supportive and developmental in quality, and ensure students receive it as fast as possible.

National student evaluation systems of the kinds used in the UK, Australia and elsewhere indicate that what students really hate about feedback is:

- Poorly written comments that are nigh on impossible to decode, especially when impenetrable acronyms or abbreviations are used, or where handwriting is in an unfamiliar alphabet and is illegible.
- Cursory and derogatory remarks that leave them feeling demoralised 'Weak argument', 'Shoddy work', 'Hopeless', 'Under-developed', and so on.
- Value judgements on them as people rather than on the work in hand.
- Vague comments which give few hints on how to improve or remediate errors: 'OK as far as it goes', 'Needs greater depth of argument', 'Inappropriate methodology used', 'Not written at the right level'.
- Feedback that arrives so late that there are no opportunities to put into practice any guidance suggested in time for the submission of the next assignment.

Therefore good feedback:

- Is dialogic, rather than mono-directional, giving students chances to respond to comments from their markers and seek clarification where necessary.
- Helps clarify what good work looks like, so students are really clear about goals, criteria and expected standards, and provides opportunities to close the gap between current and desired performance (Sadler, 2010b).

- Actively facilitates students reviewing their own work and reflecting on it, so that they become good judges of the quality of their own work.
- Doesn't just correct errors and indicate problems, potentially leaving students discouraged and demotivated, but also highlights good work and encourages them to believe they can improve and succeed.
- Delivers high-quality information to students about their achievements to date and how they can improve their future work. Where there are errors, students should be able to see what needs to be done to remediate them, and where they are undershooting in terms of achievement, they should be able to perceive how to make their work even better.
- Offers 'feed-forward' aiming to 'increase the value of feedback to the students by focusing comments not only on the past and present … but also on the future – what the student might aim to do, or do differently in the next assignment or assessment if they are to continue to do well or to do better' (Hounsell, 2008, p. 5).
- Ensures that the mark isn't the only thing that students take note of when work is returned, but that they are encouraged to read and use the advice given in feedback and apply it to future assignments.

Students working in professional contexts are particularly reliant on good feedback from placement or workplace supervisors as well as from their tutors, since they are often working day-to-day with live clients or end-users who experience the students' developing competence and autonomy at first hand. Where it is well-designed, feedback can provide a bridge between current practice and advanced work, potentially leading to progressive and incremental advances in capability. An example of how assessment can really contribute to learning by offering regular and developmental advice, guidance, praise, commentary and hints for improvement follows.

Using incremental and ongoing feedback assessment with early years student teachers in Spain

Victor M. López-Pastor, Faculty of Education, University of Valladolid, and convenor of the Network for Formative and Shared Assessment in Spain

Introduction

This account describes approaches to authentic assessment in an education faculty in Spain where third- and fourth-year students are assessed on their learning while on teaching practice in schools. This assessment works well because, in addition to evaluating students' competences, the programme requires students to demonstrate their reflection on practice and to demonstrate development over their period of study. A cohort of around 80 students in their third and fourth years spend one semester in each year in practice in schools, for 10 or 12 weeks.

Assessing practice

Much assessment in Spain is very traditional, but in this context students aren't just summatively assessed, they receive much formative assessment from regular meetings with the course tutor. These involve dialogical processes with individual students and groups of around twelve students in regular discussions with their tutor, to ensure deep learning occurs, rather than just checking-off competences. Importantly, the classroom teacher who oversees the work of the student teacher in the host school is also involved in separate discussions directly with the student and the university tutor. Capabilities which are assessed include planning and competence in teaching practice, but also include professional behaviours such as punctuality and the extent of deep engagement with the host school. A significant component of the assessment is a reflective diary which students write daily. In addition they produce an extended reflective report of around 60 pages, which is incrementally produced following classroom discussions. This includes students' analytical reviews of the scholarly literature they are reading for the seminars, and an element of action research whereby they choose an aspect of their teaching to investigate, and undertake a small-scale review in relation to it. Marks are broken down as follows: 50% for reports by host teachers on students' work in practice, 30% for students' own reflective accounts and diaries, and 20% for tutors' assessment of their contributions in seminars.

Review

Victor chooses this approach with his groups of students because he thereby ensures that students learn better and more deeply than students who do not benefit from this approach. Student opinion of the assessment approach is divided: some students really like it and feel that it helps them to learn a great deal, while others do not appreciate the high workload which involves extended reading and the demands being made on them to think deeply about their practice.

Victor regularly interviews teachers in the host schools, and they really like this approach because they perceive it as rigorous and supportive, and also because they are able in the regular visits made by the tutor to the school to immediately to resolve any problems that students are experiencing before the end of the teaching practice. This thereby also serves as in-service training, support and guidance for the teachers themselves, who are commonly not given much formal training on how to mentor students.

Victor himself appreciates this approach because, as well as benefiting students, it means he builds supportive learning partnerships with the host teachers, and they help to ensure that he maintains his own currency and

continued overleaf

Using incremental and ongoing feedback assessment with early years student teachers in Spain *continued*

authentic understanding of changing classroom practices in schools, informing his own continuous professional development. This provides a quality control over the whole process, because professionals in the classroom are contributing to the wider education of the students.

Although there is no formal evidence that students using this approach achieve better, within Victor's teaching groups, those students who fully embrace this approach get much better marks overall for their teaching, and on their evidence of practice on this module.

Problematic issues

Not all tutors on this programme adopt Victor's approach, so students on the same programme may have variable assessment experiences, and the interpretation of marking criteria across the programme is not identical.

A further emergent issue which has been addressed is the potential disparity in formative assessment experience between the majority of students on placements around Segovia, and a minority of students who undertake placements in England and Ghana as well as in cities elsewhere in Spain. This is addressed by staff making occasional visits in person when possible, but to a much greater extent by virtual support on a regular basis provided through synchronous discussions via Moodle, as well as ongoing telephone and email contact with students and tutors in host schools. The model therefore lends itself to usage in other regions and nations as well as in other professional disciplines.

Six ways of giving feedback efficiently and effectively

Recognising that giving really good formative feedback that achieves all of its aims takes a great deal of academic time, effort and resource. In the next section, I will suggest a diverse range of time-saving methods for giving feedback. By providing a variety of feedback mechanisms, it is possible, I propose, to give students the kind of help they need and encourage them to take feedback more seriously. Each of the feedback approaches suggested has merits and disadvantages, so you can choose on each occasion an approach that best suits the assignment, the level, the subject and the cohort.

1. **Collective oral reports**. In these, instead of writing detailed feedback comments on individual assignments by hand or electronically, minimal in-script comments are made and the assessor uses collective time (potentially at the start of a lecture or in a seminar but also perhaps by podcast or virtual meeting) to give an oral report to the group on the

cohort's performance, common mistakes, showing examples of good practice, asking students to judge, say, which of two introductions was considered best and why and so on. Oral feedback can allow the tone of voice, differential emphasis and body language to get key points across and set a supportive mood around feedback. Students thereby can learn from this generic feedback about their own and each others' strengths and weaknesses and they can ask questions about details they've not understood. This makes feedback a shared rather than a solitary experience and gives higher status to the commentary and critique.

In this approach, staff mark assignments giving minimal in-text comments and write grades/marks as normal on the work. In the face-to-face context, the tutor provides an overview of class performance and orally remediates errors, clarifies misunderstandings, and praises good practice. It can save a great deal of time, especially with large cohorts.

2. **Collective written reports** use a similar approach but in text form rather than orally. As with oral reports, this approach enables students to know how they are doing by comparison with the rest of the course, possibly illustrated graphically, and offers chances to demonstrate good practice. A written report can provide a greater variety of examples of good practice and can offer additional reading suggestions. Of course, it is possible to combine the two methods, providing a written report by email or online, and supplementing this with a live slot so students can interact face-to-face with the assessor. It's important to let the students know your rationale for using a collective approach, emphasising the benefits of a shared feedback experience.
3. **Model answers with 'exploded' text**. Just as handbooks for electrical appliances provide labelled diagrams so customers can identify how to use them and how they work, model answers can be designed with illustrative commentary appended to the text in hard copy or on the VLE to show how solutions have been reached and demonstrate good practice as well as illustrating problems and errors. They give students a good idea of what can be expected of them and it is sometimes easier to *show* students than *tell* them what is required. They can be very helpful to students, particularly in the early stages of a programme as the commentary can indicate why an answer is good, rather than just providing solutions, as is commonly the case with traditional model answers.

   Staff preparing an assignment can draft one or more model answers, potentially using anonymised extracts from several student's answers (with their permission). However, caution should be exercised in order to avoid students thinking that model answers provide a recipe for success if copied, or that only one approach is acceptable.

4. **Statement banks**. These comprise an extended list of comments relating to key points in a student's work that can be appended or referred to. Many of us already have a substantial repertoire of frequently-used comments and this approach harnesses a resource you already use. It avoids you writing the same comments repeatedly; allows you to give individual comments additionally to the students who really need them; can be automated with use of technology in the form of rubrics within assessment management systems e.g. Livetext or in Moodle. The tutor identifies a range of regularly used comments written on students' work. These are collated and numbered, the tutor marks the work and writes numbers on the text of the assignment where specific comments apply, or provides a written (or emailed) detailed commentary which pulls together the appropriate items into continuous prose.
5. **Assignment return proformas**. Proformas save assessors writing the same thing repeatedly, help to keep assessors' comments on track, show how criteria match up to performance and how marks are derived, help students to see what is valued and provide a useful written record. Most assessment management systems can use assignment return sheets well, criteria presented in an assignment brief can be utilised in a proforma, variations in weighting can be clearly identified, a Likert scale or boxes can be used to speed tutor's responses and space can be provided for individual comments. Figure 8.1 shows an example of an assignment return sheet.

Criterion no.	Criterion	Mark (0–5)	Tutor comments and suggestions for further work	Student response
1	Demonstrates ability to present information clearly, logically, accurately and fluently	3	This work is written reasonably fluently but there are some typos that would not slip in if spell checker used properly. Also note you don't use the definite and indefinite articles ('a' and 'the') appropriately: please refer to the language guidance 17.3 on the VLE	*This is something I've had problems with over the years but am still working on it*
2	Demonstrates ability to choose and use appropriate software	5	Made excellent choices and used it well to suit the context of the problem being addressed	*Thank you*
3	Demonstrates ability to use a range of reference materials and cite them appropriately	1	Cited only one reference and did so inaccurately Please refer to the ifs referencing guide on the VLE and ensure that you provide all the information required	*I've checked it out and see where I was going wrong*

Figure 8.1 Example of an assignment return proforma

Computer-assisted assessment to improve the efficiency of assessment

One of the principal bugbears staff complain about is the drudgery implied in repetitive marking. I suggest that we should as far as possible, **stop marking and start assessing**, by which I mean we need to radically rethink the activities we undertake when reviewing student work, and concentrate all our energies on the occasions when real judgement is needed. Using relevant and appropriate technologies can remove the necessity to get involved in activities involving routine checking against correct answers. In these contexts, it makes a lot more sense to use some form of e-assessment than for us to do this manually. Time-saving computer-assisted assessment can include using multiple-choice questions.

Multiple-choice questions (MCQs)

MCQs enable assessment to be undertaken regularly and incrementally and can save tutor time for large cohorts and repeated classes (although they are not so valuable for very small cohorts or where curriculum content changes rapidly). Well-used for many years in paper formats before e-assessment was widely used, MCQs enable students to click on what they believe to be the correct answer and receive almost instantaneous feedback on whether or not they are right. In the best systems, they are informed why particular answers are right or wrong, and given further opportunities to check their understanding. This facilitates the integration of assessment with learning and offers personalised learning, with students able to navigate through pathways directed by their responses to prior questions, with multiple opportunities for self-review. Students seem to really like having the chance to find out how they are doing, and attempt tests several times in an environment where no one else is watching how they do. For tentative students this can offer a neutral and non-exposing environment to practise and learn.

MCQ packages are often available from publishers of text books, colleagues, commercial suppliers and other sources. For example, some discipline groupings in the UK have built very large collective test banks from which partners can draw down questions and answers, enabling students to be given different tests every time without requiring high staff input in preparing them.

One of the main critiques of MCQs is that it can be easy for students to do well by guessing answers in subjects about which they know very little (indeed I have done so myself!). Some argue for penalising wrong answers, so students only record answers about which they are very confident, but a better way to prevent 'succeeding-by-guesswork' is to use a wider range of question types. e-assessment questions don't have to be just MCQs comprising a 'stem' statement or question that has one or more 'correct' responses. Other formats include:

- Drag-and-drop questions where students click and drag images or words into position on a diagram, map, table, photograph, etc.
- Cloze questions where students fill in (or select) blank sections, for example, missing key words (possibly selected from pull-down lists).
- Hotspots, where students click on a picture, graph or diagram to indicate the selected answer they believe to be correct.
- Knowledge matrices where several related MCQs are grouped together with interdependent answers, reducing the potential for students just to guess correct answers.
- Matching pairs where students match items in a list of words or statements with items in a second list.
- Pull-down lists where students match a set of statements with items in a pull-down list, or label diagrams with items and so on.
- Ranking tasks where students rank a list of choices in order numerically. For example: 'In priority order, which are the more common causes of a subarachnoid hematoma?'.

After Fisher et al., 2014, pp. 113–14

Academics using computer-based assessments don't have to design them all by themselves: in fact this is very poor practice, since three elements are necessary for good e-assessment – familiarity with subject content, familiarity with technologies to support assessment implementation and the capacity to design good questions and answers – and these are capabilities infrequently found within the same person. Testing and piloting of items is also imperative, since designing e-assessment is a tough task. More detail about using technologies to support assessment is provided in the next chapter.

Relatively quick and easy forms of e-assessment have benefits not only in enabling us to return grades and feedback to students quickly and efficiently, but also because it is easy to track who is or is not doing them, allow us to monitor what is going on across a cohort, so we can concentrate our energies either on students who are repeatedly doing badly or those who are not engaging at all in the activity.

Other forms of computer-assisted assessment

Fisher, Exley and Ciobanu (2014) mention other forms of assessment, some of which have been used for many years, where using technology can be time-efficient and enhance learning. Among these are e-portfolios, simulations of practice, and assessed blogs and wikis.

e-portfolios

An **e-portfolio** is

> 'a purposeful aggregation of digital items – ideas, evidence, reflections, feedback etc which "presents" a selected audience with evidence of a person's learning and/or ability.'
>
> Sutherland and Powell, 2007, p. 124

The major advantage of any kind of portfolio is that it allows learners to present wide-ranging evidence of achievement and to show originality and creativity alongside mastery of subject matter (Brown and Race, 2012), but they take time to mark and can be bulky and unmanageable, whether in hard-copy format or electronic. e-portfolios' advantage over paper-based versions is their ability to use video, audio and other digitised media, but as with all formats, guidance to students needs to be provided on scope and scale, otherwise the sheer act of reviewing and grading them can make more work for assessors. A real advantage of e-portfolios is that students can maintain them and show development after graduation, so long as the platform they use is accessible once they stop being students.

Simulations of professional contexts and tasks

Simulations, as Fisher et al. (op. cit.) suggest, are widely used in assessing students on professional courses and for continuous professional development (for example for surgeons and airline pilots). Where work contexts are difficult or dangerous to access, for example building sites and radioactive environments, simulations can allow rehearsal and assessment of competence in risk-reduced environments. Simulations where students are engaged in role-play scenarios involving live human beings are expensive and time-intensive to organise, and this is where simulations come into their own, for example using computer-generated wards in hospitals or production factories. Learning and assessment activities which are constructed so that students face challenges and changing scenarios as in computer-based role-play games are increasingly being used, with decision trees used to enable students to steer personalised pathways and to interact with peers. Time-saving in this context needs to be balanced with the amount of time invested in creating, developing and updating these scenarios, so work most economically when they can be re-used with large cohorts.

Assessed blogs and wikis

These enable students to work individually and collectively, enabling interactions between part- and full-time students, as well as campus-based and distance learners. Students' work for assessment can be developed iteratively over time, and can be used for critique of own or peers' work, reflection on practice, assembling and analysis of data and so on. Assessment can, in early stages, just involve ensuring that students post a minimum number of entries, but subsequently the quality and scope of postings, together with their ability to generate comments and peer dialogue can be assessed, as another means to access students' ability to generate ideas and articulate their thinking.

Choices on which e-assessment approaches to use will depend on their fitness-for-purpose, as discussed in the previous chapter, and crucially, on the extent to which they foster learning through assessment in manageable ways. The following account outlines how proprietary software systems can be used to support evidence-based approaches to assessment.

Technologies to support curriculum management and quality assurance

Victoria Guzzo, Director of Corporate Communications, LiveText, USA

Technologies that put student learning at the centre

One of the most valuable contributions anyone can make to another person's learning is constructive feedback. Feedback on performance, when effective, is widely considered to be integral to learning. People learn faster and more deeply if they know what the strengths and weaknesses of their performances are and most importantly, how to improve future performances.

We all learn from feedback: sometimes self-generated feedback from self-assessment, sometimes from the feelings of success or failure at what was attempted. Sometimes the feedback comes from the environment; and sometimes the feedback comes from another person or a group. From wherever the feedback originates, we use it to modify our future actions to either reinforce our previous behaviour or to change it for the future using the D-A-R strategy, that is **D**irect-**A**ssess-**R**edirect. This is true of all learning, from motor skills, to self-reflection, to cognition of the world around us. This concept of feedback is especially important for students at universities and colleges.

This potential to influence future performance is what is known as feed-forward. In order to generate feed-forward, *feedback* must not only identify the learner gap between actual and desired performance (by indicating the standard achieved on any given criterion for example) but also provide information needed to close that gap. When specific guidance is provided to close the gap, the feed-forward effect is even greater and the focus of feedback quickly becomes learning rather than grades or marks.

This is academic assessment, and it's an ongoing process that requires continuous re-evaluation to determine whether teaching and learning processes achieve the goals and objectives defined by faculty and administrators at the institution. When students do not achieve those goals and objectives, changes should be made. And when students succeed in achieving those goals and objectives, perhaps we can conclude that those changes in the teaching and learning process are working. The question is, how do we know? How do we do this in the most efficient way?

Part of the answer must lie in integrating supportive technology – that is, technology that systematises the often paper-based process of assessment, technology that can capture that student-teacher interaction, technology that can facilitate the feedback process immediately, technology that can at any given point report out data trends on this process so we can see how effective our teaching and curriculum delivery actually are.

Platforms are available to support such a process for higher education institutions. One example is LiveText, which is a student learning assessment management platform. Systems such as LiveText provide a web-based assessment solution that supports evidence-based learning. With e-portfolio, course, subject, and outcomes-based assessment capabilities integrated within one system, these systems allow teaching staff to communicate more easily with students on the progress of their work and provide feedback; students receive that feedback immediately and are able to stay more engaged in their learning experiences by re-thinking and applying that feedback and university administrators can collect data on this process for purposes of assessing programme effectiveness and improving programme quality.

Assessment should be viewed as a self-reflective learning tool for students and an opportunity for teachers to present concrete advice/questions/evidence for learning improvement. When technology is engaged for these purposes, we are able to more easily see a fuller picture of and trends in student learning at all levels – for individual students, within and across courses, within and across programmes, and, of course, across an entire institution. The technology is built into the teaching process, and the data that comes out of this is a natural by-product of a more systematised,

continued overleaf

Technologies to support curriculum management and quality assurance *continued*

automated process. Applying such technology here allows for the following benefits:

- Opportunities for the academic community to engage in self-reflection of its learning goals, to determine the degree to which these goals align with student and marketplace needs, and to evaluate if students' overall performances coincide with the institution's expectations.
- Ways for academic programmes to explore the dimensions of student learning when seeking to improve student achievement and the educational process.
- Evidence of student achievement for accreditation or quality assurance regulating groups. Specialised, professional, and regional accreditation bodies hold institutions responsible for providing reliable evidence of the continuous improvement of student learning.

If our ultimate goal is to make improvements so that we can increase student achievement and provide evidence of those improvements and achievement, we should more closely consider the value and role of technology in systematising the process of providing feedback, assessing student learning, and collecting data on it. Then we'll have what can truly be called a student-centred higher education experience.

Reference

Hounsell, D. (2008) The trouble with feedback: new challenges, emerging strategies. *Interchange*, Spring.

Audio feedback

It can be time-consuming to give feedback live in a studio or lab setting, and then to follow this up with written notes later, but making no record of the feedback event can result in the learning being lost. Providing feedback in audio form, with sound recorders used to capture live commentaries and then emailed to students can be both efficient and valuable.

It can also be helpful to audio record rather than write feedback on text assignments submitted on paper or virtually: academics involved in the *Sounds Good* project (JISC, 2008) reported that although it takes some time to get used to using an audio recorder rather than a pen or keyboard, once in the swing of things, it became a faster and more satisfying means of giving students a formative commentary on their work, enabling tone of voice and warmth to provide a more personalised and less threatening means of giving challenging advice. Students involved in the project were overwhelmingly positive about receiving audio feedback on their coursework. They frequently remarked approvingly about its personal nature and the detail provided, evidence that the lecturer had carefully considered their work. For students with visual impairments and dyslexia or those learning in a second (or more) language, having feedback aurally was often considered a bonus.

Many of the other methods above including model answers, assignment return proformas and statement banks rely substantially on aspects of e-assessment to make them efficient and effective. Making the best use of the platforms providing a virtual learning environment for the university can also make assessment more efficient and effective, as illustrated in the good practice account that follows.

Taking the pain out of managing assessments in higher education

Mark Glynn, Dublin City University, Ireland

Introduction

Assessment is intricately linked to teaching and learning and plays an important part in the learning process. Indeed, both summative and formative assessments inform progress and guide learning, are essential to the accreditation process, and results are used in all sorts of ways to measure outcomes and success of the student, teacher, course, or institute. Academic institutions are obliged to measure and prove that the learner has met specific learning outcomes of their course. This 'proof' is provided through assessment (Angelo and Cross, 1993). The challenge for most lecturers is to get the balance right between offering enough assessment, with appropriate levels of feedback, without overburdening the student and ourselves, which is not an easy challenge to meet. To further complicate things there needs to be communication and co-ordination between lecturers delivering different modules across the same programme to ensure that the aforementioned balance is also achieved with respect to the programme as a whole. The learning management system (LMS) is a crucial tool when it comes to addressing this challenge and here various features of how an LMS can be used to manage assessments efficiently are described.

Transparency

Good practice dictates that we should be transparent with our assessment. A lecturer can use the LMS to post key information about assignments: descriptions, deadlines, and its value towards to the final grade. If staff use the LMS properly, it will automatically create a calendar of assessments for students, and if linked up to their smart phones, they can be sent reminders directly about impending (or missed) deadlines. The LMS we use at Dublin

continued overleaf

Taking the pain out of managing assessments in HE *continued*

City University (Moodle) also enables lecturers to provide rubrics or marking guides to comment on and correct students' work. Both rubrics and marking guides can be presented to students in advance of an assessment or afterwards, thereby providing consistent structure to the lecturer's feedback, helping offer transparency for the students.

Administration

For lecturers, the simple act of collecting assignments from students can be troublesome. However Moodle can provide a 'virtual postbox' where students can submit their assignments. Then there can be no argument about whether students have submitted their assignments as all are stored in Moodle, and it also puts a timestamp on the student's submission, providing clarity for both the student and lecturer.

Using an LMS can be very helpful when managing group assignments. First, Moodle can easily allow a lecturer to either allocate students to groups or get them to choose their own, thereby removing a potentially time-consuming task for lecturers. Furthermore, when a lecturer provides a grade and feedback to one student the other students in the group are automatically given the same grade and feedback. To illustrate the power of this feature, if there are assignments with four students per group the lecturers workload is reduced by 75% if they use Moodle to manage mark distribution over doing it individually.

Calculation and issuing of grades

Moodle provides a Gradebook facility that allows lecturers to grade all assignments out of 100 and then the lecturer can choose to weight the grades before collating them all together for individual assignments and presenting the total course grade to students. Additionally, Moodle can be set up to provide feedback to the student but withhold the grade, for example, until exam boards are complete or marks moderated. This has the advantage that students tend to concentrate on the feedback rather than get distracted by the grade. In addition, a lecturer can determine which grades from a wide range of tasks count towards the final mark. Hence, a lecturer may set several assignments and/or online quizzes for revision purposes where only some of the marks obtained count towards the final course mark. Alternatively a lecturer may set several assignments and can set Moodle to only count the top three or perhaps four assignments.

Moodle has many features that can support the assessment and management of assignments, only a few of which are highlighted here: technology can be used in many ways to enhance the assessment experience for both the student and lecturer.

Reference

Angelo, T. and Cross, K. (1993) *Classroom Assessment Techniques*, New York: Jossey Bass.

Encouraging students to use feedback well

Once we have spent time on giving students feedback, it is a sad waste if students don't make good use of it. We need to explore ways to incentivise reading and using of feedback since students often don't bother, just looking at the mark given. This can be wasteful of staff effort and a missed opportunity for students who may need support to understand that the comments are not just judgements, but, in the best cases, aiming to provide developmental guidance on how to improve their future submissions (*feed-forward*). Using audio feedback as described above can be very helpful: the Sounds Good project (op. cit.) indicated that students will listen to audio feedback between one and seventeen times, since it has to be listened to in order for the student to get the mark at the end of the comments, whereas they often did not read written feedback at all. Other tutors provide feedback by email without a grade attached and students are required to read the comments and then estimate the mark which they then email back to their tutors, who awards some extra marks to students who have come within five marks of the original number as a reward for good self-evaluation.

Students who perceive that academics are working hard to ensure that they benefit from thoughtful and just feedback are likely to respond in kind to the student-centred environment if they see it as nurturing and developmental. The next section explores how we can foster a climate where fairness and good academic conduct prevail.

Fairness and good academic conduct

Developing a study climate that makes cheating and plagiarism unthinkable can help to foster loyalty to the university and to the standards it assures. If students are made aware of the efforts that a university makes to benchmark qualifications against national standards, make assessment impartial, inclusive and fair to all, and subject marking decisions to internal and external scrutiny, they may be better able to make good judgements about their own academic integrity. Students hate unfair assessment and are more inclined to cheat and plagiarise if they consider it to be happening all around them. In this section I will consider how assessment can be designed and managed fairly.

According to Flint and Johnson (2011, p. 2) student evaluations frequently reveal poor assessment practices that lack authenticity and relevance to real-world tasks, make unreasonable demands on students, are narrow in scope, have little long-term benefit for students' learning, fail to reward genuine effort, have unclear expectations and assessment criteria, fail to provide adequate feedback to students and rely heavily on factual recall rather than on higher-order thinking and problem-solving skills.

Assessing fairly

Work undertaken on what students perceived as fairness in the 1990s (Sambell et al., 1997) suggests that the issues students regard as unfair include perceived favouritism and bias, poor inter-tutor reliability, where work of the same quality receives different marks from different tutors and high marks depend on the 'luck of the draw' in terms of who marks your efforts. Other things students regard as unfair include hidden criteria and lack of transparency, lack of clarity about the rules of the game, particularly in relation to students from disadvantaged backgrounds, and complexities around terms such as 'authentic', 'original' and 'innovative'.

We need to 'play fair' with students by:

- Having ground rules to ensure equivalent (not identical) treatment of students.
- Using joint assignment design, co-marking, effective moderation, reference to agreed benchmarks and other means to assure inter-tutor reliability.
- Making assessment criteria available, accessible and understandable.
- Ensuring rules about compensation, late submission and condonement are applied equally.
- Allocating time within the curriculum to discuss and develop academic literacy in relation to contested terms.

David Boud would also have us be fair to students by avoiding what he terms 'final language' (Boud, 1995): words like 'appalling', 'disastrous', 'hopeless' and 'incompetent' give students no room to manoeuvre whereas words like 'incomparable' and 'unimprovable' don't help outstanding students to develop ipsatively either. We need to avoid destructive criticism of the person rather than the work being assessed and try not to use language that is judgemental to the point of leaving students nowhere to go.

We need also to play fair to students in relation to giving feedback too: students at the top end of the ability range sometimes feel short-changed by minimal feedback and students with many weaknesses can easily become dispirited if there is too much negative feedback. In the UK, the

Open University trains its assessors to give an *assessment sandwich.* They are taught to start with something positive, go into the detailed critique and find something nice to say at the end (to motivate students to keep reading!).

Poor academic conduct

Concerns about plagiarism and cheating have increased over the years, as academics and managers worry that mass higher education provides more opportunities for poor practice and lower chances of being caught. In former times, it was harder for students to cheat by copying the work of others, and the very act of copying manually gave students at least some contact with the material they were supposedly well-acquainted with. Nowadays wider use of communication and information technologies, especially the internet, facilitate passing off the work of others as one's own. 'The learning process is being radically reshaped, to a point where the notion of plagiarism is becoming foggier, and not one that's automatically synonymous with cheating' (Marsden, 2014, p. 49). He quotes broadcaster Vicky Beeching as saying, 'I recently heard someone refer to the internet as our "outboard brain" and now it's surely a question of making a difference in the world by applying that pool of resources'.

Changes in assessment practice, including the increased use of course work, make some aspects of cheating easier. (How many parents, for example, have experienced moral dilemmas when 'proof reading' their children's course work prior to submission and been tempted to help them improve the work in ways that verge on co-authorship?) It is also the case that students in pre-university contexts may have actually been encouraged into bad academic practices. Some schools encourage the learning and re-use of model answers in exams and in some cultures, teachers or text books are honoured sources and it isn't surprising that students are led to believe that there is nothing inappropriate about repeating their words verbatim.

Some argue that higher stakes now exist for university assessment than ever before, with students in many nations paying high fees, and thereby wanting a return on their investment. Similarly, pressure on employment opportunities increases the importance of graduates getting good grades and hence good jobs. It is possible also that there is more reported bad practice than formerly or heightened panic inflamed by press interest.

Carroll (2002) describes plagiarism as passing off someone else's work as your own, wholesale 'lifting' of entire assignments/texts, patching together bits and pieces of others' work and paraphrasing without attribution, purchasing assignments from 'essay mills' and fellow students, or commissioning others to do one's assignments. All of these are clearly reprehensible and universities use a range of means to deter, detect and punish them, but some types of plagiarism are easier than others to do so. Plagiarism detection services are widely used, including 'Turnitin' which has a traffic light system to compare electronically submitted material against a very large number of electronic sources (red = very likely to be plagiarised, green = unlikely to be plagiarised), but these can only detect material that is electronically stored and cannot detect original material written for others.

It is worth also considering that on occasions unintentional plagiarism occurs, either where the student doesn't really understand the concept or makes genuine errors. Avid readers may not always be fully conscious of how much they have absorbed from sources they fail to attribute, particularly when students read very fast and fail to keep good records of references. Many authors (myself included) can attest to the propensity to self-plagiarise accidentally (have I actually written this same paragraph word–for-word in another publication?).

Stephen Newstead and colleagues (1996) have defined cheating as a deliberate process to 'get round' the system, and have identified a whole range of behaviours which could be regarded as cheating including:

- Making up references to support assertions.
- Taking unauthorised material into exams (including paper notes, access to information on mobile phones, writing on the body and so on).
- Impersonation, whereby students get someone else to sit an exam, test or online assignment on their behalf. Press reports tell of even parents being caught doing this!
- Getting special help from a tutor which other students cannot access, either because of overt favouritism or because tutors are not scrupulous in fairly rationing their time to all students seeking help.
- Question spotting, whereby students don't bother to learn the whole curriculum but instead try to second guess what the examiner will ask, based on previous patterns of behaviour and past papers, and get an advantage over students who cover all material.
- Recycling one's own assignments previously submitted on other courses. (Some would argue that there is a problem with the assessment strategy if a student can get a better mark in the third year for an assignment submitted for a second-year course, as is anecdotally the case.)
- Getting extensions of deadlines with false claims of illness or other extenuating circumstances (again, the system is at fault if there are not proper checks and balances to prevent this).

Effective assessment design to avoid cheating and plagiarism balance using strict controls, making the rules clear and having known penalties which are rigorously applied, designing assessment instruments that make poor academic practice difficult and developing a study climate that will reduce the likelihood of cheating (McDowell and Brown, 2001).

A 'strict control' approach might include using well-invigilated, unseen, closed-book exams, using computer-based tests in a strictly monitored environment where photo-identity cards are checked against student numbers, conducting unannounced spot tests and checking for mark discrepancies over a student profile, looking for and investigating anomalies. Where clear rules and known penalties are used, it is important to brief students so they understand what is expected of them and to be honest about grey areas. It can also be helpful to publicise occurrences of cheating and associated disciplinary action (without scape-goating individuals) so students see the risks and the penalties. Some would even advocate using students to police one another (without encouraging a 'sneak' culture), but this strategy has its own risks.

Fostering good academic conduct implies designing assessment instruments that make cheating difficult, for example using assignments reliant on personal experience which are difficult to plagiarise such as reflective journals and critical incident accounts, vivas and orals, assessed presentations and differentiated assignments. If we want to avoid overreliance on factual recall, which tends to tempt students to cheat, it may help to use open-book rather than closed-book exams, where the task involves using information rather than regurgitating it. Where possible it can help to provide assignments with an element of choice and individual activity, although care must be taken to ensure that this doesn't just make it easy to buy or use an off-the-shelf assignment. It should be impossible, for example, for a candidate to get to a PhD examination with a plagiarised thesis because good supervision practice would imply incremental and regular feedback on drafts, together with discussions of key issues and arguments, and similar good practice can be used for undergraduate and masters level work. One can, for example, ask students to submit the photocopied annotated source material they've used, or hand in drafts showing text changes alongside the final assignment.

No system is completely fair, but as university teachers we need to demonstrate we are committed to institutional integrity. Students who are determined to breach good academic conduct will often find a way to do so, despite our best efforts, so we need to remain vigilant while designing good systems. We need to ensure students have trust in the fairness, justice and integrity of the academic systems within which they are working, since anecdotally it is clear that some students who see others getting away with bad academic behaviour feel justified to behave similarly.

One aspect of academic integrity is ensuring that we adopt collegial approaches to assessment design. If students feel that teaching staff don't talk to each other, they may suppose that poor academic conduct is difficult to detect. If they feel that assignments are unthinkingly being timed and set by staff with little interest in what their peers are doing, students facing competing deadlines across their modules, with several assignments to be submitted at the same time, may feel that cutting corners and taking short cuts is justified. For this reason, the next section outlines a collaborative approach to assessment design, through which curriculum designers think through planning and implementing assessment at a programme level.

▶ The big picture: towards programme-level assessment

Curriculum designers do well to move beyond a 'cantonised' curriculum, where each module or unit behaves like a semi-autonomous canton within the Swiss government, to a more federated approach where assessments are not only constructively aligned (Biggs and Tang, 2007) but also aligned with other assignments within and between levels across a whole programme of study. Programme-level assessment is integrative in nature, and assesses the knowledge, understanding and skills that represent key programme aims. It has been practised for many years, but a UK National Teaching Fellowship-funded project led by Peter Hartley has been highly influential in advancing thinking about programme-focused assessment (McDowell, 2012). The team argue that working at programme level provides for a more cohesive student experience and is more likely to enhance student retention and achievement. The project sought to redress the imbalances where assessment issues are primarily investigated and discussed at module or unit level, with some staff focusing solely on their direct responsibilities at module level, by providing evidence-based guidance and exemplars and examples to help programme leaders develop and implement effective programme-focused assessment strategies.

The major assessment problems and issues the project team set out to address include:

- Students and staff failing to see the links between elements of the programme, and treating each as a separate item, with no perceptible coherence within an atomized curriculum.
- A realisation that in many cases modules were considered to be too short to focus on and provide feedback on slowly learned literacies and/or complex learning.

- Over-assessment, with an associated potential overload of marking, data management and quality assurance procedures.
- A failure to assess overarching programme outcomes.
- Over-standardisation in regulations and the institution-wide mandating of standard procedures for module assessment which may not allow tutors flexibility to use a more appropriate range of assessment techniques for their subject area.
- Too much summative, and not enough formative, assessment.

PASS, 2012, pp. 1–2

The team argue that:

'The first and most critical point is that the assessment is specifically designed to address major programme outcomes rather than very specific or isolated components of the course. It follows then that such assessment is integrative in nature, trying to bring together understanding and skills in ways which represent key programme aims. As a result, the assessment is likely to be more authentic and meaningful to students, staff and external stakeholders.'

PASS, 2012, p. 3

Some possible solutions they suggest include:

- Having an integrated curriculum where any of the learning activities could contribute to any of the assessment strands across several years of the programme.
- Synoptic problem-based assessment and extended year-long modules.
- Capstone modules, where for example a fashion show can provide a cumulative assessment bringing together disparate elements of learning across a number of modules.
- A separation of assessment blocks and study blocks, enabling formative assessment to be given during the intensive study periods and summative assessment addressed subsequently.
- Using portfolios or e-portfolios, linked to personal and professional development.

Programme-focused assessment design can improve the quality of the student learning experience and make assessment more meaningful for the students. The Bradford team suggest that over the longer term there can be considerable savings of staff time (although in the design and early implementation stages there will need to be an investment of staff and other resources). Working at a programme level can result in more robust assessment strategies, which, by involving a team in design and implementation, can be more reliable since marking and assessment is undertaken collectively, giving benefits in quality assurance terms.

Conclusions

Taking a strategic approach to the design and implementation of assessment can pay dividends if it thereby becomes manageable, fair and co-ordinated. When working with universities at a departmental or institutional level, I am often struck by the ways in which assessment design decisions have been made in sometimes a rather *ad hoc* manner, without clarity of purpose or particular thought to how assessment practices will impact on the student experience. At validation stage, curriculum designers often (but not always) have a clear idea of what they want their chosen assessment strategy to achieve, but these aims sometimes become blurred over time, resulting frequently in over-assessment and the absence of constructive alignment. Adopting a strategic approach as advocated in this chapter can ensure that feedback becomes an engine of learning, that assessment can be effective and efficient through pragmatic and technology-supported approaches, and that a coherent approach is adopted across programmes. Since assessment impacts significantly on students' personal and career achievements, it pays dividends to get it right. As David Boud frequently argues, 'Students can avoid bad teaching, they can't avoid bad assessment': we owe it to them to design assessment meticulously, using the best available scholarship to underpin our choices, implement it justly and appropriately and to continuously review and enhance our own practices.

9 Using appropriate technologies to support learning

Introduction

This chapter ought, in some ways, to be unnecessary: as Helen Beetham reminds us, digital technology is not separate from but is systemic within higher education, and technology infuses almost all aspects of how we support and manage student learning.

> 'We are not rethinking some part or aspect of learning, we are rethinking all of learning in these new digital contexts.'
>
> Beetham, 2007

So just as we might not have wanted in the 1980s to have consideration of, say, 'learning from printed text' as the title of a chapter on higher education pedagogy, then perhaps we should just be talking about 'learning' nowadays without focusing on the enabling technologies (as indeed we do in other chapters here).

Nevertheless, digital technologies have advanced so rapidly in recent decades that some consideration of how this has impacted on university learning in this period seems appropriate. Additionally, as I have suggested in Chapter 1, we cannot assume equivalence of experience of technologies across the globe, since not all universities can provide technologically enriched learning environments, not all subject areas lend themselves equally to making extensive use of technologies to support learners, and not all students are confident and critical in their uses of information and technologies. Hence this chapter aims to explore what kinds of practices and approaches underpin successful learning in a digitally-enhanced environment.

What are the appropriate technologies?

In a rapidly moving field, it's hard to be adamant about which technologies are currently (2014) the most useful to support students' learning, or on how to future-proof decisions on technology use, so here I will concentrate on:

- technologies to support curriculum delivery;
- technologies to support assessment;
- technologies to support student engagement;
- technologies to support curriculum management and quality assurance.

Technologies to support curriculum delivery

For a number of years, universities in many nations have been encouraging their staff to make learning materials available to students through virtual learning environments (VLEs) including lecture summaries, lecture notes, videos, podcasts, audiocasts, course readers made up of copyright-cleared extracts from books and articles, electronic text books and more. It is commonplace for students to also have everything they need in terms of course information including timetables, course handbooks, Personal Development Planning (PDP) templates and so on made available through the VLE. However, putting materials up on the web and actually getting students to use the materials and information provided are two very different things. The key success factor in terms of student learning is the extent to which student engagement with materials is fostered: engagement with VLEs requires familiarity, confidence and competence whereby students engage in meaningful activities where the technologies support the purpose authentically (Beetham, 2014).

If all students arrived at university at 18 years old from a single school system within a single nation, we would be justified to some extent in assuming, as many advocates of new media do, that our students are 'digital natives' who need minimal support in using the wide range of technologies available to support their learning. But this is patently not the case because diversity of experience, social and cultural capital, digital literacy and familiarity with social media varies substantially from student to student. Some are techno-tentative, some are unwilling to reveal how weak their digital skills actually are and 'even digitally proficient learners need a solid grounding in academic practice to succeed' (Beetham, 2014). The next good practice account outlines suggestions on how to use technology to introduce students to key technologies like learning management systems (LMS).

Inducting students with diverse experience of technology

Mark Glynn, Dublin City University, Ireland

Introduction

Learning management systems (LMSs) are crucial systems for all higher education institutions. When implemented correctly they can provide a huge benefit to institutions and their students. In particular they can provide a great degree of flexibility to students with respect to their learning. Students in the information age expect this level of flexibility with on-demand anytime/anywhere high-quality learning environments accompanied by good support services. They typically want the increased flexibility that modern technologies can provide. However when incorporating technology into the classroom it is important not to isolate the students who may not be that comfortable with technology. LMSs such as Moodle are an integral part of every higher education institution, so every effort should be put in place to ensure that students are fully aware of and competent in the use of each institution's system. There are several techniques and initiatives that can be put in place to help achieve this.

Provision of instructional resources to explain the use of the various features of the LMS

Short bite-size videos accompanied by associated Microsoft® Word documents are ideal re-usable learning objects that can help students become familiar with how to use the LMS. Over time academics may build an extensive library of these resources so it's important to package them in ways that mean students can easily find the most appropriate resource at their time of need, for example by using a Frequently-Asked-Questions style database.

Providing a self-paced course for students on how to use the LMS

There are many advantages of tying such resources together into courses that a student can complete before they start college or shortly after they arrive. Providing a 'help' resource is valuable but in my experience students don't always know what they don't know and therefore may miss out on very useful and relevant features of the LMS. Incorporating the learning resources into the logical sequence of a well-designed short course can encourage them to explore the use of a LMS to discover how it can be best used to their advantage. The design of such courses is crucial, since they are typically not directly linked to a student's grade, hence courses should be easy to follow and very engaging in order to encourage participation. I recommend implementing a technique termed 'gamification' to encourage student participation. Gamification involves the incorporation of game

continued overleaf

Inducting students with diverse experience of technology *continued*

elements into non-game settings. It has huge potential in an education setting and is an area of increasing interest, specifically in the area of student retention. When students become engaged in such a course, in addition to supporting their learning directly, it shows them the various ways how an LMS can be used properly. Therefore providing such knowledge to students can empower them. When they are familiar with the potential uses of a LMS they tend to encourage lecturers who are currently not using LMS features to their full capacity to do so, for example, asking academics to emulate colleagues who use online quizzes.

Student drop-in clinics and peer mentoring

Providing resources online really does provide great flexibility for both the student and the institution but it should not eliminate the personal touch, the importance of which should not be under-estimated. Locating a student tutor with a desk and a laptop in the middle of the student canteen or some other suitable informal area can provide students with the opportunity to ask questions about the technology but also about other aspects of college life, helping them generally to settle in.

Instances

Massive Open Online Courses (MOOCs) require a significant investment in time and money from an institution. However with minimal investment, an institution can set up a Moodle 'instance' for students that is also available to members of the public. Such short bite-size courses could be used not only to share knowledge with the community but also provide avenues to attract prospective students by extensively using schools liaison programmes to make the wider community aware of what is on offer.

Using technologies to support 21st-century learning is non-negotiable, as Mark Glynn argues, but it can be difficult to know which technologies best help students to navigate the complex pathways through higher education, particularly when encountering unfamiliar modes of learning, such as distance and blended learning. Students who have previously only encountered high levels of personalised tutor support in schools and feeder colleges can falter when faced with demands for much higher levels of planning, decision-making and self-organisation, as well as self-efficacy and confidence to learn independently. Gilly Salmon's seminal model of development of the online learner (Salmon, 2000), which has influenced practices globally not only in higher education contexts but also business environments, proposes five stages of development, each of which merit support. She argues that students need supporting through these various stages to build their confidence and skills, leading ultimately towards independence and autonomy. Her work has strongly influenced the approaches used by the originators of the good practice account that follows.

A blended learning approach to an undergraduate evidence-based practice module for healthcare students

Anita O'Donovan and **Michelle Leech**, School of Medicine, Trinity College Dublin, Ireland

This good practice account describes a key pedagogical development in the BSc Radiation Therapy curriculum at the School of Medicine, Trinity College Dublin. This consists of an evidence-based practice (EBP) project in the final year (Year 4), delivered through a blended learning approach, based on a social constructivist approach to teaching and learning. The main advantage of this approach is that it enables students to carry out group work while on clinical placement in diverse locations nationwide.

The intended **learning outcome** of the EBP project is that on completion of the module the student should be able to analyse, evaluate and critique all aspects of clinical practice and the literature, with regard to a specific tumour site.

We have built our EBP project using Salmon's five-stage model as a guide (Salmon, 2000), so it was designed to comply with the different stages of development of the online learner. Rubrics are provided at each stage to provide clarity on assessment criteria. Salmon's model takes students through five stages of learning. Throughout these five stages, both e-moderating and technical support are key: the amount of interactivity is highest in the middle stages.

For the EBP module, the initial 'access and motivation' stage is addressed at the introduction to the module through a face-to-face session that deals with issues of Virtual Learning Environment (VLE) navigation. Orientation to the VLE is provided by the module co-ordinator at this introductory session, and students are invited to introduce themselves on the online discussion forum, and state their expectations of the module, as well as share a learning resource with their peers. Discussion fora are used for the majority of assigned tasks, with online web conferencing facilities employed for student feedback sessions. Each successive stage requires the student to develop different skills or competences, increasing in complexity and supported by the module co-ordinator as the module progresses. Tasks on the module include:

- An introductory face-to-face session in the computer laboratory, and login to Blackboard with instruction on navigation and introductory posting to the discussion forum.

continued overleaf

A blended learning approach to an undergraduate module for healthcare students *continued*

- An 'online socialisation' stage which consists of sending and receiving messages and involves familiarisation and bridging of gaps between cultural, social and learning environments, provided by an online journal club. Participating in the journal club involves posting a 500-word contribution to the online discussion forum, on a specific paper, and responding to one other person's post (10% marks).
- The 'information exchange' stage, where tasks involve searching and personalisation of software and where students are supported in their use of learning materials, uses a peer tutoring assignment, whereby students are assigned different topics, per group, to teach their peers. A 1,000-word synopsis is then posted to the online forum after collaboration and research. Each group then poses questions to other groups' offerings and has to re-post their topic after reflecting on their peers' contributions (10% marks).
- Individual students are then assigned a debate topic and whether they were for, or against, the motion. At the conclusion of this debate, a 'guest moderator', who is an expert in the field, views the online submissions and makes a contribution to the discussion, summing up important clinical points (10% marks). This corresponds to the 'knowledge construction' stage in Salmon's model, where students are now more confident in their ability online and more accustomed to engagement with their peers.
- The final stage corresponds to Salmon's 'development' stage, whereby students take more responsibility for their own learning and for that of the group. Critical thinking skills come to the fore and there is evidence of increasing reflection on practice. The project concludes with a group presentation and participation in the production of a collaborative group presentation. Students are advised that the discussion board should outline how the work of the group is distributed, and how each individual contributes to the final project (50% EBP module marks in total, 30% for group presentation, 20% for individual contribution).
- Reflection is encouraged throughout the module through the use of a reflective diary with entries at the beginning, mid-point and the conclusion of the module (1,000 words in total) (20% marks).

A Task Oriented Online Learning (TOOL) approach is taken (Fox and Walsh, 2007). This comprises a series of online tasks, designed to build interpersonal skills, and the ability to work collaboratively as part of a team, co-constructing knowledge in a peer learning process. These are all vital skills for a graduate radiation therapist, who works as part of a wider multidisciplinary team. Higher-order learning is promoted through the use of online discussions, which necessitates the development of a professional discourse and an ability to provide constructive criticism of peers' arguments. To mitigate the effects of non-participation, online engagement features strongly in the rubrics for each task, and there is also an individual mark awarded for students' individual contribution to the group project, as evidenced online.

To capture the full extent and complexity of the online learning environment, the Constructivist On-Line Learning Environment Survey (COLLES), devised by Taylor and Maor (Taylor and Maor, 2000) is used for module evaluation by students. This comprises 24 statements, grouped into six scales, each of which addresses a key component of the online learning environment and it investigates students' perceptions of both their preferred and actual online learning, and is designed for use with university students engaged in online learning.

Conclusion

Our evidence-based practice project for undergraduate healthcare students offers a transferable template for many related courses. It provides greater flexibility in relation to teaching and learning since this model allows the development of higher-order learning in an online 'Community of Inquiry'. Feedback demonstrates that the transition to a blended learning approach has been well received.

References

Fox, S. and Walsh, E. (2007) Task Oriented Online Learning (TOOL) – Social interaction in an online environment, *Case Studies of Good Practice in the Assessment of Student Learning in Higher Education*, 1, Dublin: AISHE/HEA.

Taylor, P. and Maor, D. (2000) *Assessing the Efficacy of Online Teaching with the Constructivist On-Line Learning Environment Survey,* paper presented at the Flexible Futures in Tertiary Teaching: 9th Annual Teaching and Learning Forum, Perth: Curtin University.

Technologies to support curriculum delivery are evolving rapidly, and one of the key developments in the last decade has been what some regard as a revolutionary approach to the ways in which universities provide education: a virtual throwing open of the doors of the academy to smash elitism and provide democratic access to higher education as exemplified by the hyper-hyped phenomenon of MOOCs.

Massive Open Online Courses (MOOCs)

MOOCs are seen by some as a panacea for all that is problematic about higher education. Making excellent learning materials from top universities available free to all online is seen by some as a way of providing higher education for the masses, particularly those who can't afford to study at conventional universities, and by others (including some Vice-Chancellors and presidents) as a way of delivering content cheaply, thereby freeing up academics for other (more or less important) duties including research and administration. The concept is at heart a good one: many providers of open educational resources, such as the Open University in the UK and the Massachusetts Institute of Technology (arguably the originators of MOOCs), did so partly as a response to the knowledge that their outstanding course readers and other materials were widely plagiarised (and there was no point trying to stop people doing this in the digital age) and partly philanthropically, in the knowledge that giving away content freely in no way detracts from the paid-for programmes and indeed often acts as a magnet for paying students. So are MOOCS actually 'Massive', 'Open', 'Online' and 'Courses'?

Massive

Some of the biggest MOOCs have hundreds of thousands of students signed up to them, certainly well beyond the number normally enrolled with traditional universities. However, some entities claiming to offer MOOCs actually only have subscribers numbering in tens or hundreds.

Open

This suggests that material is made available without payment and readily through electronic means. Many of us committed to the transformative power of widening participation – to ensure that all capable of benefiting from higher education have opportunities to study, which goes well beyond the current aim of 'fair access' initiatives (enabling the brightest from all backgrounds to gain entry to elite universities) – can see the benefits of openness. Pegler suggests that:

> 'There has so far been no fee for engagement in a MOOC and relatively relaxed limits on who can participate. Registered students based at institutions offering the MOOC are likely to be significantly outnumbered by open learners who have no affiliation with it. For example in late 2011, a MOOC on artificial intelligence taught by Stanford professor Sebastian Thrun was capped at 160,000 enrolments from 190 countries, while only 200 Stanford students enrolled on campus. The exceptional class size represents not only massive scale but massive diversity of background and motivation, adding to a distinctive feel of MOOCs as separate from mainstream education. If open education aims to remove barriers to accessing learning activity, MOOCs could be viewed as a high-profile manifestation of this potential.'
>
> Pegler, 2013, p. 152

However, while celebrating the genuine benefits of the ubiquitous accessibility of open materials, Laurillard retains a healthy scepticism about the extent to which we can assume that access implies an assurance that learning is happening.

> 'The Open Educational Resources movement has turned the web into a universal educational library of lecture materials and well-produced educational resources, available to all. This is a significant shift for education because it provides access to educational materials to anyone who has Internet access. It is a wonderful democratization of access to resources. But it is not the same as access to education.'
>
> Laurillard, 2013, p. xvii

Online

The business model for MOOCs relies on the fact that electronic provision of materials is easy, free to use (once the original fixed costs of development and uploading on the web have been covered) and readily accessible by anyone with a wifi connection. Many of the variable costs associated with traditional distance learning programmes such as printing of course materials are therefore not applicable. As students enrolling on MOOCs don't take invigilated exams or other resource-rich assessments (some offer computer-marked multiple-choice tests or quizzes), high assessment-related costs don't apply either. The power of online learning is to offer a wide range of resources including text, video, audio, animations, links to YouTube, TED talks, iTunesU and social networking sites such as Facebook.

Courses

This term implies not just access to learning materials but also the opportunity to gain accredited recognition for the learning undertaken. MOOCs by this definition are therefore usually not actually courses, they are substantially content-deliverers enabling learners to prepare for examination or other forms of assessment by other providers. Such assessment as is commonly provided by MOOCs tends to be peer commentaries on written work by fellow students on the MOOC, which many indicate they have found helpful. Otherwise assessment of learning through MOOCs can be undertaken for additional payment through test centres offered by established HE providers.

So maybe some MOOCs are all of these things, but not all are, and not all work as they should do. It seems probable that most people registering for MOOCs already have degree or near-degree level qualifications, so their transformative impact on the lives of disadvantaged people may well be exaggerated. Peter Scott in the *Guardian* on 6 August 2013 suggested that separating teaching from accreditation is highly attractive for a number of reasons: many are attracted by the open accessibility of open-access courses which are available without fees to people who traditionally don't have access to higher education. Others are attracted to the flexibility that MOOCs offer to people who don't want to commit to conventional three-year degree courses. Institutional managers are excited by the potential economies of scale. While welcoming MOOCs' potential to open up participation in higher education, others are cautious that the disadvantaged will be further disadvantaged by being offered a second-rate educational experience while elite students still continue to study in elite universities.

Nevertheless, one cannot disregard the impact that MOOCs are having all over the world in assuaging the thirst for knowledge of many who can't or won't pay for higher education programmes, and the excitement that many students feel about readily accessing the work of some of the best brains in the world from their own homes, particularly those not seeking formal accredited programmes.

> 'It seems likely that many of the learners choosing to study on MOOCs (massive open online courses) are participating in the kind of lifelong learning tradition that has always provided learning for its own sake, rather than learning that leads to qualifications.'
>
> Mayes and De Freitas, 2013, p. 25

Technologies to support student engagement: using digital and social media to support networking and collaboration

In the majority of nations, universities normally provide a web presence of some kind to support not only university systems including marketing, admissions and information-giving but also offer a VLE as a platform for communications, networking, building course cohesion, hosting wikis and blogs, fostering peer-to-peer learning, submission and return of assignments, e-portfolio building and many other purposes.

Similarly, student use of social media including Twitter, Facebook, LinkedIn and so on is ubiquitous and pervasive and this is likely to have an impact on the way students interact and learn in universities.

> 'Many students entering HE in the 21st century have never known life without the web, and its use is completely integrated with how they communicate, learn and live. This is who they are. Arguably then, the educational experiences that we design and plan have to recognise this and seek to maximise the potential of social media.'
>
> Fisher et al., 2014, p. 44

For those students comfortable with online environments, sourcing, creating, using, citing, adapting, re-versioning, sharing and 'sampling' web-based material (text, images, sound, music, video and so on) becomes an everyday and automatic practice and it behoves us to recognise this in creating and fostering student engagement. However, for those students with limited access, limited confidence or limited resources, if we make assumptions about what they know about and can do, we will be doubly disadvantaging them, so sensitivity in requiring social media use as part of learning activities, particularly in, for example, transnational contexts is needed. (See Chapter 1 for examples of the kinds of limitations some students may face.) Nevertheless, for most academics working in most universities in most countries, using digital and social media provides opportunities to engage students that we do well to use.

▶ Using Twitter for academic purposes

Twitter is a relative newcomer to the academic domain, and it has been regarded in the past as mainly a platform for people to share trivia (which indeed it is), but it can also be really helpful in academic contexts for:

- Enabling students (and staff) to locate and use articles, websites, features, videos of high currency relevant to their academic work.
- Helping students to locate and interact with peers prior to registration onto a course, during induction, throughout the programme and after graduation. (Academics can also use it for finding colleagues with shared interests at conferences and even seeking taxi shares when approaching the conference venue!)

- Providing a means to make, keep and access notes that might otherwise be ephemeral, since one's own Twitter feed is a more lasting resource for many than hand-scrawled notes.
- Using 'Storify' to collect together and preserve a number of tweets from different sources to make an accessible and more permanent record of them.
- Sharing notes with peers, both those alongside you in sessions as well as people who didn't make it to the lecture (or conference), for whom Tweets and photos can provide a window into events they can't attend.
- Asking and responding to questions where the lecturer/presenter is using a hashtag (which is ideally visible on the first slide, short and memorable, published in the course handbook/website).
- Building peer networks and communities of practice.

The next good practice account shows how social media can help to harness the power of individuals who may be working in disparate and distanced environments to build learning communities that embody social practices harnessing contemporary technologies.

Digital Arts and Humanities – Blended in Ireland research-led teaching and learning enhanced by social media

Orla Murphy, University College Cork, Ireland

> "Good morning everyone – please turn on your 'phones and computers.
> Please post your thoughts, comments and ideas to the hashtag – and where possible post links to some of the texts, theories, images and people you mention. Thanks!"

Introduction

Building an engaged community of students who do not know each other is a daunting task. When this is complicated by physical separation the difficulty is compounded. Forty students, in four separate centres means teaching 'remotely' via video link, where you have the approximation of 'liveness' but not the physical presence of being in the room. All the usual indicators of the students' understanding and following the class are gone; eye contact, body language, and a smile are impossible to capture in these circumstances.

A diverse teaching team was/is integral to such a programme, drawing on researchers and practitioners from all over Ireland in University College Cork, Trinity College Dublin, NUI Galway, and NUI Maynooth. We also wanted to create an engaged transdisciplinary group who would collaborate with each other from the outset – and the best way to achieve this was to enshrine collaboration and engagement in the teaching and learning methods we used. Each institution rotated delivery in two-hour sessions each Tuesday at 10.00am over ten weeks.

We 'attended' the lectures virtually – sitting in the video conferencing room and listening with colleagues to others' contributions. We began to consider how best to harness the collective energies in the various rooms, and most importantly engage the students in an active learning experience. One of the courses we teach is digital pedagogy, and in this course, we practised what we preached, bringing our research in creating an open collaborative virtual learning community into our teaching.

We built and shared an online space using the free tool Wordpress. Each university had a different virtual learning environment, so we needed to provide an accessible, free solution for all. The class was structured around four key questions posted in advance, with supporting readings and links for everyone to see. We then enrolled each person as an editor so that they could actively contribute to the page.

Activity, discussion, interaction and engagement were critical aspects of this approach. We did not want people sitting and listening and note-taking for two hours, as an opportunity for peer learning would have been missed. In every classroom, the variety of subjects and life-experience is the untapped potential we cannot initially know as educators: their responses, range and depth of understanding and the resonance the material may have for them is hard to capture, even in a face-to-face communication. Using these virtual and online tools we were anxious to extend this further and to capture the combined ideas of the class, and share them accessibly and widely across the group for the benefit and consideration of all, and long term to show other students in years to come.

We used Twitter to capture, share, ask and answer questions and note ideas throughout the session – all aggregated to the agreed hashtag. This meant that one student who was on a delayed train kept up with the conversation! Also the discussion extended beyond the given class time – as students read, considered and responded to each other after the class in a social media environment. They became aware of and followed the other students' Twitter accounts, further building the sense of an engaged virtual class community.

Each of the live locations broke out into groups for ten minutes, then both vocally in real time and also virtually responded to each other. Capturing the responses online allowed facilitators to measure the understanding of participants, re-engage with key questions and adjust our strategy throughout the session. We had freedom within a structure. Thirty-five online responses were posted in the months following the activity. Their links and comments augment ours. We succeeded in capturing the live exchanges for subsequent students, and made visible to ourselves, our peers, and any interested others the content of our teaching by using social media – anyone following individual Tweeters could join in the conversation – making the classroom effectively the world!

Twitter, Facebook and other media can provide additional interfaces between staff and students to enhance existing academic communication routes: however, academics might well learn from students who recognise the dangers of permeating boundaries between the academic and social worlds and have separate accounts for their personal and professional lives.

Technologies to support assessment

As discussed in the last chapter, computer-based assessment can be really useful for taking some of the drudgery out of routine marking, for example for checking of work, drills and so on. But '[t]echnology can provide a range of opportunities to assess different things in different ways, as well as doing what we have always [done] but just on a computer' (Fisher et al., 2014, p. 104). In addition to supporting marking and grading in time-efficient ways, Fisher et al. propose the following ways in which technology can support assessment processes:

- 'Question generation: for example, random generators, building question banks, etc.
- Question/task presentation and delivery to learners: for example, students sit at the computers to take the test.
- Development of standalone, self-study and self-assessment tools, such as RLOs (Reusable Learning Objects): these may take the form of self-assessment quizzes or problem-solving tasks.
- Submission of student responses.
- Providing automated feedback and further guidance.
- Detecting plagiarism.
- Analysis of (class) grades and generating statistics and evaluation reports.
- Recording and monitoring learner achievement – for example, using ePortfolios.
- Storage of assessments and student attainments for quality assurance purposes.' (p. 112).

An example follows in the next good practice account (pp. 166–8) of how software systems can help make academics' task of assessment easier and more efficient, as well as contributing to student learning.

As I've argued earlier, assessment and feedback are powerful drivers for engagement and learning, if they are strategically designed and implemented. As well as making assessment less demanding on staff time, assessment technologies can help to ensure that the principles of good assessment design proposed in Chapter 7 are implemented to truly integrate assessment with learning. The UK agency for promoting effective technologies to support teaching, learning and assessment, JISC, suggests that good e-assessment, like all assessment, should aim to:

- Engage the students with the assessment criteria so that they understand the standards they are being judged against.
- Support individual and personalised learning.
- Ensure feedback can lead to improvement.
- Focus on the students' development and progress.
- Stimulate constructive dialogue.
- Consider staff and student effort and workload. (JISC, 2010)

The nature of assignments that technologies can support can be rather different from those based on paper or in face-to-face presentations including:

- Multiple-choice tests and other kinds of e-assessment.
- Annotated bibliographies, where students provide a hard-copy or virtual folder of resources from a variety of electronic contexts, demonstrating how they found and evaluated the data, and how they plan to use it in their assignments.
- e-portfolios, which provide a repository of text, images, video and other data enabling students to demonstrate their achievement of learning outcomes in a structured and systematic way.
- Blogs, often interactive, where students can post news, commentaries and personal viewpoints or insights over a period of time allowing the development of ideas to be recorded and tracked.
- Wikis, which are web pages that can be edited by several users, allowing co-construction of text, often used to support student projects.
- Reflective accounts, which can be private, public, or published with limited permissions to access.
- Patchwork texts where work is produced incrementally by individuals or groups and stitched together for final submission.

As with all forms of assessment, if students are to benefit from the diversity of assessment methods and approaches when they are introduced as innovations, either to the programme or to new cohorts of students who might never have encountered them before, it is essential to provide briefing, training and rehearsal opportunities prior to their use for summative assessment. Twenty-first century students may well relish the opportunity to showcase their capabilities using digital and social media, but they will only do so if they feel secure, confident and comfortable in the use of the technologies that support them.

Technologies to support student engagement

The assessment methods and approaches mentioned above have the potential, when well designed, to foster student engagement by allowing students to learn by integrating theory and practice when undertaking authentic and realistic tasks. The next good practice account demonstrates how this can be implemented to support student achievement.

Effective online learning environments promote student engagement and success

Cath Fraser, **Judi Honeyfield**, **Lynette Steele** and **David Lyon**, Bay of Plenty Polytechnic, Tauranga, New Zealand

Background

Learning environments in the 21st century are less about bricks and mortar than they are about learning climate and culture. Certainly on a campus, the physical classroom and the design of the learning space are important features, but in today's world of multi-modal literacies, increasing use of technology has supported a widening interpretation of learning environments.

Learning in higher education online environments is equally reliant on the core tenets of good adult education as traditional environments; core principles include supporting empowerment, critical reflection, using experience, fostering collaboration and recognising that learning models should inform learning activities and design. Essential conditions incorporate:

- an atmosphere of inclusion and respect;
- relevant activities to reinforce motivation and persistence;
- challenging learning experiences which engage with the learner's perspectives and values;
- authentic assessment that connects learning experiences to real-life needs;
- teaching delivery which is interactive and learner-centred.

(For an extended discussion, see, for example, Brookfield, 2005; Cercone, 2008; Honeyfield and Fraser, 2013.)

Successful strategies

A graduate course at a New Zealand polytechnic which began in the latter half of 2012 offers an example of a number of strategies which are proving highly effective in establishing an online environment of student engagement, success and achievement. Key features are innovative problem-solving, strong stakeholder networks and a 21st-century sensibility.

The Graduate Certificate in New Zealand Immigration Advice (GCNZIA) has been designed to meet the academic and experiential requirements to gain a licence to practise as an Immigration Adviser for New Zealand, and from its inception has been delivered totally online. New Zealand is one of the few countries that allow non-New Zealand citizens or residents to become licensed as immigration advisers; consequently the programme of study must be globally accessible and support students' individual choices about where, when and how they want to work.

A key strength is that a course design which addressed the needs of distance students has always been central to the offering, rather than being added on, as so often occurs in the adaptation of campus-based to eLearning formats. A second strength related to the context is the collaboration with stakeholders: the GCNZIA was developed after our organisation secured a tender from the New Zealand Government. An integral aspect of the submission was the inclusion as partners of two universities as well as the industry representative, the Immigration Advisers Authority (IAA). A wide consulting base and steering body, together with industry involvement has led to a holistic yet pragmatic business model; the course of study is needed by industry, leads directly to a professional credential and will provide graduates with genuine skills and opportunities for future employment.

Selection of the software platform for development and delivery required the input of several units across the organisation: Information Systems, Teaching and Learning, Student Support as well as the Legal Studies teaching and management team. After some trial and error, Adobe Connect web conferencing software was added into the existing Moodle learning management system to allow face-to-face real-time tutorials with students across New Zealand and around the world.

The Adobe Connect tool has allowed extensive flexibility with instructional design and the enactment of a student-centred teaching and learning pedagogy. The GCNZIA instructional practices are creative and flexible, incorporating threaded discussions, blog posts, narrated PowerPoints, group work, synchronous and asynchronous chats, quizzes, and online formative assessment with automated feedback and marking (final examinations are conducted face-to-face in locations where the students are resident; scripts are scanned and e-mailed to Tauranga, New Zealand for marking). There are plenty of opportunities for collaboration and peer review as well as ample contact with tutors.

continued overleaf

Effective online learning environments promote student engagement and success *continued*

One example of the pedagogy in action is that all live feed visual images are presented the same way. While the tutor is the first face viewed, due to opening the session, there is no distinction between the tutor's screen allocation and the students'; all have equal status. Another example is the adjustment GCNZIA teachers have made to their own teaching personas, as many traditional face-to-face teaching methods are not suited for online delivery. With the split screen configuration, there's no talking to the whiteboard, or standing at the front of the class. Teaching staff can be simultaneously managing several functions: introducing topics, managing class interactions and overseeing group activities in Adobe Connect's break-out rooms.

Developing a new course through a co-operative process which involves widespread consultation, and keeps learners' interests and end goals to the forefront has been challenging at times, but has allowed us to put into practice the principles identified in the literature as emblematic of effective learning environments – being inclusive, relevant, challenging and connected. Students from the first delivery have enjoyed a high level of success, with an 89.7% completion rate, and evaluations are extremely positive.

References

Brookfield, S. (2005) *The Power of Critical Theory: Liberating adult learning and teaching*, San Francisco: Jossey-Bass.

Cercone, K. (2008) Characteristics of adult learners with implications for online learning design, *AACE Journal*, 16(2), pp. 137–59.

Honeyfield, J. and Fraser, C. (2013) *Goalposts: A professional development resource for new tertiary teachers in their first year* [Handbook]. Available from https://akoaotearoa.ac.nz/

An excellent way to help build a learning community among students and staff is to use web conferencing or web seminars ('webinars') in real time in a virtual classroom, enabling students who are located in other areas, including other countries, to share learning experiences using multimedia technologies (Cornelius et al., 2014). Live online learning offers a facilitated space in which small and large groups of students can interact with each other and with academics or 'guest facilitators' for discussion, debate, co-viewing and co-creating resources and for assessment activities. Webinars offer flexibility of access and interaction, with students able to speak, hear, comment publicly and privately, draw on whiteboards, annotate diagrams and participate to the level that they feel comfortable, either actively engaging or more passively absorbing others' contributions. Where the purpose of the web conference/webinar is building cohort cohesion and fostering a learning community, 'lurking' without participation may be acceptable and even encouraged as people find their feet, but where it is being used as a means of assessment, ground rules for engagement need to be set and enforced. As more and more universities offer programmes in multiple modes (for example, Central Queensland University in Australia offers all its programmes in face-to-face, mixed mode and distance formats), using web conferencing/webinars may be the only viable approach to curriculum delivery and engagement.

Technologies to support curriculum management and quality assurance

Potentially one of the greatest savers of time, energy and resource in universities is the use of data management systems to save repetitive data entry, to avoid overuse of multiple spreadsheets and for data analytics that describe how students progress through a sequence of learning activities.

Earlier I have commented on how technologies can be used to detect when collusion, cheating and plagiarism have occurred, and both commercial and internally-developed software packages to help do this have been available for some time. For example, at Sheffield Hallam University in the UK, software entitled 'Assignment handler' enables academics to mark and give feedback on assignments but hold back information about marks awarded until students have posted online learning points derived from the feedback, encouraging students to take notice of the hard-won comments their assessors have provided (Fisher et al., op. cit., p. 136).

Perhaps the best known of the systems, 'Turnitin' (see http://submit.ac.uk/), uses an internet-based text-matching system which allows academics to judge whether or not submitted assignments contain material that is likely to have been plagiarised, using a massive content database enabling assignments to be compared against new and existing content. Unoriginal content is highlighted and colour-coded, and the original source appears on screen for the marker together with the percentage of content originating from that source. It is highly efficient at doing this, but is not a universal panacea since it doesn't identify material not on the database, work written to order, or work that has been translated back and forth between languages and then smoothed. Some argue that Turnitin can provide false confidence in students' academic integrity, since it is all too easy for academics to say that, because they use the system, plagiarism cannot occur. However, in an era when students use internet resources very readily to provide components of their assignments, often without proper attribution of sources, Turnitin provides a first-line resource to tackle the problems.

Increasingly academics are encouraging students to check their own work through Turnitin (or similar software) to help those who might not have much familiarity with academic conventions understand where they are indulging in risky academic behaviour (Rolfe, 2010). As the software offered by Turnitin, Moodle and others is being developed, newer features are being added, including the opportunity to provide rich feedback on assignments in a wide range of subject areas in diverse formats including spreadsheets, images and html code as well as text through the use of rubrics, with voice comments as well as text-based comments. Comments from a statement bank can be dragged and dropped into electronic copies of student work, potentially saving a great deal of time once the personalised systems have been set up.

Peer review comments and assessment can be supported using such systems, with electronic distribution enabling anonymous or named comments, with the potential to help students learn from the work of others and develop their own critical faculties by learning sensitively, fairly and accurately to critique peers' submissions. Most systems also provide platforms for the location, assessment and maintenance of e-portfolios which can be personalised and shared and for supporting students, often at significant distances, on placements and internships. LiveText student learning assessment software is one example of a system that supports these functions.

LiveText, Tasksteam and other systems can also provide multi-functional software, not only to support assignment submission and return as Turnitin and Moodle do, but also to support curriculum design in preparation for accreditation and periodic review – checking alignment with PSRB requirements through the use of templates and proformas. They enable course designers to map programme-level learning outcomes against strategic plans, to manage versioning problems during the design process and to keep documentation well-organised and accessible through using a single institutional repository, rather than multiple spreadsheets. By keeping course data in one place, they make it easier to analyse data at course, programme and institutional levels, as well as to track trends and thereby inform and contribute to the quality enhancement initiatives that will guide future planning.

In choosing whether to buy in a system or to develop one in-house, institutions have to balance the potential for having to invest huge amounts of time and resource in developing idiosyncratic systems in-house against the possibility that commercial systems are nearly but not quite right for a particular institution, especially if it is developed in one country and then sold (with or without local customisation) to other countries. The option of not having some kind of digital support for curriculum development and quality assurance is not really a viable one, however.

Conclusions

No one could have reasonably foreseen the advances that have been made in technologies to enhance and support student learning that we have witnessed in recent years, which have altered the learning landscape profoundly by making possible educational and social practices which continue to evolve. When in 1994 Tim Berners-Lee founded the World Wide Web Consortium, few envisaged its pervasive impact on all aspects of life and particularly on education patterns, expectations, structures, systems and indeed the nature of learning itself. Few predicted the availability of computer-mediated information in one's handbag or pocket, free to access 24/7/365, nor indeed the information overload this has brought about. In this respect, it is hard to predict what will happen in the next decade, let alone over a longer period. In educational contexts today, it is the interaction of the individual learner with teachers, peers and resources that remains a constant feature, whether this is directly mediated by an organisation such as a university or disintermediated by learners finding and using information directly. For academics as practitioners, our role has changed and is changing further, as we find new ways to help learners learn, supported by technologies, but still with the student at the very heart of the process.

10 Fostering students' employability and community engagement

Introduction

Much has been written about the connections between higher education and the economy, with rhetoric nowadays increasingly describing the principal or sole purpose of higher education as being to train an educated workforce and to contribute to the market economy by supplying a continuous stream of graduates to plug gaps in the job market. While many of us would rebel against such a *dirigiste* and instrumental perspective, we nonetheless recognise the importance of fostering employability among our graduates, and this chapter explores how we as educators can do so, while at the same time helping students to become fulfilled and capable members of society.

Employers continue to seek graduates who can bring to the workplace capabilities and knowledge that can help them fit straightaway into a modern workforce, and it continues to be the case that employers regularly bemoan the lack of 'work-readiness' of many starting work, often indicating that the behaviours and attributes they seek have to be inculcated within new employees by the companies and professions themselves. It is worth considering what might be going wrong here and what can be done to remediate the situation.

Determining and developing relevant and transferable graduate attributes

As Race argues:

> 'For the last two decades and more, there has been a lot of discussion about the balance we need to strike in our educational provision between deepening learners' knowledge and understanding of the subjects they are studying and developing the skills they will need for their careers, and indeed the rest of their lives.'
>
> Race, 2010, p. 192

It is clear that employers expect a range of generic graduate skills on top of the essential subject knowledge provided by various degree programmes: over the years these have been termed Core Skills, Key Skills, Graduate Attributes, Key Competences, Transferable Skills, Capabilities, Soft Skills and other terms. Most lists involve:

- Team work, leadership and working effectively in groups.
- Interpersonal communication, emotional literacy, social skills, social competence, self-efficacy.
- Writing and speaking fluently and accurately in a variety of contexts relevant to their professions and workplaces.
- Problem-solving.
- Essential numeracy relevant to the job.
- Competence in the uses of information technologies; digital literacy; the ability effectively and confidently to use basic packages like Microsoft® Word, Excel and PowerPoint, Prezi; confidence in appropriate uses of social media.
- Autonomy, independence, self-management, time management and diary management.
- The ability to think creatively and 'out of the box'.

Race (2010) would add to these:

- Having demonstrable intellectual curiosity, generosity of spirit, understanding of purpose, and adaptability.
- Being positive, responsive, thoughtful, well informed, organised, sociable and, above all, able to listen and try to fit in while also contributing to the workplace.
- The ability to interpret appropriately your role within an organisation.

Since almost every university aims to attract students through offering enhanced employability, to stand out from the crowd universities need to ensure their offers are relevant and special. For example, Deakin University in Australia have made a commitment to the development of employability skills that they term the eight Deakin Graduate Learning Outcomes: Discipline knowledge and capabilities, Communication, Digital literacy, Critical thinking, Problemsolving, Self-management, Teamwork and Global citizenship. They say that they are concerned with:

> 'educating learners for effective citizenship and employability through courses enhanced for highly personal, engaging and relevant learning experiences through premium cloud and located learning. We focus on

> clear expectations and standards, evidence of learning, personal and connected learning experiences and enhancing courses (rather than focusing predominantly on units).'
>
> O'Brien and Oliver, 2013

They suggest that

> 'excellent student learning is most likely to be achieved when:
>
> 1. Learning outcomes are clearly articulated and relevant to graduate destinations;
> 2. Assessment and feedback are carefully designed opportunities to enable students to demonstrate, improve and evidence achievement of graduate learning outcomes;
> 3. Educators engage, enthuse and inspire;
> 4. Learning experiences, on location or in the cloud, are highly personal, interactive and focused on engaging learners in authentic tasks and work-integrated challenges.'

In many nations students' evaluations of their university experiences are regarded as key data by their governments, and issues around employability are of high importance for students and their families paying fees. In the UK, universities are committed to seeking feedback from students through the National Student Survey (NSS) which indirectly reflects their perceptions of their own employability through the questions in the section entitled 'personal development' comprising these statements.

19. The course has helped me to present myself with confidence.
20. My communications skills have improved.
21. As a result of the course, I feel confident in tackling unfamiliar problems.

It behoves us therefore as educators to do our very best to help all students, not just those from advantaged backgrounds to build the kinds of self-efficacy and resilience that can make them employable. The next part of the chapter will outline a number of ways in which these ambitions can become actualities within the curriculum and its assessment.

Demonstrating evidence of employability

As Yorke (2004) argues, employability is not the same as employment, many students achieve employment of some kind that may or may not match up to their levels of qualification. Employability, he suggests, 'implies something about the capacity of the graduate to function in a job and be able to move between jobs, thus remaining employable throughout their life.' (p. 7), that is having the capability to work at the right level, and have 'know-how' and 'know-why' as well as 'know-what'. Students leaving university with a degree have credentials that say they are able to study successfully at higher education level, but among employers there is often an expressed view that graduates don't bring to the workplace nearly enough of the work-ready capabilities they would like to see in evidence. Many students on programmes that include placements, secondments, internships or 'sandwich years' out are required to demonstrate the capabilities developed during these opportunities (although it is still possible to find institutions where learning outside the university is largely disregarded!). Where such experiences count, assessment is usually through various assignments, including logs, blogs, reflective diaries and so on, but these have tended only to be internal documents for use within the university system, and therefore have limited value in demonstrating employability. For this reason, universities are seeking a variety of ways to provide additional enhancements to the degree certificate, leading their students to curate and carry forward rich digital evidence which can include:

- Requiring students to build and maintain throughout a degree programme an **e-portfolio of evidence of achievement** that can be used during interview and selection processes to structure a dialogue about their competences, and, if not dependent on a university's own digital platform, can be portable and used post-graduation as a record of continuous professional development (see Chapter 8).
- **Offering Digital or Open Badges** is a concept derived from games technologies and provides a validated indicator of accomplishment, skill, quality or interest that can be earned in various learning environments and which provide micro-credentials that can be gained (rather like Girl Guide badges) as endorsements of learning activity. They can be used to motivate students by evidencing success in a variety of contexts, and can help them set achievable goals which on achievement can be readily and quickly recognised. They can be particularly useful as part of a formative assessment process, providing constant feedback and tracking of what has been learned and what the next step should be.
- **Becoming a certified training establishment** for the particular software or system company (for example, Sage Accounting, whereby students are able to achieve industry standard certificated qualifications within or alongside a degree).

- Offering **assignments that link to live employment contexts**, particularly in the case of part-time students and those seconded by their employers.

The good practice account that follows provides an example of how all of these things work in practice.

Involving recent graduates in offering assessments linked to life

James Derounian, University of Gloucestershire, UK

Background

Designing assignments based in real-world rather than simulated contexts provides a golden opportunity to connect graduates and your alumni currently in employment, since they can offer projects, placements, internships, research and evaluations. Involvement of (recent) graduates has advantages since they are likely to be able to remember what being a student was like and therefore can tailor inputs accordingly. They can offer role models for current students, giving them something to aspire to and can provide up-to-the-minute inputs, giving a different 'voice' from the lecturer.

This practice can enable students to address real issues and opportunities in communities, through their assignments, meaning that students can gain skills in dealing with real-world problems, such as problem-solving, time management and working with others, whilst communities effectively benefit from free consultancy.

Students scattered across considerable distances, and perhaps studying via blended learning (relying on web-based interaction, workbooks, and occasional residential schools) can tailor assignments to their own individual and community circumstances. At a time of climate change and pursuit of education for sustainability, this emphasis on a student's locality for assignments, ties in with the work of American researchers DeLind and Link:

> 'Before losing themselves in the virtual or plunging ... into the international, students need to carefully and critically examine what exists ... outside their front (and back) doors.'
>
> DeLind and Link, 2004

Assignments completed at the students' home or place of work can save both travel and carbon emissions and can contribute to sustainability by triggering local community action.

The key features that make this practice effective are that it is simple and purposeful. The use of live projects, policies and initiatives local to a student means that individuals are genuinely motivated to undertake assessments because they stand a chance of making a real change (and perhaps even directly benefiting themselves). For example, a student researching a venture for a module on 'Community Projects' could select the establishment of a play area or skateboard park for their village, neighbourhood or town. By undertaking a needs assessment and resource plan, they can determine whether such projects could and should proceed, and in what ways; whilst at the same time gaining academic credit.

As a spin-off, this kind of customised assessment, tailored to the needs of the individual student, means that plagiarism is virtually impossible! The particularities of developing a community hall will not be the same as those for a community-run bus service or shop, in very different locations and settlements.

Snags, issues and how to deal with them

This approach lends itself particularly to study by part-time (mature) students, whose 'day job' focuses on development of policies, programmes and projects. For full-time students, especially those entering university direct from school, the prospect of linking to outside agencies and real projects, where views may be contested and discussion heated, may well require intensive staff facilitation, support and encouragement (particularly at the outset). In contrast, with a part-time student employed in an area directly linked to the course or module (e.g. *Community Engagement and Local Governance*), a teenager, straight from school will potentially need extra guidance and nurturing to make the most of such live opportunities.

One way to deal with this is to mix part- and full-time students to undertake assessments in small groups. This has a benefit that younger ones can often assist older students to optimise use of technologies (Skype, Twitter, Facebook etc.), and the mature students can frequently help younger colleagues get to grips with time management, planning and getting the best from external agencies and staff. Another issue relates to the types of evidence and literature presented: part-time students used to working in employer-based contexts may be used to report writing and deploying practice sources but may need additional steering and reminding of the importance of using academic materials.

The applicability of this approach in other national contexts will depend on whether its use of real issues and possibilities for assessments fit with the overall aim and constituent (learning) objectives for a module and/or course. If it seems purposeful and appropriate for the context, it is worth trying out.

Reference

DeLind, L. and Link, T. (2004) 'Place as the nexus of a sustainable future: a course for all of us', in P.F. Barlett and G.W. Chase (eds) *Sustainability on Campus: Stories and strategies for change*, Cambridge, Mass: MIT Press.

Working closely and effectively with employers is crucial in ensuring that learning beyond the university can form a coherent and relevant part of university and college study. While, as Yorke argues (2004, p. 7), curricular processes may facilitate the development of prerequisites appropriate to employment, they do not guarantee it. The next good practice account describes how co-operative education, which is very commonly used in N. America, can be implemented to good effect.

Co-operative education

Celia Popovic and **Kathleen Winningham**, York University, Toronto, Canada

Co-operative education combines meaningful work experience with university-level study in a way that integrates both the study and the work experience. This approach to learning is not restricted to the university sector, it is very successful at the community college level, and is available to high school students although in that context it is unpaid.

The key characteristics of Co-op are that the work experience is approved by the programme of study, the employer is involved in monitoring the student's progress, the student is paid for their work and the total amount of work-based experience totals at least 30% of the time spent in academic study. The student typically spends a total of at least one year in a co-op position. The co-op work terms alternate with the academic terms and each builds on the other to enable maximum learning in both areas.

Co-op is most closely associated with programmes such as Engineering, Business and Science, however it is not restricted to these areas. It is possible to integrate co-op into virtually any field of study. The University of Waterloo is well known for its provision of co-op programmes as it provides more than 120 programmes of study with over half of all undergraduate students taking part. Other universities in Canada are less ambitious in their scope but most have some provision of this sort and most are intending to expand as this has proved to be so popular with students keen to get the edge in gaining employment post-graduation. Co-op is distinct from an unpaid practicum, such as is common in Education and Health programmes.

The advantages of co-op are many. Not least that the necessary link between industry or the work place and academia leads to greater understanding between the two sectors. Students are able to relate their studies to practice, which not only leads to greater motivation and deeper understanding, but also enhances the classroom with multiple up-to-date examples of practice which can be related to theory. Thus students share the benefits of their peers' experience as well as their own. Students recognise the value of co-op such that programmes that offer this opportunity are more popular than those that do not, it is thus a valuable recruitment tool for institutions competing for the most able students. Studies show that co-op graduates find full-time employment more quickly and can command a higher salary than non-co-op graduates from the same field of study.

A key obstacle to establishing a co-op programme is in finding sufficient employers in relevant fields. In Canada competition for employers between institutions is fierce. In a large well-established programme such as the one at Waterloo, relationships are built up over time. Student expectations, both in terms of what they will do and what will be expected of them, can be ironed out by drawing on the experiences of previous students. When setting up co-op for the first time these expectations may evolve as the employer learns from each successive placement, as do the programme team.

Possibly the biggest obstacle to running successful co-op programmes is the cost to the institution and the challenges involved in getting institutional support and buy-in when launching a programme. Co-op programmes are very expensive to run as the employers need to be nurtured, relationships developed and the process of matching students and employers is significant in time and resources.

Anyone considering launching a co-op programme would be well advised to conduct an internal and external SWOT analysis to identify the key issues in a given environment. This should include an environmental scan to establish local support for the approach. All stakeholders (employers, potential students, institutional management) should be consulted, as it is vital to gain employer buy-in prior to launch as well as complete institutional support from management and faculty. Students rarely need to be persuaded of the benefits.

Yorke (2004, p. 2) argues that employability derives from complex learning, and is a concept of wider range than those of 'core' and 'key' skills. He suggests that it is not merely an attribute of the new graduate. It needs to be continuously refreshed throughout a person's working life. The approach taken in the next good practice account suggests that a powerful approach is to integrate learning through work in a more holistic way, which may provide some challenges for both staff and students, but ultimately adds value to graduates' learning.

Work-integrated learning (WIL) experience approach in New Zealand

Susan F. Stevenson and **Kishwer Kingschild**, The New Zealand Curriculum Design Institute

In New Zealand, the work-integrated learning (WIL) approach is progressively becoming better understood and more widely utilised by higher and tertiary institutions as they come under increasing pressure from government and employers to produce work-ready graduates. Extensively

continued overleaf

Work-integrated learning (WIL) experience approach in New Zealand *continued*

used internationally, WIL has been applied in practice for many years in New Zealand, especially in teacher education. WIL may include many approaches and activities. However the key factor distinguishing WIL from these other approaches is the philosophically and theoretically equity value WIL ascribes to new knowledge and learning drawn from the practice-work contexts as opposed to traditional research. As Garnett stated:

> 'the integration of learning and work is not a new concept. From the middle ages, professions such as medicine and law developed their skills in practice and then took their learning into the academy to codify and transmit a body of professional knowledge. Since then, WIL has been adopted by other professions such as engineering, nursing and teaching, often starting as an apprenticeship model, but increasingly moving into delivery by higher education with universities defining the curriculum. Today, WIL at higher education level acknowledges not only that work has learning needs (i.e., workers require specific knowledge and skills) but also that high-level learning can take place at work, through undertaking work and for the specific purposes of work. WIL has a focus on higher education level knowledge, skill acquisition and application; this distinguishes it from simple work experience, which is not necessarily integrated into theoretical and research-based university programmes.'
>
> Garnett, 2009, p. 165

The main strength of WIL is that it describes curricular, andragogic and assessment practices, across a range of academic disciplines that can integrate formal learning and real workplace or professional practice challenges, problems and situations. WIL supports learners to integrate theoretical and research-based knowledge with the real-life challenges, problems and scenarios and to make the transition into complex and challenging professional work roles. A critical feature of authentic WIL is that it focuses on work as a learning activity and not just an opportunity to do or apply what has been learned in a higher education sector. Its key strength is that it recognises the potential of work and professional practice as complex and dynamic activities that have the capacity to develop higher and associative-level knowledge and skills.

The New Zealand Curriculum Design Institute (NZCDI) utilises forms of WIL throughout its higher education programmes. WIL may occur in classrooms but classroom experiences are principally designed to integrate and constantly include authentic real-life work challenges and scenarios. A wide range of learning activities can be included in WIL-based programmes including: field trips, visiting speakers, examination of case studies, clinical placements, practicum, work-based, project-based learning projects, negotiated assessments, problem-based learning, utilisation of authentic real-world problems, simulations, role plays, case study analyses, 'what if' scenario games, business presentations, business plan preparation, scenario reports, observations and so on.

When well-facilitated WIL is effective in increasing the depth, meaning and authenticity of learning experiences and has also been associated with increasing motivation and 'inspiring' heightened efforts by learners. In New Zealand it has been more recently applied to support professional development and learning through work undertaken by higher education teachers. It supports staff and learners to adjust to the realities and requirements of the 'real world' professional workplace and can foster independent, continuous improvement-orientated and reflective learning. Defined as a 'process whereby students learn through experiences which draw upon real life experiences in educational and practice settings' (Billett, 2011), WIL is a powerful approach especially when integrated throughout a whole programme by developing authentic and real life understandings, procedures and dispositions, including the criticality and reflexivity required for effective professional practice.

Key challenges staff are likely to encounter when initially utilising WIL may include how best to develop high-level educational facilitation, relational and communication capabilities that will enable students to authentically experience work or professional practice, setting experiences themselves. Staff need to build appropriate advanced-level knowledge, skills, attitudes and values in pre-requisite educational facilitation programmes to successfully implement WIL-based programmes. As Brodie (in Hunt and Chalmers, 2012) indicated, good facilitation skills are crucial to success. 'Facilitators help learners to manage the learning process: the facilitator does not lead, but guides' by helping learners and teams to clarify and establish their own direction while still making sure learning outcomes are achieved. Facilitators of WIL need the capacity to scaffold learning and learner capabilities and an equity orientation. Issues new staff in higher-tertiary education may meet when embarking on offering authentic WIL experiences may include encountering scepticism:

- from their institution and colleagues about utilising a learning approach that shares knowledge creation power with the professional or lay work context;
- about their embarking on further education in order to become a 'professional educational facilitator' who can effectively provide rich WIL experiences; and
- about them personally experiencing authentic professional or lay work place needs, challenges and requirements.

The key strategies NZCDI recommends for overcoming the above challenges are to both communicate about the WIL approach within institutions and to colleagues and to comprehensively research and evaluate longitudinally the multiple end-user outcomes of any WIL programmes you lead.

continued overleaf

Work-integrated learning (WIL) experience approach in New Zealand *continued*

Authentic WIL programme learners are also encouraged to develop, propose, negotiate and then undertake projects and assessment tasks in consultation with their Educational Facilitators; this truly learner-centred approach requires a flexible and secure disposition by those who facilitate such programmes.

Power is equitably shared with learners in WIL-based programmes as they advance and become increasingly independent. Learners in WIL-based programmes need a wide-ranging choice especially of assessment task options and opportunities to resolve real-world work challenges that have personal meaning, application and relevance to them. At NZCDI we would strongly recommend those planning to utilise the WIL approach, plan comprehensively and undertake advanced professional Educational Facilitator education before or while delivering the WIL approach.

References

Billett, S. (2011) *Final Report: Curriculum and pedagogic bases for effectively integrating practice-based experiences*. Australia: Griffith University.

Brodie, L. (2012) 'Problem-based learning', in L. Hunt and D. Chalmers (eds) *University Teaching in Focus: A learner-centred approach*. Melbourne: ACER Press.

Garnett, J. (2009) 'Contributing to the intellectual capital in organisations', in J. Garnett, C. Costley and B. Workman (eds) *Work Based Learning: Journeys to the core of higher education*. London: Middlesex University Press.

Hunt, L and Chalmers, D. (eds) (2012) *University Teaching in Focus: A learner-centred approach*. Melbourne: ACER Press.

Community engagement

Beyond elite universities, where 'town' and 'gown' represent different worlds, students have much to offer and much to gain if they engage productively with the communities in which they are studying. University study isn't just all about fostering employability and competences to enable graduates to fit into the workplace: students growing in confidence and capability through their learning experiences have important roles to play as citizens in their local and national communities as well as in the wider world. The next good practice account reviews how universities can provide a transformative agenda within their national communities, fostering active citizenship and working towards redressing disadvantage.

Building community engagement into higher education in the Bolivarian Republic of Venezuela

Mike Cole, University of East London, UK

Introduction

Having closely followed social transformation in Venezuela for many years, and having worked briefly in higher education there, I have been impressed by the ways in which universities cope with massification, which has transformed the university system, while demonstrating a strong commitment to student engagement and redressing disadvantage. Academics work with substantial student cohorts in a system underpinned by socialist principles to benefit not just the individual students but also the communities in which they live and work.

Since the late Hugo Chávez's first presidency, following a landslide election victory in 1999, this growth is demonstrated by frequent references to Venezuela's now being ranked second in Latin America (behind Cuba) and fifth worldwide in university enrolment rates, as reported by UNESCO in September 2010 (Ramírez, 2010, cited in Griffiths, 2013). This expansion has resulted in a nearly 200% increase from 1999 to 2009, from under 900,000 to over 2 million students (Ramírez, 2010, cited in Griffiths, 2013).

The transformative process, founded on socialist principles, seeks to build students' social and political consciousness in order to undertake work in the interests of the local community, the society and the Bolivarian Republic.

> 'A particular feature of the envisaged transformation is the intent to directly link higher education to the project of national endogenous development, under the banner of reconnecting universities to local communities, and to concrete social problems and their resolution, thus connecting theory with social practice.'
>
> Griffiths, 2013, p. 92

Redressing disadvantage

The Bolivarian University (UBV) was founded in 2003 as part of a major attempt to extend access to higher education, and is free to all students. It 'seeks to fundamentally challenge the elitism of many of the traditional universities' (Griffiths and Williams, 2009, p. 209). Social justice and equality are 'at the core of all educational content and delivery,' and all courses taken at UBV use Participatory Action Research (PAR) methodology, a multidisciplinary approach linking practice and theory. Based on the work of Orlando Fals Borda, PAR emphasises grassroots communities as full partners and co-researchers; is receptive to counter-narratives as opposed to elitist versions of history; recovers local values and beliefs; and shares knowledge in an accessible way (Gott, 2008). PAR bases students in their

continued overleaf

Building community engagement into higher education in the Bolivarian Republic of Venezuela *continued*

local communities, working alongside mentors on a community project, which are a core part of their formal studies (Griffiths and Williams, 2009). Examples of this described by Griffiths and Williams include Community Health students working with doctors within the *Barrio Adentro* health mission, Legal Studies students establishing a community legal centre to advise and support families with civil law issues, and Education students working with a teacher/mentor in schools in their local community.

All UBV students relate theory learned within the university to their working on project. As Griffiths and Williams explain:

> 'The approach is designed to place day-to-day decision-making and problem solving in the hands of local communities, as part of the broader societal reconstruction underway, with all participants gaining skills through the process. The intent is that the PAR methodology places researchers in positions of political leadership, but with the projects being democratically controlled and driven by the communities themselves and their own leaders, and aimed at realising the objectives of the community based organisations.'
>
> ibid., pp. 43–4

I taught at UBV for a short while. Standards there I found very high – with seminar discussions and debate comparing more than favourably with universities I have taught at in the UK and around the world. One thing that symbolises the Bolivarian Revolution for me was the way in which, at the start of my last seminar at UBV, one of the caretakers arrived to unlock the seminar room, and then sat down, listened to, and actively contributed to the seminar.

Griffiths and Williams conclude that, while the discussions at UBV are interesting, what is most important is *who* is taking part in them. This is not only, they argue, social and economic inclusion but also *political* inclusion, with educational decision-making in the hands of staff, students, parents/carers *and the community at large.*

In higher education as in other sectors in Venezuela there are serious shortcomings that need addressing, particularly in terms of the prevalent transmissive modes of teaching, and organisational issues, highly centralised governance structures and practices which can lead to the appointment (rather than election) of university authorities. Problems experienced in Venezuela include casualisation of the academic workforce and extremely high attrition rates accompanying the expanded enrolments in some universities, caused partly by inadequate funding and resources to support these expanded numbers. While these shortcomings mirror the situation in many countries worldwide, and reflect the onward march of neoliberal capitalism, in Venezuela, unlike in most countries in the global north, there is a long-standing, well-established and very large mass of people committed to socialist transformation (Cole, 2014).

References

Cole, M. (2014) 'The Bolivarian Republic of Venezuela', in S.C. Motta and M. Cole, *Constructing Twenty-first Century Socialism in Latin America: The role of radical education,* New York and Basingstoke: Palgrave Macmillan.

Gott, R. (2008) 'Orlando Fals Borda: Sociologist and activist who defined peasant politics in Colombia', *The Guardian,* August 26. www.guardian.co.uk/world/2008/aug/26/colombia.sociology.

Griffiths, T. (2013) 'Higher education for socialism in Venezuela: massification, development and transformation', in T.G. Griffiths and Z. Millei (eds) *Logics of Socialist Education: Engaging with crisis, insecurity and uncertainty,* Dordrecht: Springer.

Griffiths, T.G. and Williams, J. (2009) Mass schooling for socialist transformation in Cuba and Venezuela, *Journal for Critical Education Policy Studies,* 7(2), pp. 30–50.

Ramírez, E. (2010) Venezuela posee la quinta matrícula universitaria más alta del mundo, *Correo de Orinoco.*

Conclusions

If universities seek to fulfil their aspirations and those of their students to provide learning experiences that offer a foundation for lifelong and life-wide satisfaction, community engagement, productivity and employment, then the approaches deployed in curriculum design, delivery and assessment must work at the level of the whole person, rather than just trying to instil particular knowledge, skills, capabilities and behaviours. Employability implies all of these things, but also implies a mindset and an orientation that is reflective and committed to ongoing self-development. As Yorke suggests:

> 'Employability goes well beyond the simplistic notion of key skills, and is evidenced in the application of a mix of personal qualities and beliefs, understandings, skilful practices and the ability to reflect productively on experience.'
>
> Yorke, 2004, p. 14

In a changing global environment, as educators, we need ourselves to be fleet of foot and relentless in seeking out opportunities to help our graduates achieve not just jobs but also work satisfaction, not just credentials but also a deeply embedded spirit of enquiry, not just a determination to succeed in their career but also a commitment to be good citizens. It's a tall order, but what we must do if university education is to be not just a private good but a public one too.

11 Supporting those who deliver good learning, teaching and assessment

Introduction

In many nations, there is increasing recognition that learning to teach and assess in universities doesn't just happen by osmosis, and that academics need some support and training in order to help students learn. Before about the 1970s, most universities tended to assume that highly qualified people would be able to teach fellow adults without much in the way of training, emulating the styles by which they themselves had been taught. In this chapter, I will review how this perspective has changed in many nations as part of the shift towards recognising university teaching as a profession in its own right.

Initial training for those new to university teaching

Since those early days, the emergent professional group of educational developers (Brown, 2013) has fostered a range of developmental activities for those new to teaching in higher education, from half-day inductions, where the basics of lecturing and seminars are discussed, to more thorough year-long courses of part-time study, leading to a Post-Graduate Certificate in Higher Education (PGCHE) or similar, of the kind commonly offered in the UK, Australia and many other nations. PGCHE courses normally offer both hints and practical tips on classroom management, curriculum design, good assessment practice, effective lecturing and so on as well as an introduction to the scholarly literature in higher education pedagogy and to reflective practice.

Some of these courses can be extended by additional study to a Diploma, and then lead to a Masters qualification, often through an extended project or dissertation. In the first instance, these courses focused mainly on supporting full-time teaching staff, but over the years it has been recognised that many students have a significant proportion of their university classes taught by **fractional** staff, regularly working a proportion of a week often on a permanent contract, **sessional** staff teaching occasional or irregular sessions, often usefully bringing into the classroom current professional perspectives, and undertaking marking duties, and **doctoral** and other students, for whom teaching, leading seminars, and assessment form a small but important part of their relationship with their university. Learning support staff are increasingly engaging with professional development in this area too. Many agree that all of these groups require some level of support so that the quality of the student learning experience can be assured. For example, fractional staff are often welcomed onto PGCHEs, sessional staff invited for one- or two-day induction events and/or provided with introductory texts, like the *In at the Deep End* booklet produced at Leeds Metropolitan University (Race, 2006a).

The next good practice account describes a training programme in the Netherlands for fractional/sessional teachers.

Piloting a professionalisation programme for novice teachers

Bernadette van de Rijt and **Mirjam Bastings**, Faculty of Social Sciences, Utrecht University, Netherlands

Introduction

The Faculty of Social Sciences at Utrecht University works with a large number of temporary, novice teachers who are initially appointed to support the lecture programme by giving seminars. In general, they are given one-year appointments which may be extended for up to six academic years. Many are young people who recently received their Master of Arts in social sciences, but do not have an educational background or training in teaching. Assessment interviews are conducted with these temporary teachers and a clear message emerges from these conversations: they feel they are thrown in at the deep end!

At the content level, these novice teachers receive plenty of guidance but at the didactical and organisational level we consider it insufficient. A questionnaire, conducted among novice teachers, confirms this impression. Hence we started a professionalisation program for novice teachers, supported by the Centre for Teaching and Learning Utrecht (COLUU). The main aim of the programme is to equip teachers with basic teaching skills, which we consider essential within the first two years of appointment. It contains several required components.

continued overleaf

Piloting a professionalisation programme for novice teachers *continued*

Year one

Introductory meeting (two four-hour-sessions). Here we explain the Utrecht educational model and the novice teachers receive general information about the faculty. In addition, common problems or situations that a novice teacher may encounter will be discussed. Furthermore, the study advisor introduces himself and one of the teachers talks about his or her experiences as a novice teacher. Also, a digital manual for new teachers (including a Faculty A to Z) is introduced and they are given a first introduction to higher education teaching.

Peer review. Every three months, novice teachers attend mandatory peer review meetings within groups that remain constant. The first two sessions, within the first six months, take place under the guidance of an educational expert. Subsequently over the next six months, groups will work independently. In first instance, group composition is by discipline, if possible.

Basic didactical course (three four-hour sessions). During the first session, novice teachers are introduced to didactic issues including what is good education and how we can explain things in a questioning way. The second session focuses on the important topic of managing student behaviour, including motivating and guiding students. The last session focuses on learning in seminars, especially their purposes and organisation.

Coaching. During the first year, novice teachers work with coaches three times, with the coach visiting novice teachers during seminars and providing feedback on their teaching skills. The coach, who is a senior lecturer, functions as a first contact so novice teachers can ask all kinds of questions.

Year two

The second year includes a further four one-hour basic didactic sessions where the focus addresses learning goals, learning and teaching styles, and their impact on education, both for students and for teachers themselves. Throughout the year, novice teachers continue to attend peer-review meetings every three months, focusing on the issues they face during their work. Continuity in coaching is provided with the same coach as in year one offering novice teachers guidance, visiting teaching sessions and being available as needed. The novice teachers also discuss video-taped classroom situations of each other in small groups and visit peers for class observations in order to learn from each other.

Review

The programme is currently being piloted and the preliminary results are promising. Participating novice teachers suggest that they have been given a thorough understanding of the faculty's structure and their own position within such a large organisation. In addition, they feel they have become more skilled in teaching compared to entry to the programme. They say they feel less insecure in their teaching situations, better able to approach students, and have an enhanced overview of various educational options. A frequently-mentioned result is that novice teachers say they experience reduced pressure. Consequently, the Faculty of Social Sciences in Utrecht has provided structural funding to enable continuation of this professionalisation programme.

Not all academics have the opportunity to benefit from systematic professional development of this kind. In many nations, a great deal of teaching and assessment is undertaken by the so-called 'precariat', that is, staff employed on temporary and zero-hours contracts, with no job security, few employment rights and usually less access than full-time staff to academic support (Grove, 2013). A positive approach to offering training for sessional staff is described in the next good practice account.

Ensuring quality standards for learning and teaching with sessional staff

Marina Harvey, Macquarie University, Australia

Background

Ensuring quality standards for learning and teaching with sessionals is a good practice issue for many universities. The term 'sessional staff' refers to those non-permanent, or non-tenure tracked, teachers in universities and encompasses casual and short-term contract tutors, lecturers, demonstrators and markers. The BLASST (Benchmarking Leadership for the Advancement of Standards for Sessional Teaching) framework, a project funded by the Australian Government Office for Learning and Teaching to support and enhance quality teaching by sessional staff in higher education, is effective as it establishes evidence-based 'criteria and standards by which we may evaluate current practice in quality learning and teaching, in management and administrative policy procedures and systems affecting Sessional Staff' (BLASST, 2013, p. 2), primarily through benchmarking.

Sessional staff provide the majority of teaching throughout Australian (May et al., 2013) as well as across American and UK universities (Bryson, 2013). The nature of their employment and the associated risks to the sector in terms of assuring and enhancing quality learning and teaching have been captured by the many terms used to describe this cohort: throw away academics, the invisible faculty, frustrated careerists, career casuals, treadmill academics, tenuous periphery.

continued overleaf

Ensuring quality standards for learning and teaching with sessional staff *continued*

In Australia, developing policy to support and enhance quality learning and teaching with sessional staff had not proved to be efficacious in reducing the risks as the ways in which these staff work and the needs of each department, faculty, discipline and institution vary widely. An approach that provided a better fit for the sector was that of national standards. The standards had to be flexible enough for multi-level, multidisciplinary and cross-institutional application, while offering the ability to identify effective practices and share them more widely. This process of refining and validating national standards to support and enhance quality learning and teaching by sessional staff evolved over a decade and was informed by a series of previous projects.

There are three main principles which underpin the BLASST standards (BLASST, 2013, p. 4):

- **Quality Learning and Teaching**. This principle refers to those issues that affect the quality of teaching and learning with Sessional Staff. These issues include institutional and intra-institutional commitment to quality learning and teaching, to good practice learning and teaching approaches and values, principles and priorities, inclusivity and inclusion, and to professional development.
- **Support for Sessional Staff**. This principle refers to the need for recruitment, employment, administration and academic systems that are consistent, appropriate and inclusive of Sessional Staff. It states the importance of support for Sessional Staff in the form of dedicated infrastructure and other resourcing in order for all staff to undertake their roles effectively and professionally.
- **Sustainability** This principle refers to the need for workforce planning that includes Sessional Staff, at all levels of the institution. The principle is associated with practices that enable retention of good sessional teachers, reduce turnover of Sessional Staff, and encourage Sessional Staff in the pursuit and development of quality teaching. It also acknowledges that this can be achieved by recognising and rewarding Sessional Staff for the contribution they make. This principle also recognises the need for appropriate resources to underpin processes, and the minimisation of the administrative load on all staff (including academic, administrative and human resources).

The framework is designed to stimulate reflection and action, and enable institutions, faculties, departments and individuals to evaluate and lead good practice with regard to sessional staff. Participants assess the standard of their practices, by a series of criteria, and need to supply evidence to support their assessment.

The online tool and associated guide enable this benchmarking process to be undertaken efficiently, making it possible to complete the exercise in one day. The colour-coded report that is generated by the online tool provides an evidenced-based foundation for reflective decision-making and can be used to inform practices, priorities and action plans.

To achieve the best outcomes from a benchmarking exercise it is recommended that a workshop approach be used. In particular, participants from all levels of the institution should participate if true whole-of-institution learning is to be achieved, and action plans emerging systematised, resourced and supported. The good practice of regular benchmarking with BLASST should be aligned with the organisation's quality framework cycles.

A challenge for the approach may be achieving multi-level participation. To overcome this, it is necessary to:

- plan in advance so that calendar invitations are secured;
- provide catering at the benchmarking workshop;
- make use of telecommunications to include participants from regional or satellite campuses; and
- pay sessional staff for their participation.

Any university teacher can engage with the BLASST framework as a starting point for reflecting on their institution's standards. They can lead a benchmarking workshop at the department, faculty or institutional level. The standards have been piloted across Australia and are now offered more widely as a potential strategy for:

- educating the sector and disseminating minimum and aspirational standards and good practice in learning and teaching for sessional staff,
- measuring enhancements over time, and
- supporting sector-wide awareness of sessional staff issues (Harvey, 2013).

References

BLASST (2013). *The BLASST Guide. Benchmarking with the sessional staff standards framework.* http://www.blasst.edu.au/docs/A413_008_BLASST_Benchmark_Guide.pdf

Bryson, C. (2013) Supporting sessional teaching staff in the UK – to what extent is there real progress?, *Journal of University Teaching and Learning Practice*, 10(3), art. 2. Woolangong, University of Woolangong

Harvey, M. (2013) Setting the standards for sessional staff: quality learning and teaching, *Journal of University Teaching and Learning Practice*, 10(3). http://ro.uow.edu.au/jutlp/vol10/iss3/4

May et al. (2013) cited in F. Beaton and A. Gilbert (eds) *Developing Effective Part-time Teachers in Higher Education*, Abingdon: Routledge.

Many PGCHEs originally focused on what might be termed educational instruction practices, but progressively they have grown to encompass the wider range of duties that teachers perform in support of student learning, including assessment. The UK Quality Assurance Agency in its Code of practice for assessment and the recognition of prior learning insists that 'Higher education providers assure themselves that everyone involved in the assessment of student work, including prior learning, and associated assessment processes is competent to undertake their roles and responsibilities' (QAA, 2013, p. 11) and that HEIs should consider offering development and training on:

- 'promoting understanding of the theory and practice of assessment and its implementation, including the different purposes of formative and summative assessment;
- effective ways to evaluate the extent to which learning outcomes have been achieved;
- effective ways to engage with students to enable and promote dialogue about, and reflective use of, feedback;
- raising awareness of staff about the importance of designing assessments that minimise opportunities for plagiarism and other forms of unacceptable academic practice;
- enabling staff to learn about new approaches to assessment and devise new methods, as well as the best ways to operate existing methods;
- raising staff awareness of the assessment implications of the diversity of students, including cultural diversity, differences in learning methods and the need for inclusivity.'

QAA, op. cit., p. 12

This may seem a challenging set of requirements, but actually contains a great deal of common sense to assure standards of assessment practice.

Beyond initial training

Continuous professional development (CPD) is crucial to assuring capability and refreshing teaching and assessment practices. Short workshops and training events are provided in universities worldwide to offer new perspectives, provide training on technological innovations and to rekindle enthusiasm among those with long careers working with students. In

Phil Race's good practice account here, he describes how the principles of good learning, teaching and assessment described throughout this book can be applied to one-off or short-series CPD sessions.

Designing participant-centred Staff Development Workshops

Phil Race, independent consultant, UK

Workshops on a broad range of aspects of assessment, learning and teaching are widely used as continuing professional development for staff. Workshops, which typically last for two or three hours or even full days, should not be just presentations. The content of a successful workshop needs to be continuously adjusted in the light of the experience and wishes of those present, and not just 'gone through rigidly' as predetermined by the facilitator in advance. Here I suggest a sequence of three elements of effective workshops, which are likely to increase the impact carried forward by participants into their subsequent practice.

Find out where participants are starting from

Getting people engaged from the outset, for example, by giving everyone a Post-it™ sticky note, asking them to jot down short completions of a starter-statement, such as (in a workshop about assessment, for example) 'Assessing students' work would be much better for me if only I ...' and then asking them to randomly swap sticky notes, enables you to gauge the interests and priorities of those in the room. You can then next ask a few volunteers to read out, maybe with passion and drama, the sticky note they now have. Finally you could ask for all the sticky notes to be stuck to a flipchart, or wall, and provide the whole group with a few highlights of things that weren't read out from others' sticky notes. This allows the main needs of the participants to be probed gently, in their own words, and serves as an exhibit and agenda to steer the rest of the workshop.

Present, adjust and prioritise possible intended outcomes of the workshop

I find it works best to draft no more than five such outcomes for a half-day workshop, indicating what participants may realistically hope to gain by the end of the workshop. I then present these, numbered on a slide, and ask participants mentally to put them in order of preference (or importance) then to vote on them as follows: 'As I call out '1' to '5' in turn, raise two hands (two votes) for the outcome you most want to achieve, then one hand (your remaining vote) for the one second in your order of preference'. From this you can establish the respective relevance of different intended outcomes. This process gives participants a sense of ownership of the agenda for the workshop, and it enables you to decide how much time and energy will be given to the main ingredients of the session.

continued overleaf

Designing participant-centred Staff Development Workshops *continued*

Choose from a range of activities which link to the chosen outcomes

Some people meticulously plan every element of a workshop and then get flustered if anything knocks it off course. The approach suggested here allows for a greater degree of flexibility in following the interests of group participants. While it may be necessary to give short elements of presentation about the topics of successive themes, to avoid it being excessively focused on the facilitator's words and ideas, the main thrust of a successful workshop is getting participants 'learning by doing' by undertaking activities relating to each selected intended outcome in turn. Sometimes tasks can be individual ones, followed by pair discussions, and short report-back elements. Alternatively tasks can be designed for groups of 4–6, randomly rotating group membership for successive tasks, so that all participants can share their experiences and ideas. It can be useful for each task to culminate in some brief recommendations from participants, which can be collated and prioritised at the workshop, and which they can then take away after the event. Workshops have most impact when the report-back relates directly to the priorities of the participants, with outputs then shared online after the event. Participants then retain the feeling that 'this was *our* workshop' rather than it just having been a 'standard' event.

Therefore when planning a workshop, it is useful for facilitators already to have designed a range of possible tasks and activities (and to have presentation snippets and resource materials readily available), from which they can select elements at the event itself, matching as far as possible what the participants had earlier prioritised. In practice, it is important not to try to cover everything you've prepared, but to go deeper and more flexibly into aspects highlighted as priorities for those present on the day.

Many HEIs offer advanced professional support for those teaching and managing teaching in higher education and in the last twenty years, efforts have been made to undertake this systematically.

Over time, it has become more common for quality assurers at a local or national level to seek confirmation that university students are not being taught by unqualified staff and in the UK, for example, the UK Professional Standards Framework has established four levels of Fellowship through which university teachers can demonstrate their commitment to professional practice. Many advertised posts in UK HEIs now specify HEA recognition for appointment and there is an expectation that HEIs should make public the proportion of staff who have done so as part of the institutional Key Information Set (KIS) data required by Government to be available on each university's website.

> 'The UK Professional Standards Framework
>
> 1. Supports the initial and continuing professional development of staff engaged in teaching and supporting learning;
> 2. Fosters dynamic approaches to teaching and learning through creativity, innovation and continuous development in diverse academic and/or professional settings;
> 3. Demonstrates to students and other stakeholders the professionalism that staff and institutions bring to teaching and support for student learning;
> 4. Acknowledges the variety and quality of teaching, learning and assessment practices that support and underpin student learning;
> 5. Facilitates individuals and institutions in gaining formal recognition for quality enhanced approaches to teaching and supporting learning, often as part of wider responsibilities that may include research and/or management activities.'
>
> HEA, 2012b

There are three dimensions of the framework covering areas of activity, core knowledge and values, and applicants for all levels of Fellowship (Associate Fellow, Fellow, Senior Fellow and Principal Fellow) are required to demonstrate these, together with their educational impact proportionate to their status, through an account of professional practice, supported by external referees or advocates. The framework provides a route for university teachers and supporters of learning to demonstrate evidence of their educational impact, and in the case of Principal Fellowships which are aimed at academic middle to senior managers, their advocacy and championing of good educational practices.

The next good practice account, overleaf, describes a long-standing programme aimed at middle managers in the Netherlands.

The final good practice account in this chapter then describes how the course leaders managed, learned from and resolved a problematic phase within the history of a course designed to help new lecturing staff be innovative within a traditional context, by fostering a community of practice to engage those who at one point seemed to be hampering the implementation of student-centred teaching.

Enhancement opportunities for experienced teachers in the Netherlands

Hetty Grunefeld, Utrecht University, Netherlands

Background

The Utrecht University has a strong research record and also takes teaching and learning very seriously. The university, like others in the Netherlands, offers a University Teaching Qualification (UTQ) to up-skill those starting to teach in higher education, and these qualifications are mutually recognised. Professional development for our academics starts with acquiring a basic research qualification (a PhD), followed by the UTQ. To become an Associate Professor, academics need a senior qualification in either research or teaching, which can be obtained by assembling an assessed portfolio including descriptions of experiences and reflections. Full Professors need a senior qualification in both research and teaching. Seniority in teaching for Utrecht University means being responsible for courses, involvement in co-ordinating programmes and in quality assurance, together with, at least for some, curriculum leadership of teaching and learning.

Beyond the basics

Since 2012 universities across the Netherlands have been discussing follow-ups to the basic teaching courses, the main issues being whether there should be an agreement between our universities about what such a programme might contain and whether there should be a national agreement to mutually recognise it. This could, like ours, be centred on leadership, responsibilities for courses and enhancing the quality of teaching and learning, leading to a senior teaching qualification certificate. Some universities currently promote a system of ongoing education that requires academics to participate in continuous professional development (CPD), recording and registering their activities. In others, the next step beyond the basic UTQ is a range of development activities working towards excellence by becoming better as a teacher.

Leading educational change

At Utrecht University a special Educational Leadership course is offered to a small group of selected academics who are leaders of educational change and (future) Directors of Education within faculties. Since 2000 we have been running a year-long programme which typically involves eight 24-hour residential workshops where colleagues work intensively to explore pedagogic and change-management issues. The precise programme each year is devised to build on the expressed interests of participants, but each year there are inputs from nationally and internationally recognised experts, for example in curriculum design or assessment, together with presentations of individual teaching and learning related projects and a study trip to universities beyond the Netherlands where particular expertise can be found. The programme is not formally accredited but has been highly successful and many who have completed the course now hold senior responsibilities for enhancement of teaching and learning. The course has in no way been detrimental to their position in research as many have been awarded research grants and professorships.

Utrecht University was the first in the Netherlands with this initiative, and subsequently several other universities have followed, some with their own programmes and some working with the Utrecht University to offer our programme for their staff.

Sharing our learning

What works particularly well within this programme is that it:

- Combines both theoretical and practical elements, making best use of international pedagogic scholarship.
- Provides colleagues with perspectives from beyond their own university and nation. Participants particularly benefit from the international field trips, where host universities and particular contacts are sought to match the interests, disciplines and pedagogic themes identified in the early sessions.
- Offers participants a community of practice, within which they can develop and extend their interests within a safe and supportive environment. The residential elements of the programme are seen as particularly valuable in building this cohort cohesion that lasts well beyond the extent of the study period.
- Provides the university with a critical mass of highly developed pedagogic leaders with some shared perspectives and ways of working to bring about productive innovation.

Reference

Grunefeld, H. (2005) *Effecten van de leergang Onderwijskundig leiderschap (Effects of the Educational Leadership Programme)*. Internal report. Utrecht University, Centre for Teaching and Learning.

Ensuring sustainability of junior lecturer-led student-centred teaching practice improvements using an inherent sense of a community culture

Shrinika Weerakoon, Staff Development Centre, University of Colombo, Sri Lanka, and **Suki Ekaratne**, Centre for the Enhancement of Teaching and Learning, The University of Hong Kong, Hong Kong

Introduction

Teaching development training became mandatory for all new higher education lecturers in Sri Lanka from 1997, coinciding with the establishment of Sri Lanka's first Staff Development Centre at Colombo University and the first PGCHE. Its early challenge was to re-orient participants' thinking towards practising a student-centred learning (SCL) approach in their classrooms. We used evidence-based SCL pedagogic practices from Western literature, together with reflective practice as in many PGCHEs. We adopted a four-step conceptual change process, as generating;

- 'dissatisfaction with an existing conception;
- intelligibility of a new conception;
- appearance of an initial plausibility;
- the suggestive possibility of the new concept as a fruitful future programme'

Posner et al., 1982

The 'dissatisfaction with an existing conception' (*viz.*, teacher-centred approach) was generated by making dissatisfaction shared, facilitated mainly through peer discussions of previously-failed reflection-on-action teaching-learning experiences. Next, the SCL concept replaced the pre-existing teacher-centred conception by discussing tutor and peer-mediated SCL teaching possibilities for it to become 'intelligible as a new conception'. Then, the tutor showcased SCL pedagogic practices which former course-trainees had implemented, provided peer-discussion opportunities with dialogic feedback, to confer an 'appearance of an initial plausibility' on SCL. Finally, supported by further dialogic feedback, participants self-selected previously-failed incidents they now considered feasible to try out to improve SCL. These became 'critical incidents' to pilot classroom change through a Learning Contract (LC) between tutor and participants and which participants used to plan their classroom-change implementations. When trainee-lecturers experienced the success of their implemented changes, they became committed change agents for the new SCL conceptions by elevating SCL change into a 'self-suggested possibility as a fruitful future programme' of their own making. Thus, using the four-step model worked well during the course with the community of practice built by peer and tutor dialogue becoming close-knit to fuel lecturer enthusiasm to sustain their actions as change agents. This also fostered increased self-confidence, closer student rapport and teacher respect. The course always ended with celebratory parting and with future visions of sustaining change improvements.

The problematic phase

These visions however were short-lived and soon after ending the first course iterations, there was intense frustration. As former tutors, we received calls for renewed support by lecturers as their continued change efforts were now frowned upon by seniors and colleagues who had not followed this training themselves. We, together with the trained lecturers, began to feel growing feelings of deep disappointment as, with each passing cohort, lecturers had to move further away from SCL practices and their beliefs. Indeed, these lecturers felt a reciprocal resentment swelling in being thwarted from implementing what they regarded as beneficial to their students. It was then that we all realised that the trained lecturers had only been 'allowed' to implement teaching changes to enable them to pass their mandatory courses, but that subsequently their effectiveness was viewed as a professional threat by other departmental colleagues and seniors. Sustaining their enthusiasm and that for the teaching improvement change process was impossible and, worse still, we felt we had contributed to the demoralisation of a well-meaning generation of younger lecturers. We hadn't anticipated this sad situation and it prompted us to much soul-searching and eventually to a Strengths, Weaknesses, Opportunities and Threats (SWOT) analysis.

Building a wider Community of Practice (CoP)

In this analysis we saw that the real strength of the course was in developing a strong supportive CoP based on a genuine national sense of community and the course had developed a coterie of effective individuals with whom the larger group of academics who hadn't done the course could not identify. We needed to find a way to involve those departmental colleagues in this effective CoP through a sense of themselves also contributing to enhancement. We did this by getting the seniors and colleagues in the departments to act as mentors involved in reviewing the Learning Contracts for their junior lecturers and therefore becoming stakeholders in the teaching enhancements of their junior staff. In this way senior colleagues became part of a larger CoP from the start of the course. This process took a couple of years to take root, but as it did, the teaching improvements became sustained, and this larger CoP became embedded.

Reference

Posner, G.J., Strike, K.A., Hewson, P.W. and Gertzog, W.A. (1982) Accommodation of a scientific conception: Towards a theory of conceptual change, *Science Education*, 66(2), pp. 211–29.

Conclusions

Some talented amateurs teach really well, but many Graduate Teaching Assistants, Post-Doctoral students and new academics, thrown in at the deep end and left to sink or swim, may take years or even decades to hone their capabilities before they become the teachers they would ultimately hope to be. Meanwhile generations of students may be experiencing sub-optimal university teaching, which they are likely to resent, particularly if they are paying high tuition fees. A tiny minority of university academics hold their students (and teaching itself) in contempt, but the vast majority really want to give inspiring and highly proficient lectures, practical classes, tutorials, seminars and online learning sessions. Toolkits, guides and collections of teaching tips are invaluable while new and quite new university teachers are finding their feet, but advanced practitioners need, I would argue, access to the kind of live or virtual learning community of peers that are offered by the kinds of programmes described here, alongside empathy and humility to reflect deeply on one's own teaching in a continuous quest to keep abreast of new ideas and to improve. Together with the authors of the good practice accounts in this chapter, that is what I aim to achieve for myself and others.

12 Conclusions: key pedagogic issues in global higher education

> 'Dramatic demographic changes in the cultural and linguistic diversity of people are occurring in many nations throughout the world. These changes have challenged higher education institutions to modify their curricula and instructional strategies to meet the needs of diverse learners and to prepare all graduates to have the awareness, knowledge, and skills to be effective in a diverse society ... to prepare students to succeed in the culturally diverse, globally interdependent world.'
>
> Morey, 2000

In this book I have set out to explore what kinds of progressive strategies are being implemented in higher education teaching, learning and assessment within the international context. I nevertheless recognise that there are few absolute pedagogic innovations, only practices that are new to the context, the mode of delivery, the students' level of study, the subject area, the university or the nation. These innovations are being put in place at a time when the very nature of teaching, and indeed learning, is changing beyond recognition, spurred by rapidly shifting perspectives on knowledge production and assimilation, especially in the light of the ubiquitous availability of information and technologies to access and process it.

> 'In all countries, the new global context has prompted a greater demand for education and is forcing institutions for higher learning to reconsider their missions, tasks, and responsibilities as well as to develop innovative strategies to improve their relevance and function.'
>
> Gacel-Avila, 2005

This book includes good practice from nations on six continents, including Australia, Bangladesh, Belarus, Canada, China, Egypt, Hong Kong, Iceland, India, Ireland, Malaysia, the Netherlands, New Zealand, South Africa, Sri Lanka, Venezuela, the United States of America and the United

Kingdom. The diversity evidenced has astonished and delighted me, and bringing these examples together here has been a profound and humbling learning experience. I look forward to being made aware of yet more rich examples in the coming years. In a brief coda to this book, building on this learning from others I will conclude by offering some thoughts on global higher education, which summarises what I believe to be the key issues we face in tertiary pedagogy in the 21st century globally. This is not a 'universal declaration' of self-evident truths, but I trust that these personal assertions are at least reasonably convincing.

No university or indeed national higher education system can behave as if it is not working in a global environment. Student and staff mobility, the impact of transnational education, a readiness by some nations to teach undergraduates as well as postgraduates in a language other than their own to protect and enhance recruitment, and the ubiquity of international software and platform providers all mitigate against drawing up the barricades around our own national university systems. We have to behave inter-culturally and cross-culturally to survive, and dominant cultures must be sensitive about not imposing their cultural, pedagogic and academic mores on other parts of the world.

Education is transformative and can be either a locus for redressing disadvantage or conversely for reinforcing elitism. Studies on the earning power of graduates compared to others have hugely variable outcomes but certainly completing a course of higher education gives life-advantages to those who succeed. These are not just pecuniary, but also tend to include improved self-efficacy and confidence, enhanced global perspectives, mature competences and professional status. This places a heavy burden on those who select, teach, support and assess students, since graduation whether at graduate or post-graduate level is likely to have high impact on lifelong achievements. The choices we make and the actions we take have social, political and economic impact on both individuals and society, and I argue we have a moral duty to act wisely and thoughtfully.

Education in universities needs to be a joint endeavour in which learners and teachers work in partnership. This can never be an equal partnership, as the requirement for academics to make professional judgements on the achievements of students means there will always be a power imbalance between the two groups. Nevertheless, the balance of power is shifting, and a recognition of the importance of co-working, communicating effectively, and recognising the drivers that prompt the actions of both is essential. Students in many nations take important roles within quality assurance activities and contribute actively to curriculum design.

We need to balance tensions between the cost effectiveness of various teaching and assessment approaches with their effectiveness in making learning happen. Mass delivery of content by electronic means is cheap but will not be cost effective if the paradigm in use neglects the importance of student engagement. Poor quality computer-based assessment is also cheap, but good CBA requires teamwork, by technically competent systems designers, advanced subject experts and knowledgeable educational developers who understand how question design works well, and this, with certain honourable exceptions including the UK's Open University, is by no means ubiquitous. We ignore at our peril five decades of research into what works well in university teaching if we go for quick fixes.

No sensible university teacher can behave as if we don't live in a digital age. As McLoughlin and Lee (2010) suggest, students want 'an active learning experience that is social, participatory and supported by rich media' where the learning experiences are 'active, process based, anchored in and driven by learners' interests, and therefore have the potential to cultivate self regulated, independent learning.' Current mores 'challenge traditional pedagogies where the teacher is the celebrated expert, dispensing knowledge and prescribing learning resources and activities' instead requiring us to be flexible, friendly, and focused on ensuring learning takes place.

The future of teaching and learning in higher education globally is unpredictable. Efforts to predict how it would change the last five decades have fallen well short of accuracy, and some of the expectations we had about academic pedagogies – the take-over of classrooms by teaching machines, the redundancy of the role of university teachers, the much heralded imminent death of the lecture – now seem faintly ludicrous, although elements of each of these predictions have a ring of truth about them. The trick is to be able to spot emergent trends and act accordingly and quickly.

In conclusion

> 'The significant problems we face cannot be solved at the same level of thinking we were at when we created them.'
>
> Attributed to Albert Einstein

Higher education students and those who teach them alike need to be able to face challenges and uncertainty with confidence, a broad repertoire of coping strategies and an advanced skill-set that equips them to become autonomous, self-directed, continuously self-developing learners. They need to be proactive thinkers, equipped not just with knowledge but also with scholarly frameworks on which they can build advanced understandings of emergent concepts and new ideas. They need to engage with the technologies and social practices of their age and prepare for those coming forward. They need to be socially-skilled and culturally-literate citizens, able to live, work and thrive in a global environment. A university education cannot possibly provide all of these things, but in working towards these goals, those of us engaged in assessment, learning and teaching know that our task is meaningful, productive and ultimately of high value to society and the communities in which we practise our profession.

References and further reading

Angelo, T. and Cross, K. (1993) *Classroom Assessment Techniques*, New York: Jossey Bass.

Assessment for Learning: http://www.northumbria.ac.uk/sd/central/ar/academy/cetl_afl/

Assessment Reform Group (1999) *Assessment for Learning: Beyond the black box,* Cambridge: University of Cambridge School of Education.

Bain, K. (2004) *What the Best College Teachers Do,* Cambridge, Mass: Harvard University Press. www.vetmed.wsu.edu/courses-jmgay/documents/SynopsisWhatBestCollegeTeachersDo.pdf

Barber, M., Donelly, K. and Rizvi, S. (2013) *An Avalanche is Coming: Higher Education and the revolution ahead*, London: UK Institute for Public Policy Research (IPPR) report.

Beetham, H. (2007) 'Active learning in technology-rich contexts', in H. Beetham and R. Sharpe, *Rethinking Pedagogy for a Digital Age: Designing for 21st century learning,* Abingdon: Routledge.

Beetham, H. (2014) Keynote to the HE Learning Futures conference in Sydney.

Beetham, H. and Sharpe, R. (2013) *Rethinking Pedagogy for a Digital Age: Designing for 21st century learning,* 2nd edn, Abingdon: Routledge.

Biggs, J. (2003a) *Aligning Teaching for Constructing Learning,* Higher Education Academy. Available at: www.heacademy.ac.uk/resources/detail/resource_database/id477_aligning_teaching_for_constructing_learning (accessed 22 August 2013).

Biggs, J.B. (2003b) *Teaching for Quality Learning at University*, 2nd edn, Maidenhead: Open University Press.

Biggs, J. and Tang, C. (2007) *Teaching for Quality Learning at University*, 3rd edn, Maidenhead: SRHE/Open University Press.

Biggs, J. and Tang, C. (2011) *Teaching for Quality Learning at University*, 4th edn, Maidenhead: SRHE/Open University Press.

Billett, S. (2011) *Final Report: Curriculum and pedagogic bases for effectively integrating practice-based experiences*, Australia: Griffith University.

BLASST (2013) *The BLASST Guide. Benchmarking with the sessional staff standards framework*. www.blasst.edu.au/docs/A413_008_BLASST_Benchmark_Guide.pdf.

Bloxham, S. and Boyd, P. (2007) *Developing Effective Assessment in Higher Education: A practical guide*, Maidenhead: Open University Press.

Boud, D. (1988) (ed.) *Developing Student Autonomy in Learning*, 2nd edn, London: Kogan Page.

Boud, D. (1995) *Enhancing Learning through Self-assessment*, Abingdon: Routledge.

Boud, D. (2007) 'Reframing assessment as if learning were important', in D. Boud and N. Falchikov (eds) *Rethinking Assessment in Higher Education: Learning for the longer term*, Abingdon: Routledge.

Boud, D. and associates (2010) *Assessment 2020: Seven propositions for assessment reform in higher education*, Sydney: Australian Learning and Teaching Council.

Bourdieu, P. (1992) 'The purpose of reflexive sociology', in P. Bourdieu and L. Waquant (eds) *An Invitation to Reflexive Sociology*, Cambridge: Polity.

Bowl, M. (2003) *Non-Traditional Entrants to Higher Education: 'They talk about people like me'*, Stoke-on-Trent: Trentham Books.

Boyer, E.L. (1990, reprinted 1997) *Scholarship Reconsidered: Priorities of the professoriate*, San Francisco: Jossey Bass/The Carnegie Foundation for the Advancement of Teaching.

Boyle, A., Maguire, S., Martin, A., Milsom, C., Nash, R., Rawlinson, S., Turner, A., Wurthmann, S. and Conchie, S. (2007) Fieldwork is good: The student perception and the affective domain, *Journal of Geography in Higher Education*, 31(2), pp. 299–317.

Brodie, L. (2012) 'Problem-based learning', in L. Hunt and D. Chalmers (eds) *University Teaching in Focus: A learner-centred approach*, Melbourne: ACER Press.

Brookfield, S. (2005) *The Power of Critical Theory: Liberating adult learning and teaching*, San Francisco: Jossey-Bass.

Brown, G. with Bull, J. and Pendlebury, M. (1997) *Assessing Student Learning in Higher Education*, Abingdon: Routledge.

Brown, S. (2011) Bringing about positive change in higher education; a case study, *Quality Assurance in Education*, 19(3), pp. 195–207.

Brown, S. (2012) Managing change in universities: a Sisyphean task?, *Quality in Higher Education*, 18(1), pp. 139–46.

Brown, S. (2013) The twenty books that influenced educational developers' thinking in the last twenty years: opinion piece, *Innovations in Education and Teaching International*, 50(4), pp. 321–30

Brown, S. and Denton, S. (2010) 'Leading the university beyond bureaucracy', in S. Denton and S. Brown (eds) *A Practical Guide to University and College Management*, New York and Abingdon: Routledge.

Brown, S. and Glasner, A. (eds) (1999) *Assessment Matters in Higher Education, Choosing and using diverse approaches*, Buckingham: Open University Press.

Brown, S. and Knight, P. (1994) *Assessing Learners in Higher Education*, London: Kogan Page.

Brown, S. and Race, P. (2002) *Lecturing: A practical guide*, London: Kogan Page.

Brown, S. and Race, P. (2012) 'Using effective assessment to promote learning', in L. Hunt and D. Chalmers (eds) *University Teaching in Focus: A learning-centred approach*, Victoria, Australia: Acer Press and Abingdon: Routledge.

Brown, S., Rust, C. and Gibbs, G. (1994) *Strategies for Diversifying Assessment*, Oxford: Oxford Centre for Staff Development.

Browne, J. (2010) *Securing a Sustainable Future for Higher Education*. www.gov.uk/government/uploads/system/uploads/attachment_data/file/31999/10-1208-securing-sustainable-higher-education-browne-report.pdf (accessed 7 June 2014).

Bruner, J.S., Goodnow, J.J. and Austen, G.A. (1956) *A Study of Thinking,* New York: Wiley.

Bryson, C. (2013) Supporting sessional teaching staff in the UK – to what extent is there real progress?, *Journal of University Teaching and Learning Practice*, 10(3), art. 2. Woolangong, University of Woolangong

Carless, D., Joughin, G. and Ngar-Fun, L. (2006) *How Assessment Supports Learning: Learning orientated assessment in action,* Hong Kong: Hong Kong University Press.

Carroll, J. (2002) *A Handbook for Deterring Plagiarism in Higher Education*, Oxford: Oxford Centre for Staff and Learning Development.

Carroll, J. and Ryan, J. (2005) *Teaching International Students: Improving learning for all,* Abingdon: Routledge.

Cejda, B.D. and Hensel, N. (2009) *Undergraduate Research at Community Colleges*, USA: Council on Undergraduate Research. Available at www.cur.org/urcc/ (accessed 24 March 2014).

Cercone, K. (2008) Characteristics of adult learners with implications for online learning design, *AACE Journal*, 16(2), pp. 137–59.

CIBER (2008) *Information Behaviour of the Researcher of the Future*. Available at www.jisc.ac.uk/media/documents/programmes/reppres/gg_final_keynote_11012008.pdf (accessed 22 August 2013).

Cole, M. (2014) 'The Bolivarian Republic of Venezuela', in S.C. Motta and M. Cole, *Constructing Twenty-first Century Socialism in Latin America: The role of radical education,* New York and Basingstoke: Palgrave Macmillan.

Cornelius, S., Gordon, C. and Schyma, J. (2014) *Live Online Learning: Strategies for the web conferencing classroom*, Basingstoke: Palgrave Macmillan.

Council of Europe (2012) *Common European Framework of Reference for Languages: Learning, teaching, assessment.* Available at www.coe.int/t/dg4/linguistic/cadre1_en.asp (accessed 1 December 2013).

Crooks, T. (1988, reprinted 1994) *Assessing Student Performance,* Australia: HERDSA Green Guide No. 8.

Crosling, G., Thomas, L. and Heagney, M. (2008) *Improving Student Retention in Higher Education*. London and New York: Routledge.

Davidowitz, B. and Rollnick, M. (2001) Effectiveness of flow diagrams as a strategy for learning in laboratories, *Australian Journal of Education in Chemistry*, 57(2001), pp. 18–24.

Deem, R. and Brehony, K.J. (2000) Doctoral students' access to research cultures – are some more unequal than others?, *Studies in Higher Education*, 25(2), p. 157.

DeLind, L. and Link, T. (2004) 'Place as the nexus of a sustainable future: a course for all of us', in P.F. Barlett and G.W. Chase (eds) *Sustainability on Campus: Stories and strategies for change*, Cambridge, Mass: MIT Press.

Ellis, R.C.T., Dickinson, I., Green, M. and Smith, M. (2006) *The Implementation and Evaluation of an Undergraduate Virtual Reality Surveying Application*, Leeds: Leeds Metropolitan University repository, http://repository-intralibrary.leedsmet.ac.uk/open_virtual_file_path/i3128n169122t/P27_Robert_Ellis.pdf.

Entwistle, N. (2009) *Teaching for Understanding at University*, Basingstoke: Palgrave Macmillan.

ERA (Excellence for Research in Australia) (2010) *Submission Guidelines*, Commonwealth of Australia.

ETF (European Training Foundation) (2011) *Building a Competitiveness Framework for Education and Training in Egypt,* Working paper.

European Commission (2013) *Improving the Quality of Teaching and Learning in Europe's HE Institutions* (Report of the High Level group on the Modernisation of Higher Education). http://ec.europa.eu/education/library/reports/modernisation_en.pdf (accessed 7 June 2014).

Exley, K. and Gibbs, G. (1994) *Course Design for Resource Based Learning: Science*, Oxford: Oxford Centre for Staff Development.

Falchikov, N. (2004) *Improving Assessment through Student Involvement: Practical solutions for aiding learning in higher and further education,* Abingdon: Routledge.

Fisher, A., Exley, K. and Ciobanu, D. (2014) *Using Technology to Support Learning and Teaching,* Abingdon: Routledge.

Flint, N.R. and Johnson, B. (2011) *Towards Fairer University Assessment: Addressing the concerns of students*, Abingdon: Routledge.

Fox, S. and Walsh, E. (2007) Task Oriented Online Learning (TOOL) – Social Interaction in an Online Environment, *Case Studies of Good Practice in the Assessment of Student Learning in Higher Education*, Vol. 1, Dublin: AISHE/HEA.

Gacel-Avila, J. (2005) The internationalisation of higher education: a paradigm for global citizenry, *Journal of Studies in International Education*, 9(2), pp. 121–36.

Garnett, J. (2009) 'Contributing to the intellectual capital in organisations', in J. Garnett, C. Costley and B. Workman (eds) *Work Based Learning: Journeys to the core of higher education*. London: Middlesex University Press.

Geisler, C. (2013) *Academic Literacy and the Nature of Expertise: Reading, writing, and knowing in academic philosophy*, Abingdon: Routledge.

Gibbs, G. (1999) 'Using assessment strategically to change the way students learn', in S. Brown and A. Glasner (eds) *Assessment Matters in Higher Education: Choosing and using diverse approaches,* Maidenhead: SRHE/Open University Press.

Gibbs, G. (2008) *Designing Assessment to Support Student Learning,* Keynote at Leeds Metropolitan Staff Development Festival.

Gibbs, G. (2010) *Using Assessment to Support Student Learning*, Leeds: Leeds Metropolitan University.

Gibbs, G. and Jenkins, A. (eds) (1992) *Teaching Large Classes in Higher Education: How to maintain quality with reduced resources*. London: Kogan Page.

Gibbs, G. and Simpson, C. (2005) Conditions under which assessment supports students' learning, *Learning and Teaching in Higher Education*, 1, Gloucester: University of Gloucestershire.

Godfrey, J. (2013a) PowerPoint presentation given at IATEFL Conference 2013, Liverpool, UK. Available at jeannegodfrey.com/sitebuildercontent/sitebuilderfiles/presiateflf.pptx.

Godfrey, J. (2013b) *The Student Phrase Book: Vocabulary for writing at university,* Basingstoke: Palgrave Macmillan.

Gott, R. (2008) Orlando Fals Borda: Sociologist and Activist Who Defined Peasant Politics in Colombia, *The Guardian*, 26 August. www.guardian.co.uk/world/2008/aug/26/colombia.sociology

Grace, S. and Gravestock, P. (2009) *Inclusion and Diversity: Meeting the needs of all students*, Abingdon: Routledge.

Griffiths, T. (2013) 'Higher education for socialism in Venezuela: massification, development and transformation', in T.G. Griffiths and Z. Millei (eds) *Logics of Socialist Education: Engaging with crisis, insecurity and uncertainty*, Dordrecht: Springer.

Griffiths, T.G. and Williams, J. (2009) Mass schooling for socialist transformation in Cuba and Venezuela, *Journal for Critical Education Policy Studies*, 7(2), pp. 30–50. www.jceps.com/index.phppageID=article&articleID=160.

Grove, J. (2013) Zero hours, infinite anxiety, *Times Higher Educational Supplement*, 13 March, originally published as 'Pending arrangements', accessed online March 2012.

Grunefeld, H. (2005) *Effecten van de leergang Onderwijskundig leiderschap (Effects of the Educational Leadership Programme)*, Internal report, Netherlands: Utrecht University, Centre for teaching and learning.

Gundara, J. (1997) 'Intercultural issues and doctoral studies', in N. Graves and V. Varma (eds) *Working for a Doctorate*, Abingdon: Routledge.

Hall, T., Healey, M. and Harrison, M. (2002) Fieldwork and disabled students: discourses of exclusion and inclusion, *Transactions of the Institute of British Geographers*, 27, pp. 213–31.

Harland, T. (2003) Vygotsky's zone of proximal development and problem-based learning: linking a theoretical concept with practice through action research, *Teaching in Higher Education*, 8(2), pp. 263–72.

Harvey, M. (2013) Setting the standards for sessional staff: quality learning and teaching. *Journal of University Teaching and Learning Practice*, 10(3). http://ro.uow.edu.au/jutlp/vol10/iss3/4

HEA (2012a) *A Marked Improvement: Transforming assessment in higher education*, York: Higher Education Academy, www.heacademy.ac.uk/assets/documents/assessment/A_Marked_Improvement.pdf

HEA (2012b) *UK Professional Standards Framework*, www.heacademy.ac.uk/professional-recognition.

Hill, G. (2001) Educational cabaret, *ALAR*, 6(1).

Hilton, A. (2003) *Saving our Students (SoS): Embedding successful projects across institutions*, Project Report, York: Higher Education Academy.

Hofstede, G. (1991) *Cultures and Organizations: Software of the mind*, New York: McGraw-Hill.

Honeyfield, J. and Fraser, C. (2013) *Goalposts: A professional development resource for new tertiary teachers in their first year*, New Zealand. Available from https://akoaotearoa.ac.nz/.

Hounsell, D. (2008). The trouble with feedback: new challenges, emerging strategies, *Interchange*, Spring, Accessed at www.tla.ed.ac.uk/interchange.

Humfrey, C. (1999) *Managing International Students*, Buckingham: Open University Press.

Hunt, L. and Chalmers, D. (eds) (2012) *University Teaching in Focus: A learner-centred approach*, Melbourne: ACER Press and Abingdon: Routledge.

Illeris, K. (ed.) (2009) *Contemporary Theories of Learning*, Abingdon: Routledge.

Jarvis, P. (1987) *Adult Learning in the Social Context*, London: Croom Helm.

Jarvis, P. (2009) 'Learning to be a person in society', in K. Illeris (ed.) *Contemporary Theories of Learning*, Abingdon: Routledge.

JISC (2007) *Effective Practice with e-Assessment: An overview of technologies, policies and practice in further and higher education*, www.jisc.ac.uk/publications/.

JISC (2008) *Sounds Good: Quicker, better assessment using audio feedback*, www.jisc.ac.uk/publications/reports/2009/soundsgoodfinalreport.aspx.

JISC (2010) *Effective Assessment in a Digital Age: A guide to technology-enhanced assessment and feedback*, www.jisc.ac.uk/publications/programmerelated/2010/digiassess.

Jones, E. and Killick, D. (2007) 'Internationalisation of the curriculum', in E. Jones and S. Brown (eds) *Internationalising Higher Education*, Abingdon: Routledge.

Jones, J. (2010) Building pedagogic excellence: learning and teaching fellowships within communities of practice, *Innovations in Education and Teaching International*, 47(3), pp. 271–82.

Kegan, R. (2009) 'What "form" transforms', in K. Illeris (ed.) *Contemporary Theories of Learning*, Abingdon: Routledge.

Kneale, P.E. (1997) 'The rise of the "strategic student": how can we adapt to cope?', in S. Armstrong, G. Thompson and S. Brown (eds) *Facing up to Radical Changes in Universities and Colleges*, London: Kogan Page.

Knight, P. and Yorke, M. (2003) *Assessment, Learning and Employability*, Maidenhead: SRHE/Open University Press.

Kolb, D. (1984) *Experiential Learning: Experience as the source of learning and development*, Englewood Cliffs, NJ: Prentice-Hall.

Laurillard, D. (2013) 'Foreword to the second edition', in H. Beetham and R. Sharpe (eds) *Rethinking Pedagogy for a Digital Age*, 2nd edn, Abingdon: Routledge.

Lave, J. (2009) 'The practice of learning', in K. Illeris (ed.) *Contemporary Theories of Learning*, Abingdon: Routledge.

Leask, B. (2007) 'International teachers and international learning', in E. Jones and S. Brown (eds) *Internationalising Higher Education*, Abingdon: Routledge.

Leonard, D. (1997) 'Gender issues in doctoral studies', in N. Graves and V. Varma (eds) *Working for a Doctorate*, Abingdon: Routledge.

Livetext website: www.livetext.com/overview/admin-overview.html.

Lortie, D.C. (1975) *Schoolteacher: A sociological study*, Chicago: University of Chicago Press.

Marsden, R. (2014) *Guardian Review*, 22 March, p. 49.

Martinez, Y. and Trees, J. (2013) *Thought Experiments in Graphic Design Education*, Books from the Future.

May et al. (2013) cited in F. Beaton and A. Gilbert (eds) *Developing Effective Part-time Teachers in Higher Education*, Abingdon: Routledge.

Mayes, T. and de Freitas, S. (2013) 'Technology enhanced learning', in H. Beetham and R. Sharpe (eds) *Rethinking Pedagogy for a Digital Age: Designing for 21st century learning*, 2nd edn, Abingdon: Routledge.

McDowell, L. (2012) *Programme Focussed Assessment*, Bradford: Bradford University www.pass.brad.ac.uk/short-guide.pdf.

McDowell, L. and Brown, S. (2001) *Assessing Students: Cheating and plagiarism*, Higher Education Academy. www.heacademy.ac.uk/assets/York/documents/resources/resourcedatabase/id430_cheating_and_plagiarism.pdf.

McKeachie, W.J. ([1951]/1994) *Teaching Tips: Strategies, research and theory for college and university teachers*, Lexington, Mass: D.C. Heath & Company.

McLoughlin, C. and Lee, M. (2010) Personalised and self regulated learning in the Web 2.0 era: international exemplars of innovative pedagogy using social software, *Australasian Journal of Educational Technology*, 26(1), pp. 28–43.

Mentkowski, M. and associates (2000) *Learning that Lasts: Integrating learning development and performance in college and beyond*, San Francisco: Jossey-Bass.

Merseth, K. and Lacey, C.A. (1993) Weaving stronger fabric: the pedagogical promise of hypermedia and case methods in teacher education, *Teacher and Teacher Education*, 9(3), pp. 283–99.

Meyer, J. and Land, R. (2003) *Threshold Concepts and Troublesome Knowledge: Linkages to ways of thinking and practising within the disciplines*, Edinburgh: University of Edinburgh.

Ministry of Education of People's Republic China (2012) *Current Situation of Higher Education Institutions in China*, www.chinaeducenter.com/en/cedu/hedu.php, accessed 31 March 2014.

Morey, A.I. (2000) Changing higher education curricula for a global and multicultural world, *Higher Education in Europe*, 25(1), p. 25.

Morgan, M. (ed.) (2011) *Improving the Student Experience: A practical guide*, Abingdon, Routledge.

Mortiboys, A. (2005) *Teaching with Emotional Intelligence*, Abingdon: Routledge.

Mulryan-Kyne, C. (2010) Teaching large classes at college and university level: challenges and opportunities, *Teaching in Higher Education*, 15(2), pp. 175–85.

Newstead, S.E., Franklyn-Stokes, A. and Armistead, P. (1996) Individual differences in student cheating, *Journal of Educational Psychology*, 88, pp. 229–41.

Nicol, D.J. and Macfarlane-Dick, D. (2006) Formative assessment and self-regulated learning: a model and seven principles of good feedback practice, *Studies in Higher Education*, 31(2), pp. 199–218.

Northedge, A. (2003a) Enabling participation in academic discourse, *Teaching in Higher Education*, 8(2), pp. 169–80.

Northedge, A. (2003b) Rethinking teaching in the context of diversity, *Teaching in Higher Education*, 8(1), www.kent.ac.uk/teaching/documents/qualifications/rethinkingteaching.pdf.

Nutt, D. (2008) *Times Higher Educational Supplement*, 21 February.

O'Brien, K. and Oliver, B. (2013) *Live the Future – Agenda 2020: Assuring graduate capabilities: evidencing levels of achievement for graduate employability*, www.som.uq.edu.au/media/377101/Prof%20Kylie%20OBrien%20and%20Prof%20Beverley%20Oliver.pdf

OECD (2002) *Frascati Manual: Proposed standard practice for surveys on research and experimental development*, 6th edn, OECD.

PASS (2012) *The Case for Programme Focused Assessment : PASS Position Paper*, www.pass.brad.ac.uk/position-paper.pdf.

Pegler, C. (2013) in H. Beetham and R. Sharpe (eds) *Rethinking Pedagogy for a Digital Age*, 2nd edn, London: Routledge.

Peelo, M. and Wareham, T. (eds) (2002) *Failing Students in Higher Education*, Maidenhead: SRHE/Open University Press.

Pickford, R. (2009) *Designing First-Year Assessment and Feedback: A guide for university staff*, Leeds: Leeds Metropolitan University Press.

Pickford, R. and Brown, S. (2006) *Assessing Skills and Practice,* Abingdon: Routledge.

Posner, G.J., Strike, K.A., Hewson, P.W. and Gertzog, W.A. (1982) Accommodation of a scientific conception: Towards a theory of conceptual change, *Science Education,* 66(2), pp. 211–29.

Price, M., Rust, C., Donovan, B., and Handley, K. with Bryant, R. (2012) *Assessment Literacy: The foundation for improving student learning,* Oxford: Oxford Centre for Staff and Learning Development.

QAA (2013) *UK Quality Code for Higher Education: Chapter B6: Assessment of students and recognition of prior learning,* www.qaa.ac.uk/publications/informationand guidance/pages/quality-code-b6.aspx

Race, P. (2001) *A Briefing on Self, Peer and Group Assessment,* in LTSN Generic Centre Assessment Series No. 9, York: HEA/LTSN.

Race, P. (2006a) *In at the Deep End – Starting to teach in higher education,* Leeds: Leeds Metropolitan University, http://phil-race.co.uk/wp-content/uploads/downloads/2013/05/In-at-the-Deep-End.pdf. Also available in Arabic: http://phil-race.co.uk/wp-content/uploads/downloads/2013/05/Arabic-translation-of-in-at-the-deep-end.pdf.

Race, P. (2006b) *The Lecturer's Toolkit*, 3rd edn, Abingdon: Routledge.

Race, P. (2010) *Making Learning Happen,* 2nd edn, London: Sage

Race, P. (2014) *Making Learning Happen*, 3rd edn, London: Sage.

Race, P. (2015, in press) *The Lecturer's Toolkit*, 4th edn, Abingdon: Routledge.

Race, P. and Leeds Met Teaching Fellows (2009) *Using Peer Observation to Enhance Teaching*, Leeds: Leeds Metropolitan Press, www.leedsmet.ac.uk/publications/files/090505-36477_PeerObsTeaching_LoRes.pdf.

Race, P. and Pickford, R. (2007) *Making Teaching Work: Teaching smarter in post-compulsory education*, London: Sage.

Ramírez, E. (2010) Venezuela posee la quinta matrícula universitaria más alta del mundo, *Correo de Orinoco.*

Ramsden, P. (2003) *Learning to Teach in Higher Education*, 2nd edn, Abingdon: Routledge.

Robinson, C. (2013) Writers should take a year off, and give us all a break, *Guardian,* 17 August.

Rolfe, V. (2010) Can Turnitin be used to provide instant formative feedback?, *British Journal of Educational Technology*, 42(4).

Rotheram, B. (2009) *Sounds Good,* JISC project, www.jisc.ac.uk/whatwedo/programmes/usersandinnovation/soundsgood.aspx.

Rust, C., Price, M. and O'Donovan, B. (2003) Improving students' learning by developing their understanding of assessment criteria and processes, *Assessment and Evaluation in Higher Education*, 28 (2), pp. 147–64.

Ryan, J. (2000) *A Guide to Teaching International Students,* Oxford: Oxford Centre for Staff and Learning Development.

Sadler, D.R. (1989) Formative assessment and the design of instructional systems, *Instructional Science*, 18, pp. 119–44.

Sadler, D.R. (1998) Formative assessment: revisiting the territory, *Assessment in Education: Principles, Policy and Practice*, 5, pp. 77–8.

Sadler, D.R. (2010a) 'Assessment in higher education', in P. Peterson, E. Baker and B. McGaw (eds) *International Encyclopedia of Education*, vol. 3, Oxford: Elsevier.

Sadler, D.R. (2010b) Beyond feedback: Developing student capability in complex appraisal, *Assessment and Evaluation in Higher Education*, 35(5), pp. 535–50.

Salmon, G. (2000) *E-moderating: The key to teaching and learning online*, London: Taylor & Francis.

Salovey, P. and Meyer, J. (1990) Emotional Intelligence, *Imagination, Cognition and Personality*, 9(3), pp. 185–211.

Sambell, K. (2013) 'Engaging students through assessment', in E. Dunne and D. Owen (eds) *The Student Engagement Handbook: Practice in higher education*, Bingley: Emerald.

Sambell, K. and Hubbard, A. (2004) The role of formative 'low-stakes' assessment in supporting non-traditional students' retention and progression in higher education: student perspectives, *Widening Participation and Lifelong Learning*, 6(2), pp. 25–36.

Sambell, K., McDowell, L. and Brown, S. (1997) 'But is it fair?': An exploratory study of student perceptions of the consequential validity of assessment, *Studies in Educational Evaluation*, 23(4), pp. 349–71.

Sambell, K., McDowell, L. and Montgomery, C. (2012) *Assessment for Learning in Higher Education* Abingdon, Routledge.

Santos, B. de Sousa (2012) Public sphere and epistemologies of the south, *Africa Development*, XXXVII(1), pp. 43–67.

Shulman, L. (2004) 'Just in case: reflections on learning from experience', in S.M. Wilson, *The Wisdom of Practice. Essays on teaching, learning and learning to teach*, San Francisco: Jossey-Bass.

Smagorinsky, P., Cook, L.S. and Johnson, T.S. (2003) The twisting path of concept development in learning to teach, *Teachers College Record*, 105(8), pp. 1399–436. Available at www.tcrecord.org/content.asp?contentid=11552 (accessed 9 August 2012).

Stefani, L. and Carroll, J. (2001) *A Briefing on Plagiarism (LTSN Generic Centre Assessment Series)*, York: Higher Education Academy.

Stewart, M. (2012) 'Understanding learning theories and critique', in L. Hunt and D. Chalmers (eds) *University Teaching in Focus: A learning-centred approach*, Abingdon: Routledge.

Sutherland, S. and Powell, A. (2007) 'Cetis SIG mailing list discussions', cited in A. Fisher, K. Exley and D. Ciobanu (2014) *Using Technology to Support Learning and Teaching*, Abingdon: Routledge.

Tan, O.S. (2003) *Problem-based Learning Innovation: Using problems to power learning in the 21st century*, Singapore: Thomson Learning.

Taskstream website: https://www1.taskstream.com.

Taylor, P. and Maor, D. (2000) *Assessing the Efficacy of Online Teaching with the Constructivist On-Line Learning Environment Survey,* paper presented at the Flexible Futures in Tertiary Teaching: 9th Annual Teaching and Learning Forum, Perth: Curtin University.

Times of India (2013) 'Harvard scientists have proof yoga, meditation work', *Times of India*, Mumbai, 24 November, p. 17. Available at http://timesofindia.indiatimes.com/home/science/Harvard-scientists-have-proof-yoga-meditation-work/articleshow/26288574.cms (accessed 23 May 2014).

Turnitin website: http://turnitin.com/en_us/features/overview.

Walsh, A. and Coonan, E. (eds) (2013) *Only Connect ... Discovery Pathways, Library Explorations, and the Information Adventure*, Huddersfield: Innovative Libraries.

Wenger, E. (1998) *Communities of Practice: Learning, meaning and identity*, Cambridge, Mass: Harvard University Press.

Yorke, M. (1999) *Leaving Early: Undergraduate non-completion in higher education*, Abingdon: Routledge.

Yorke, M. (2004) *Employability in Higher Education: What it is – what it is not* (Vol. 1). York LTSN Generic Centre. Available at the Higher Education Academy website: www.heacademy.ac.uk/assets/was%20York%20-%20delete%20this%20soon/documents/ourwork/tla/employability/id116_employability_in_higher_education_336.pdf.

Yorke, M. and Longden, B. (2004) *Retention and Student Success in Higher Education*, Maidenhead, Open University Press.

Index